WOW! EARTH

LONDON, NEW YORK,
MELBOURNE, MUNICH, AND DELHI

For Tall Tree Ltd:
Editors Rob Colson, David John, and Jon Richards
Designers Ben Ruocco, Ed Simkins, and Jonathan Vipond

For Dorling Kindersley:
Senior editor Victoria Heyworth-Dunne
Senior designer Smiljka Surla

Managing editor Linda Esposito
Managing art editor Diane Thistlethwaite

Creative retouching Steve Willis
Picture research Nic Dean

Publishing manager Andrew Macintyre
Category publisher Laura Buller

DK picture researchers Claire Bowers, Emma Shepherd
Production editor Hitesh Patel
Senior production controller Angela Graef

Jacket design Akiko Kato, Junkichi Tatsuki
Jacket editor Mariza O'Keeffe
Design development manager Sophia M Tampakopoulos Turner

First published in Great Britain in 2009 by
Dorling Kindersley Limited,
80 Strand, London, WC2R 0RL

2 4 6 8 10 9 7 5 3 1
WD207 – 04/09

A CIP catalogue record for this book is available from the British Library

ISBN: 978-1-40534-157-8

Printed and bound by Leo, China

WOW! EARTH

Written by:
John Woodward
Consultant:
Kim Bryan

1

2

3

Contents

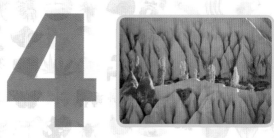

VOLCANIC LIGHTNING
Lightning crackles through a plume of volcanic ash erupted from the Chaiten volcano in Chile during a storm. Such spectacular events are dramatic evidence of the titanic forces that have shaped our planet.

Planet Earth

OUR GALAXY

The Universe contains at least 100 billion galaxies, each with billions of stars – most of which probably have orbiting planets. Our own galaxy, the Milky Way, consists of about 500 billion stars, including all the ones that we can see in the night sky, as well as large clouds of gas and dust, some of which form new stars. The Milky Way is a flat disc with a central bulge and bright spiral arms. Our Sun is a medium-sized star in one of the spiral arms, about two-thirds of the way out from the centre. From Earth, we look out across the galaxy's disc, so the densely packed stars at its centre look like a milky band of light across the night sky.

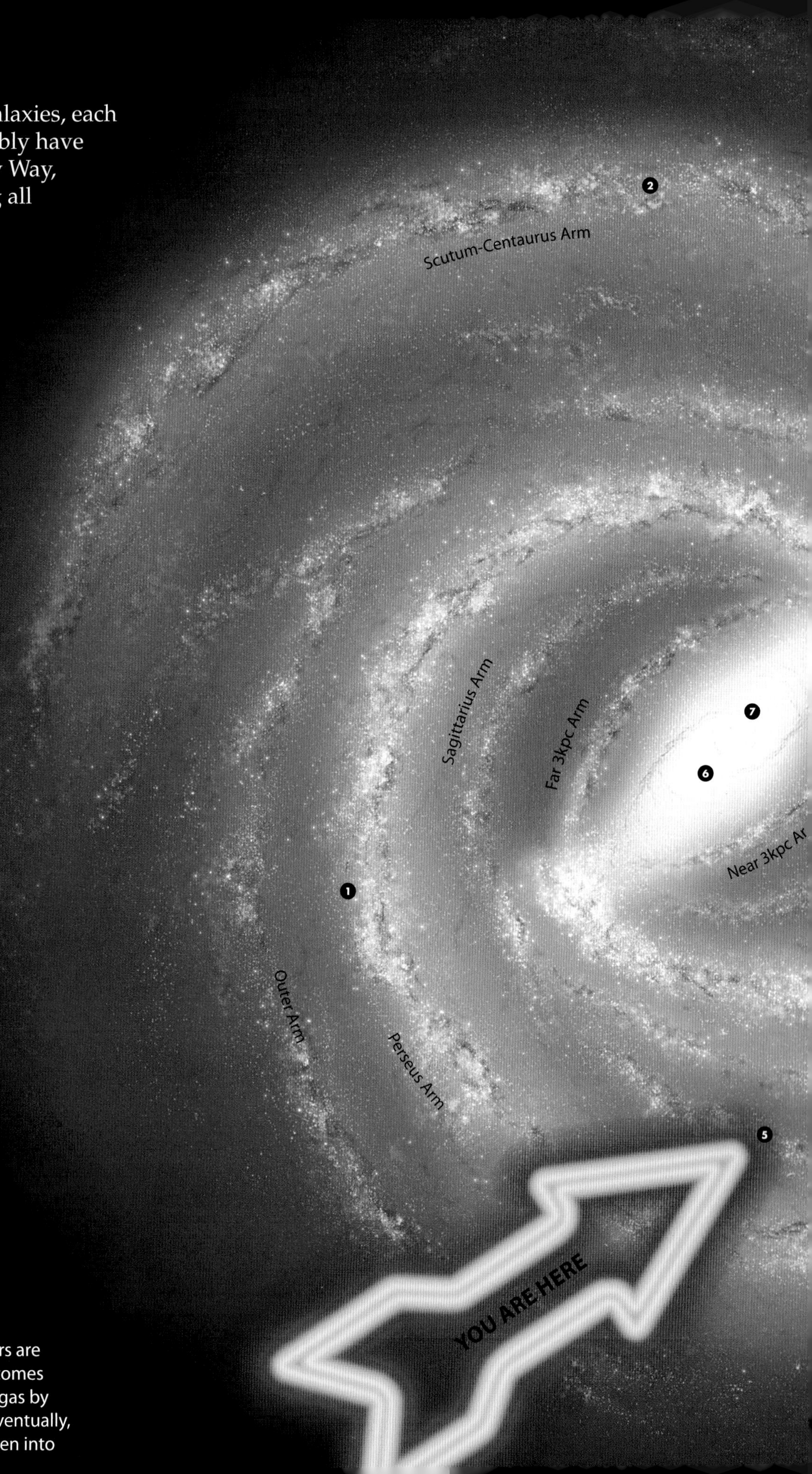

1 GAS AND DUST
The galaxy contains masses of gas and dust particles that are thrown out by the explosions of giant stars. During their lives, these stars generate energy by nuclear fusion, turning lighter elements into heavier ones. The biggest stars contain many of the elements that form new stars, planets, and even life on Earth. These elements are scattered into space when dying stars explode.

2 SPIRAL ARMS
The Milky Way galaxy has a pattern of spiral arms swirling out from its central bulge. These arms are made up of young, bright blue stars and slightly older, whiter stars, as well as clouds of dust and gas. Other stars lie between the arms, but they are not as bright. All these stars are slowly orbiting the central bulge. Each follows its own route, and takes several hundred million years to complete its orbit.

3 STAR NURSERY
The pink patches on this image mark regions where stars are created within clouds of hydrogen gas. Part of a cloud comes together to form a dense ball of gas. This attracts more gas by gravity, squeezing the ball into a tighter, hotter mass. Eventually, this triggers a nuclear fusion reaction that turns hydrogen into helium gas and radiates energy as brilliant starlight

❹ HOT BLUE STAR

Stars glow with colour, just like hot steel. Some glow red-hot, while hotter ones like our Sun glow yellow. Many even hotter stars glow white-hot, but the hottest, brightest stars are an intense blue. As stars get older they cool down and change colour. Most eventually swell up to form "red giants" of dispersing gas. Some of the very biggest stars end their lives in vast explosions called supernovas.

❺ SOLAR SYSTEM

The Sun is a ball of hot gas that acts as a nuclear fusion reactor. It squeezes together hydrogen atoms to form helium atoms, and this releases massive amounts of energy, which we experience as light and heat. Gas and dust left over from the Sun's creation 4.6 billion years ago have clumped together to form the planets, asteroids, and comets that make up the Solar System.

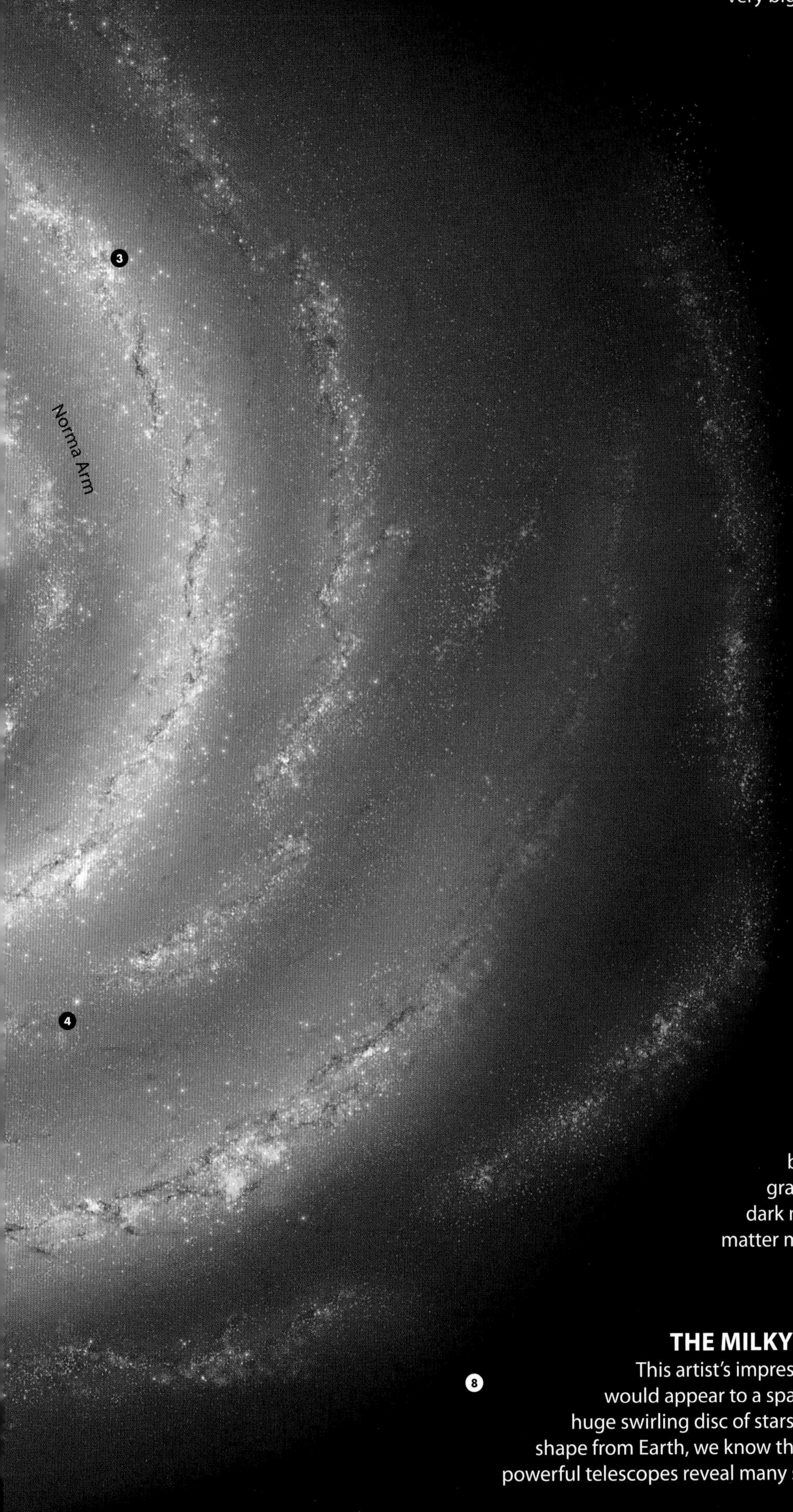

❻ CENTRAL BULGE

The hub of the galaxy is packed with stars that radiate yellow or red light. This shows that they are cooler and older than the blue, white, or pale yellow stars found in the spiral arms. These older stars form the vast central bulge of the galactic disc, which we see from Earth as the brightest part of the Milky Way. The bulge also contains a huge amount of gas that forms a ring around the centre.

❼ BLACK HOLE

At the heart of the central bulge lies a supermassive black hole. Black holes have such colossal gravity that even light cannot escape them. Most are formed by the collapse of giant stars, but a supermassive black hole is created by the collapse of many stars, which are sucked into the hole like water swirling down a drain. The violence of this process generates intense energy that makes the region glow white-hot.

❽ DARK MATTER

Galaxies glow with the light generated by stars, but they also contain a lot of gas and dust that does not emit light. Something also exists in the apparent voids between galaxies, because galaxies interact in ways that can be explained only by the gravity of material that we cannot see. Astronomers call this material dark matter and are unsure about what it is exactly. However, dark matter may account for about 23 per cent of the Universe.

THE MILKY WAY

This artist's impression shows the Milky Way galaxy as it would appear to a space traveller approaching from above the huge swirling disc of stars. Although we cannot see our galaxy's shape from Earth, we know that it has this form – partly because powerful telescopes reveal many similar spiral galaxies in deep space.

THE SOLAR SYSTEM

The Sun is a vast ball of hot gas that formed from a spinning cloud of gas and dust about 4.6 billion years ago. Some of this material spread out as a spinning disc, and clumped together to create the orbiting planets of the Solar System.

The four small inner planets are balls of rock. The much bigger outer planets are mainly gas and ice, although they have many rocky moons. There are also a few dwarf planets and billions of small rocky asteroids.

Near vertical ring around Uranus shows that the planet spins on its side
Surface features hidden by atmosphere are revealed by radar
1
2
3
4
Great Red Spot is a huge storm, wider than the Earth
Surface of Mercury is pitted with impact craters

❶ URANUS

A distant, cold world, Uranus is made mainly of water-ice and frozen gases, such as methane and ammonia. However, it does have a rocky core and a hydrogen-rich atmosphere. It also has 27 moons and a ring of dust particles that orbit the planet from top to bottom. This is because the planet is spinning on its side, on an almost horizontal axis.

❷ JUPITER

The fifth planet from the Sun is more than twice the size of all the other planets put together. Its rocky core is surrounded by thick layers of hydrogen and helium gas that are continually rising and falling in currents that form colourful swirling bands. This gas giant has 63 moons, although only four are easily visible from Earth through telescopes.

❸ VENUS

Similar in size to Earth, but orbiting nearer the Sun, Venus is a rocky planet peppered with giant, extinct volcanoes. Its surface is hidden by a thick cloudy atmosphere rich in carbon dioxide. This traps heat, making Venus the hottest of the planets with a surface temperature of 464°C (867°F) – hot enough to melt lead.

❹ MERCURY

Mercury is the smallest of the inner planets, and the closest to the Sun. Its rocky surface is covered with craters, and it has a thin atmosphere. This allows the Sun to build up scorching surface temperatures of up to 430°C (806°F) by day. At night the heat escapes and temperatures plunge as low as -180°C (-292°F).

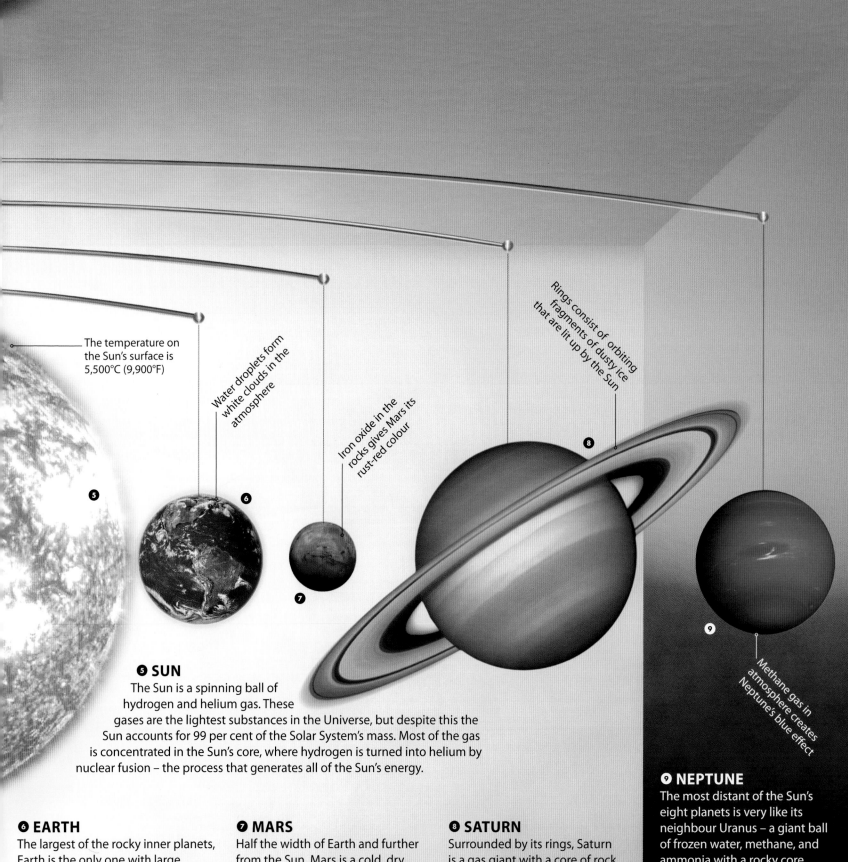

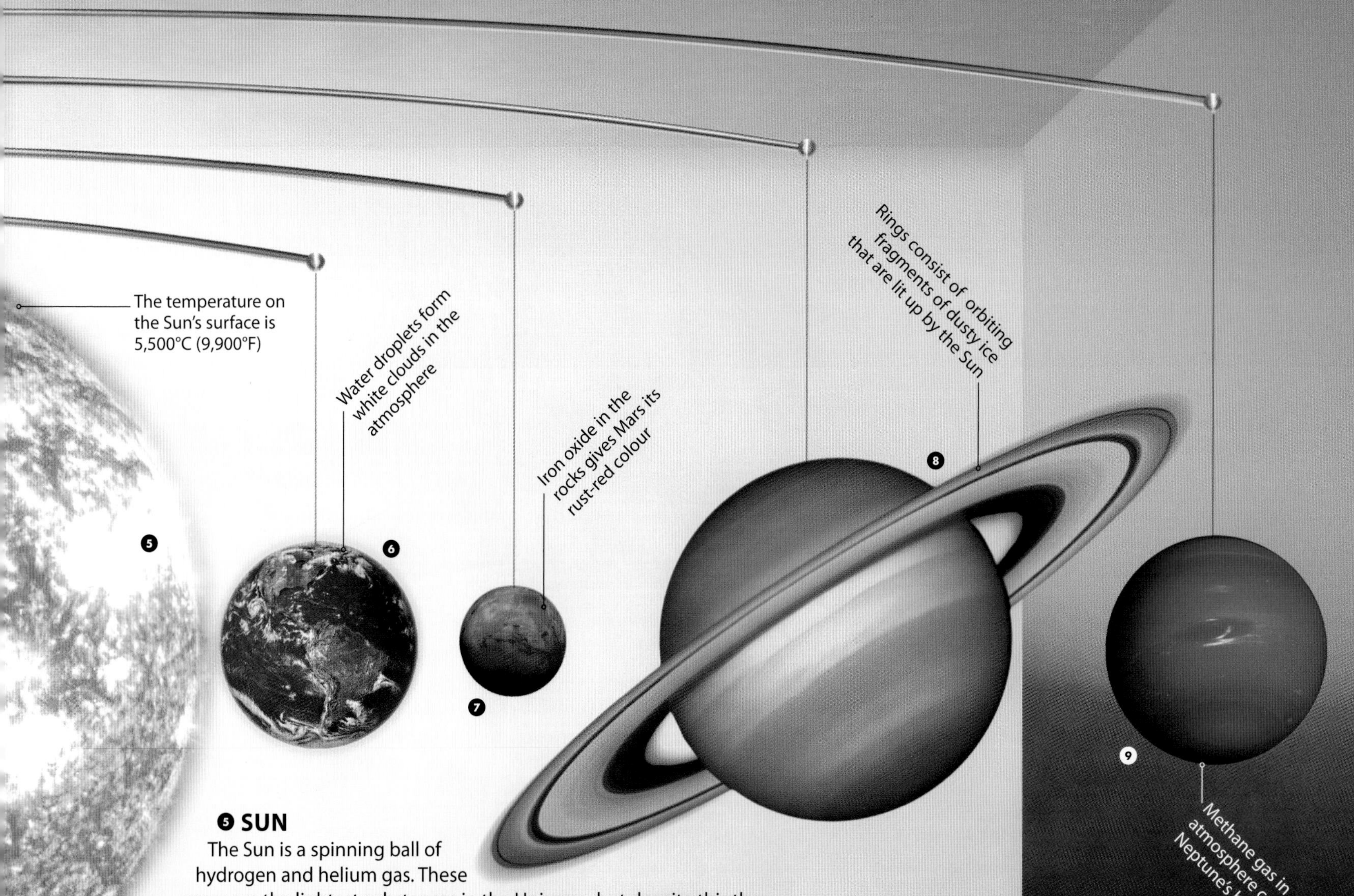

The temperature on the Sun's surface is 5,500°C (9,900°F)
Water droplets form white clouds in the atmosphere
Iron oxide in the rocks gives Mars its rust-red colour
Rings consist of orbiting fragments of dusty ice that are lit up by the Sun
Methane gas in atmosphere creates Neptune's blue effect
5
6
7
8
9

5 SUN

The Sun is a spinning ball of hydrogen and helium gas. These gases are the lightest substances in the Universe, but despite this the Sun accounts for 99 per cent of the Solar System's mass. Most of the gas is concentrated in the Sun's core, where hydrogen is turned into helium by nuclear fusion – the process that generates all of the Sun's energy.

6 EARTH

The largest of the rocky inner planets, Earth is the only one with large amounts of liquid water, and this allows life to flourish. One reason for this is that Earth's atmosphere acts like a blanket, keeping the planet warm enough to stop the water from freezing solid. Most of the water forms broad oceans that cover nearly two-thirds of the planet.

7 MARS

Half the width of Earth and further from the Sun, Mars is a cold, dry world of reddish rock. Its thin atmosphere is mostly carbon dioxide, as on Venus. Three billion years ago, the atmosphere was thicker and it kept the planet warm enough for rivers of water to flow on the surface. Nearly all the water on Mars has now turned to ice.

8 SATURN

Surrounded by its rings, Saturn is a gas giant with a core of rock and ice, second only in size to Jupiter and with at least 60 small moons. Like Jupiter, Saturn is made mainly of hydrogen and helium. However, both planets are too small for their gravity to trigger the nuclear reactions that would turn them into stars.

9 NEPTUNE

The most distant of the Sun's eight planets is very like its neighbour Uranus – a giant ball of frozen water, methane, and ammonia with a rocky core. Neptune is so far from the Sun that its surface temperature is roughly -200°C (-320°F), and it takes 165 years to complete one orbit. It has one large moon, Triton, and 12 much smaller ones.

ASTEROIDS, METEORITES, AND COMETS

As well as the big planets, the Solar System contains many billions of smaller orbiting objects. Many of these are lumps of rock, iron, and nickel left over from the formation of the planets. These include the asteroids that mainly orbit the Sun between Mars and Jupiter. There are also comets – big chunks of ice and dust that loop around the Sun before vanishing into the far reaches of the Solar System. Smaller pieces of rock and ice shoot through Earth's sky as meteors. Some of these pieces may even fall to Earth as meteorites.

▶ IMPACT CRATERS

This crater in Arizona is one of about 170 that have been found on Earth. Formed by an asteroid strike about 50,000 years ago, it is 1.2 km (0.75 miles) across. The impact would have caused a colossal explosion, killing everything in the region. Luckily, these large impacts are very rare. The last occurred in 1908, when an asteroid exploded high above a remote region of Siberia called Tunguska.

▼ ASTEROIDS

The Asteroid Belt between the orbits of Mars and Jupiter contains vast numbers of asteroids. Most are too small to have names, but a few, such as Gaspra and Ida, are big enough to have been photographed by passing space probes. Some asteroids orbit outside the main belt, including Eros, which passes within 22 million km (14 million miles) of Earth.

GASPRA

Discovery date	1916
Length	18 km (11 miles)
Orbital period	1,200 days
Orbital speed	20 km (12 miles) per sec

IDA

Discovery date	1884
Length	53 km (33 miles)
Orbital period	1,768 days
Orbital speed	18 km (11 miles) per sec

EROS

Discovery date	1898
Length	33 km (20 miles)
Orbital period	643 days
Orbital speed	24 km (15 miles) per sec

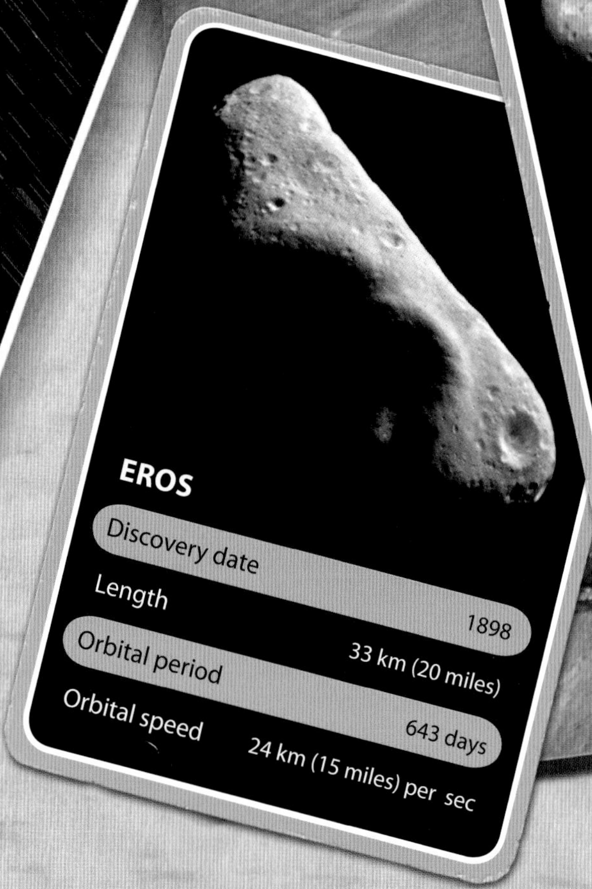

▲ COMETS

There are billions of comets in the Oort Cloud, a region of the Solar System beyond the orbit of Neptune. A few of these icy bodies travel close to the Sun. As they approach, they are blasted by solar radiation that makes them trail long tails of glowing dust and gas. After several weeks, the comets vanish, but some reappear many years later. This is Halley's Comet, which orbits the Sun every 76 years.

▼ METEOR SHOWER

Particles attracted by Earth's gravity streak through the atmosphere and are heated by friction until they glow white hot. Most of these meteors burn up high above the surface, but a few reach the ground as meteorites. Showers of meteors occur very year when Earth passes through trails of space dust left by comets.

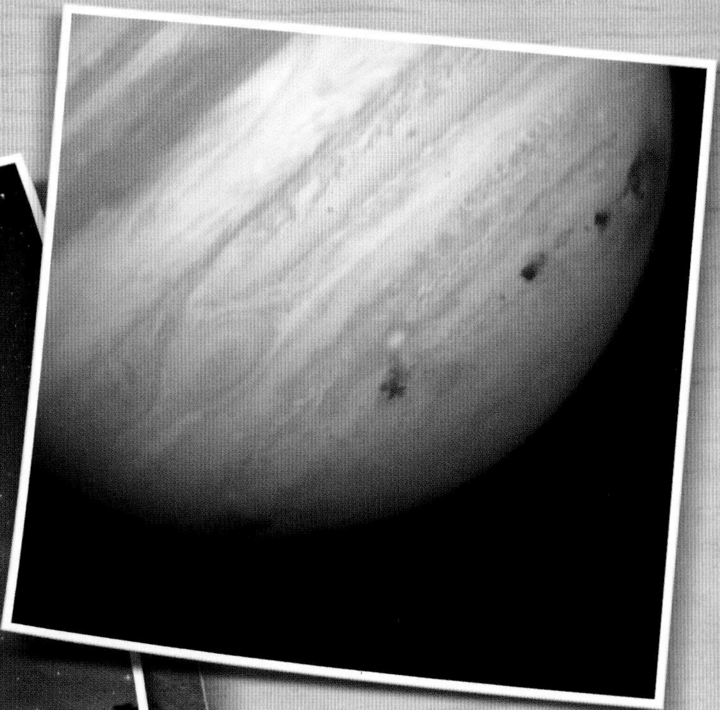

▲ PROTECTIVE JUPITER

Many of the asteroids and comets that might hit Earth are dragged off course by the intense gravity of Jupiter. This has probably saved us from many catastrophic impacts in the past. In 1994, scientists watched as parts of the comet Shoemaker-Levy 9 plunged into the giant planet, creating a series of huge dark scars in its thick atmosphere – some as big as Earth itself.

Meteorite fragment

Nakhla meteorite

Shargottite Sayh al Uhaymir 008 meteorite

▶ METEORITES

Thousands of meteorites hit Earth every year, although few are big enough to be dangerous. Most are stony, but others are largely made of iron or – rarely – a mixture of the two. Many are fragments of asteroids, and some are made of the material that formed the planets. A few, like the Nakhla meteorite, have been blasted from the surface of Mars by other impacts, and others have come from the Moon.

THE MOON

Our Moon was created when an object the size of Mars crashed into Earth some 4.5 billion years ago. The impact melted part of Earth's rocky mantle, and the molten rock burst out and clumped together to form the Moon. Unlike Earth, the Moon does not have a big, heavy core of iron, which is why it does not have enough gravity to have an atmosphere. However, it does attract asteroids, and their impacts have left it pockmarked with craters. It is a dry, sterile world, quite unlike its closest neighbour.

▼SPINNING PARTNERS

The Moon is trapped in Earth orbit by Earth's gravity, which stops it spinning away into space. But the Moon also has gravity, and this pulls on the water in Earth's oceans, creating the rising and falling tides.

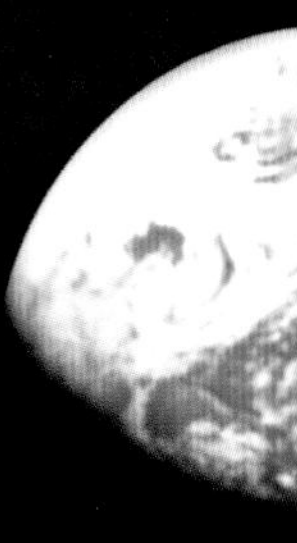

▲LUNAR LANDSCAPES

The Moon's surface is covered with dust and rocks blasted from asteroid impact craters during the first 750 million years of its history. The biggest craters are more than 150 km (90 miles) across, and their rims form the Moon's pale uplands. The darker "seas" are big craters that have flooded with dark volcanic rock.

Solar panels collected sunlight to generate power for the probe
Antenna sent and received data
Antenna beamed images to Earth
American *Surveyor 1* (landed in June 1966)
Russian *Lunokhod 2* (landed in January 1973)
Eight wheels carried probe over lunar terrain
Spring-loaded legs cushioned landing

◀UNMANNED PROBES

The first spacecraft sent to the Moon were robots, which analysed the surface conditions, gathered images, and beamed the data back to Earth. The information they collected was vital to the safety of the first astronauts to visit the Moon in the late 1960s. Since then, further unmanned missions have provided scientists with a steady stream of information about the Moon.

▼MOON ROCK

The boulders that litter the Moon are made of rock that is very old by Earth standards. Pale moon rock is 4.5 billion years old – as old as the Moon itself – and the dark lava that fills some of the larger craters is at least 3.2 billion years old. This is because, apart from a few asteroid impacts, all geological activity on the Moon stopped long ago.

Boulder lies where it fell after being blasted from a crater

APOLLO 11

Apollo 11: The first humans to step on the Moon were Neil Armstrong and Buzz Aldrin on 20 July 1969. They spent 2.5 hours on the surface.

MOON MISSIONS

In 1969, as part of the Apollo project, the United States sent the first manned mission to land on the Moon. Six similar missions followed, only one of which was unsuccessful, and a total of 12 Apollo astronauts explored the lunar surface.

◄ON THE SURFACE

There is no air on the Moon, and no atmosphere of any kind to create a pale sky and soften the harsh sunlight. The temperature can rise to 120°C (240°F) in the sunlight, but plummets to -150°C (-240°F) in the dark because there is no atmosphere to stop the heat escaping into space. Since the Moon takes 27.3 Earth days to complete one spin, more than 320 hours of daylight are followed by the same period of darkness.

Apollo astronaut's suit gave protection against intense solar radiation

Lunar cycle
The Moon takes nearly four weeks to orbit Earth. It spins at the same rate, so the same side always faces Earth. During this time, the Sun lights up different amounts of the side we see, creating the lunar phases.

Apollo 12: This was the first mission to carry scientific equipment to the Moon. Earthquake and magnetism detectors were left on the surface.

Apollo 13: An explosion on the spacecraft prevented a Moon landing, but the crew managed to return to Earth.

Apollo 14: This mission landed in a hilly region of the Moon in February 1971. It was led by Alan Shepard, who had also been the first American in space.

Apollo 15: Landing in July 1971, the crew took a lunar rover vehicle that allowed them to explore much more of the surface.

Apollo 16: In April 1972 this mission used another lunar rover to explore the Descartes Highlands region and carry out experiments.

Apollo 17: The last Apollo mission in December 1972 included the only scientist to visit the Moon – geologist Harrison Schmitt.

EARLY EARTH

Earth was created from pieces of dust and rubble orbiting the young star that became the Sun. These gradually clumped together to form a planet in a process called accretion. The process began slowly but, as the planet grew, its increasing gravity attracted more fragments of space rock. Eventually the whole mass melted, and the heavier iron and nickel in the molten rock sank towards the centre of the planet to form its core. The rest formed the thick, hot mantle and the relatively thin, cool, brittle crust.

Colliding at colossal speed, two rock fragments melt into each other

▶ACCRETION

Made by nuclear fusion in giant exploding stars, heavy elements such as silicon and iron formed clouds of space dust and rock in the region of the galaxy where the Sun was born. As the pieces of dust and rock orbited the star, they were pulled together by their own gravity, and the energy of these collisions was transformed into heat. This heat welded the rocks together, forming larger and larger chunks and eventually creating the "proto-planet" that became Earth.

◀BOMBARDMENT

While the young Earth was surrounded by rocky debris, the planet was bombarded by all kinds of objects. The energy of each impact was converted into heat that ultimately melted the entire planet and created its layered structure. As the bombardment slowed down, Earth cooled, but radioactivity near the core still generates heat that causes volcanoes and earthquakes.

Big impacts created vast craters, later erased by geological events

▼EARTH'S MAGNETISM

Earth's core is a mass of molten iron, nickel, and sulphur, with a ball of solid metal at its heart. Intense heat causes swirling currents in the molten outer core, which interact with the planet's spin to generate an electromagnetic field. This makes the planet act as a giant magnet, and is why a compass can be used to find magnetic north.

Rivers of red-hot lava pour from the craters of giant volcanoes

▲MASSIVE VOLCANISM

As the early Earth became hotter and hotter, and its metallic core started to form, chemical reactions released vast amounts of carbon dioxide, sulphur dioxide, and water vapour. These gases boiled to the surface and erupted from colossal volcanoes, along with masses of molten rock. The gases formed the first atmosphere, and the water vapour turned into torrential rain that filled the first oceans.

EARTH'S STRUCTURE

If we could cut down through Earth to its centre and take out a slice, it would reveal that the planet is made up of distinct layers. At its heart lies the solid inner core, surrounded by a liquid outer core. Both are made mainly of heavy iron. The outer core is enclosed by a deep layer of heavy, very hot, yet solid rock called the mantle. The cool shell of the mantle forms the oceanic crust beneath the ocean floors, while vast slabs of lighter rock form thicker continental crust. Scientists have deduced much of this from the way shock waves generated by earthquakes travel through the planet.

❶ CORE

Earth's metallic heart consists of a solid inner core about 2,440 km (1,515 miles) across and a liquid outer core some 2,250 km (1,400 miles) thick. The inner core is about 80 per cent iron and 20 per cent nickel. It has a temperature of about 7,000°C (12,600°F), but intense pressure stops it melting. The outer core is 88 per cent molten iron and 12 per cent sulphur.

❷ MANTLE

At 2,900 km (1,800 miles) thick, the mantle makes up most of the planet. It is mostly made of heavy, dark rock called peridotite, and although its temperature ranges from 1,000°C (1,800°F) to 3,500°C (6,300°F), colossal pressure keeps it solid. Despite this, heat currents rising through the mantle keep the rock moving very slowly, and this movement is the root cause of earthquakes.

❸ OCEAN FLOORS

At the top of the mantle, movement in the rock creates cracks that reduce pressure, allowing the peridotite rock to melt. It erupts through the cracks and solidifies as basalt, a slightly lighter rock that forms the ocean floors. This oceanic crust is roughly 8 km (5 miles) thick. It is constantly being recycled and renewed, so no part of the ocean floor is more than 200 million years old.

Mountains form as crust is squeezed and folded

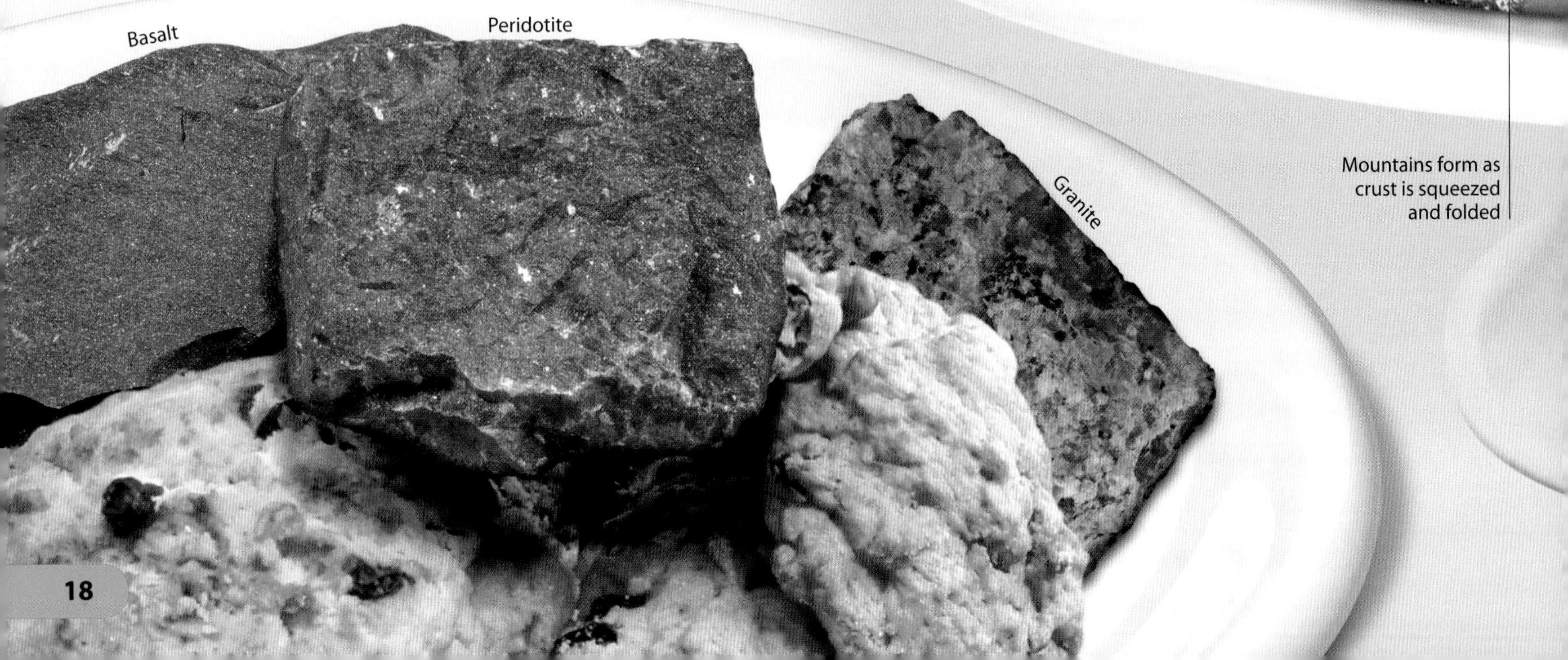

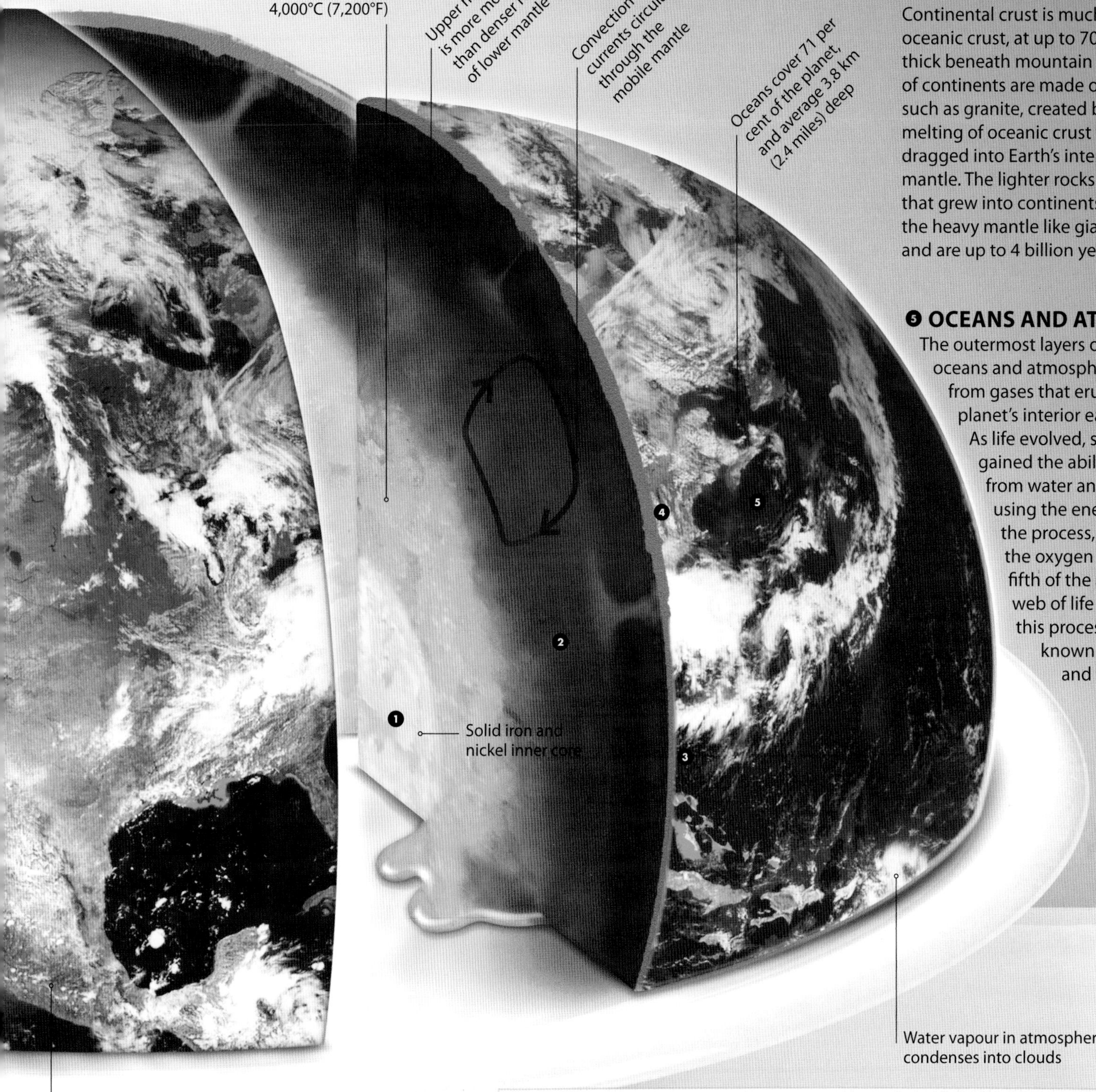
Molten outer core has a temperature of roughly 4,000°C (7,200°F)
Upper mantle is more mobile than denser rock of lower mantle
Convection currents circulate through the mobile mantle
Oceans cover 71 per cent of the planet, and average 3.8 km (2.4 miles) deep
Solid iron and nickel inner core
Water vapour in atmosphere condenses into clouds
Plants, animals, and other life make up the biosphere

❹ CONTINENTS

Continental crust is much thicker than oceanic crust, at up to 70 km (45 miles) thick beneath mountain ranges. The cores of continents are made of lighter rocks such as granite, created by the partial melting of oceanic crust where it is being dragged into Earth's interior by the mobile mantle. The lighter rocks formed islands that grew into continents. These float on the heavy mantle like giant rocky rafts and are up to 4 billion years old.

❺ OCEANS AND ATMOSPHERE

The outermost layers of Earth are the oceans and atmosphere, both formed from gases that erupted from the planet's interior early in its history. As life evolved, some organisms gained the ability to make food from water and carbon dioxide using the energy of sunlight. In the process, they produced all the oxygen that now forms a fifth of the atmosphere. The web of life that depends on this process is sometimes known as the biosphere and is unique to Earth.

❻ PROBING THE PLANET

The planet's structure is revealed by the behaviour of shock waves generated by earthquakes. Rippling S-waves are blocked by the liquid outer core, forming a shadow zone where they cannot be detected. Pressure-type P-waves pass through the core, but are deflected in ways that indicate the nature of the core and mantle.

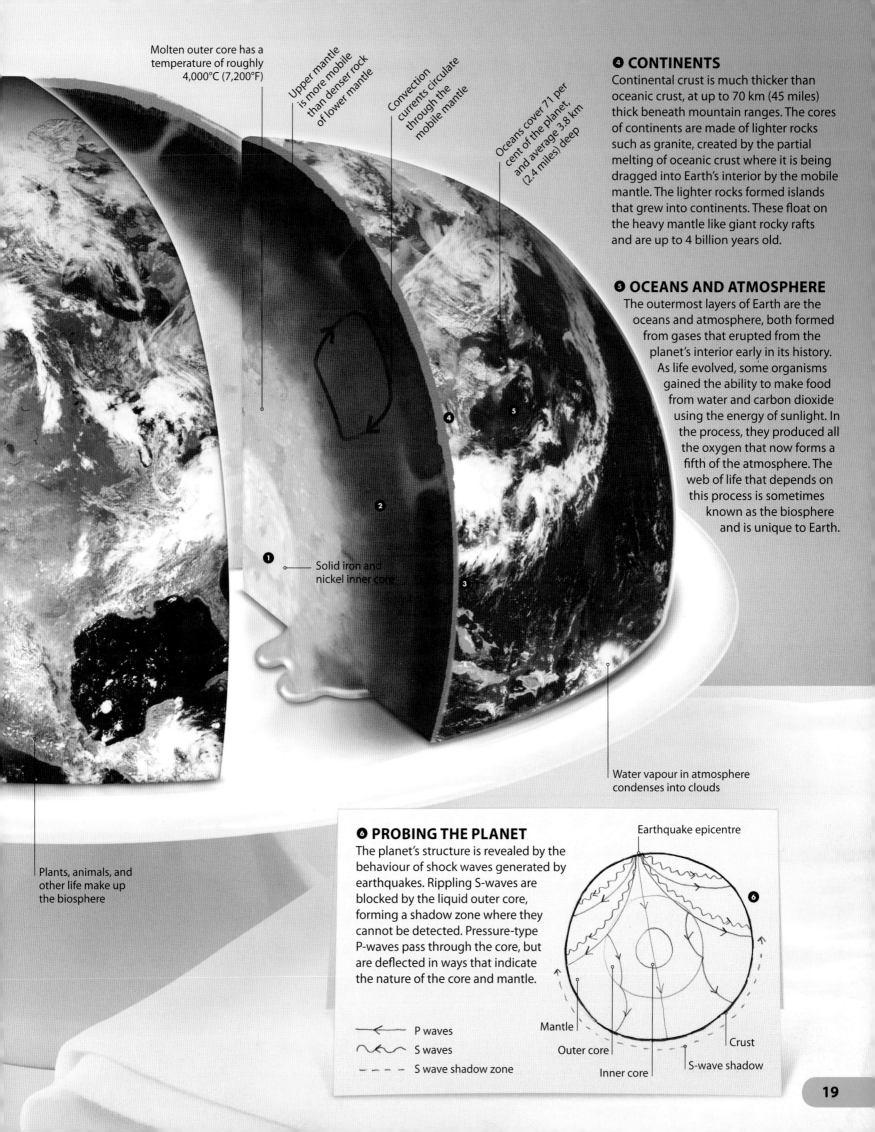

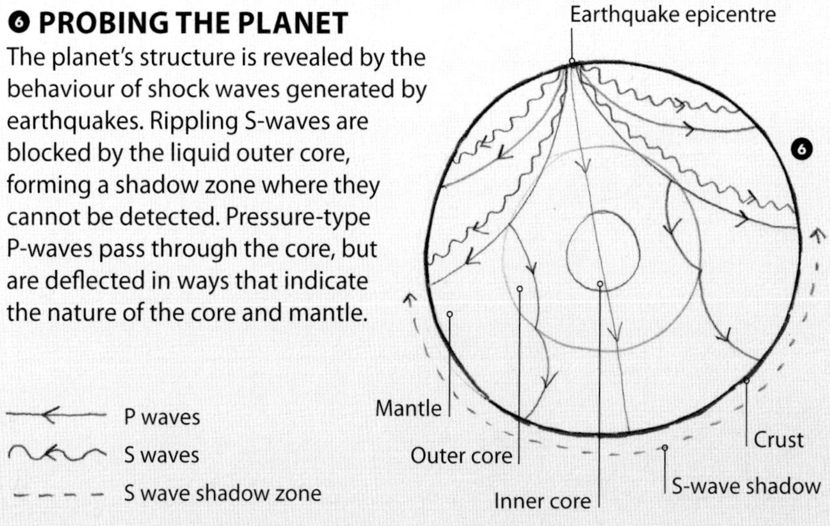
Earthquake epicentre
Mantle
Outer core
Inner core
Crust
S-wave shadow
P waves
S waves
S wave shadow zone

PLATE TECTONICS

Radioactive rocks deep inside the planet generate heat, which rises through the mantle. This creates convection currents that make the hot rock flow at roughly the rate your fingernails grow. It flows sideways near the surface, dragging sections of the crust with it and splitting the crust into curved plates. Where two plates pull apart, they form a rift. Where they push together, one plate slips beneath another, causing earthquakes and volcanic eruptions. This process is known as plate tectonics.

1 SUBDUCTION ZONES

The plate boundaries where one plate of the crust is diving beneath another are known as subduction zones. As the crust is dragged down, often creating a deep ocean trench, part of it melts and erupts, forming chains of volcanoes. The movement also triggers earthquakes. In some subduction zones, one plate of ocean floor is slipping beneath another. In others, oceanic crust is grinding beneath continents and pushing up mountains.

2 SPREADING RIFTS

Where plates are being pulled apart at oceanic spreading rifts, the pressure beneath the crust is reduced, allowing the hot mantle rock to melt and erupt as basalt lava. As the rift widens, more lava erupts and hardens, adding new rock to the ocean floor. These boundaries are marked by a network of mid-ocean ridges. Similar spreading rifts can divide continents, forming seas such as the Red Sea, which may eventually grow into oceans.

4 San Andreas Fault

This notorious earthquake zone in California is a transform fault that marks the boundary where the Pacific plate is moving northwest against the North American plate. The movement is frequent and gentle on some sections of the fault line, but rare and violent on others.

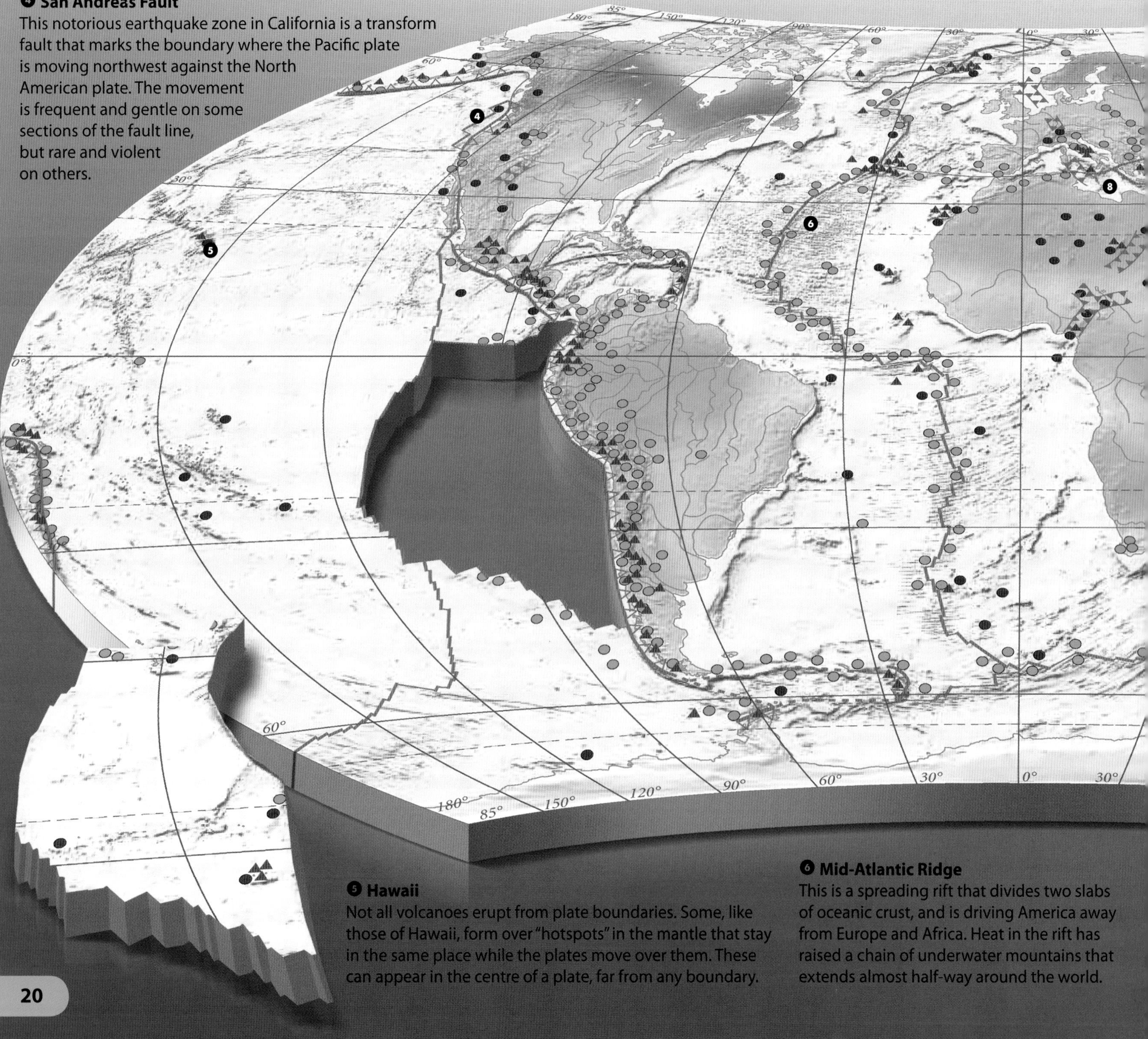

5 Hawaii

Not all volcanoes erupt from plate boundaries. Some, like those of Hawaii, form over "hotspots" in the mantle that stay in the same place while the plates move over them. These can appear in the centre of a plate, far from any boundary.

6 Mid-Atlantic Ridge

This is a spreading rift that divides two slabs of oceanic crust, and is driving America away from Europe and Africa. Heat in the rift has raised a chain of underwater mountains that extends almost half-way around the world.

❸ TRANSFORM FAULTS

The zigzags that interrupt the lines of the spreading mid-ocean ridges and other rifts on this map are transform faults – parts of the plate boundaries where plates are simply sliding past each other. Because of this, crust is neither destroyed nor created. But the movement can still be destructive, because the two sides of the fault often lock together, build up tension, and then snap in a sudden movement that causes an earthquake.

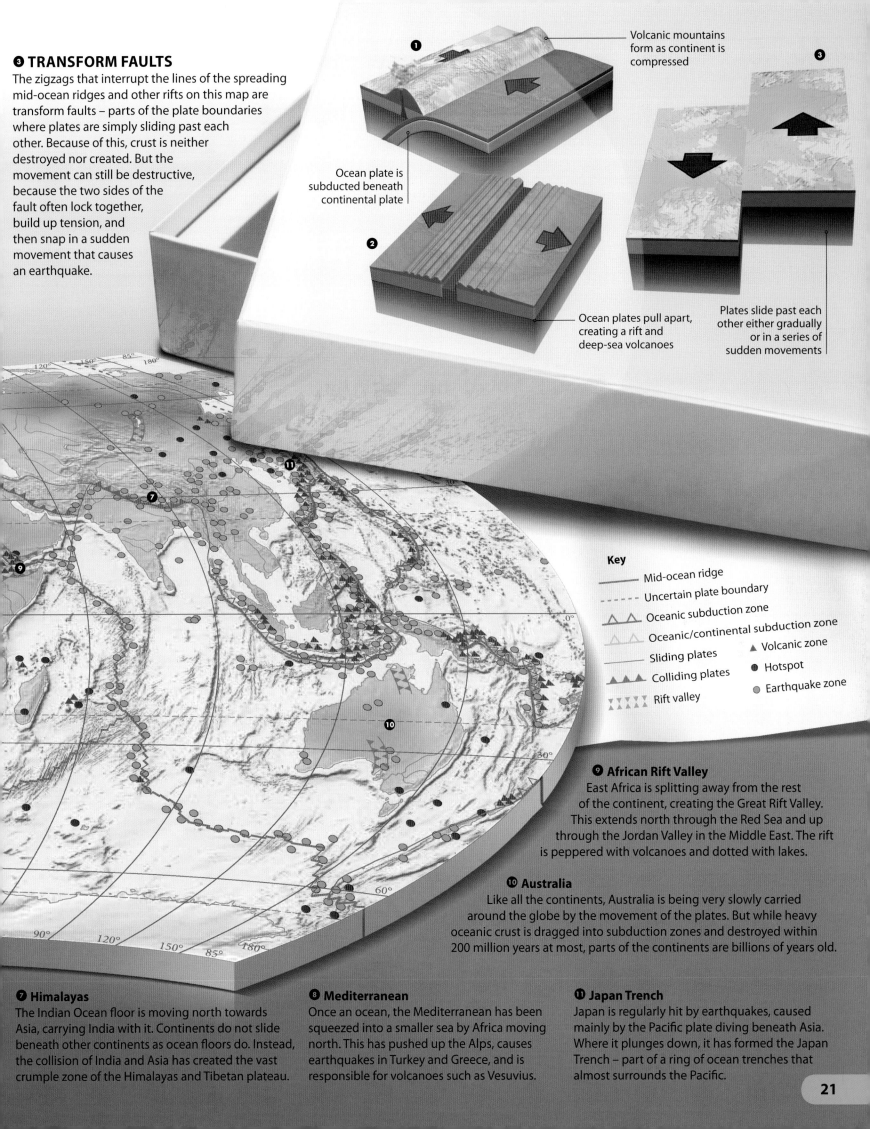

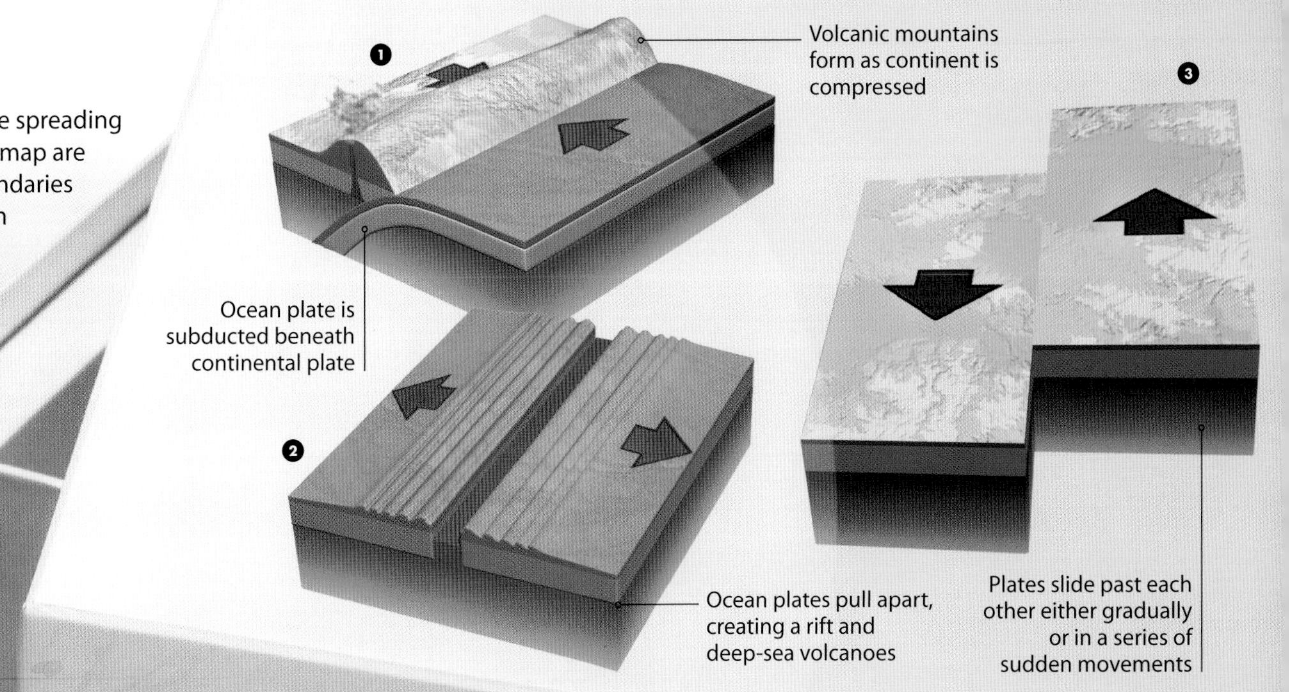

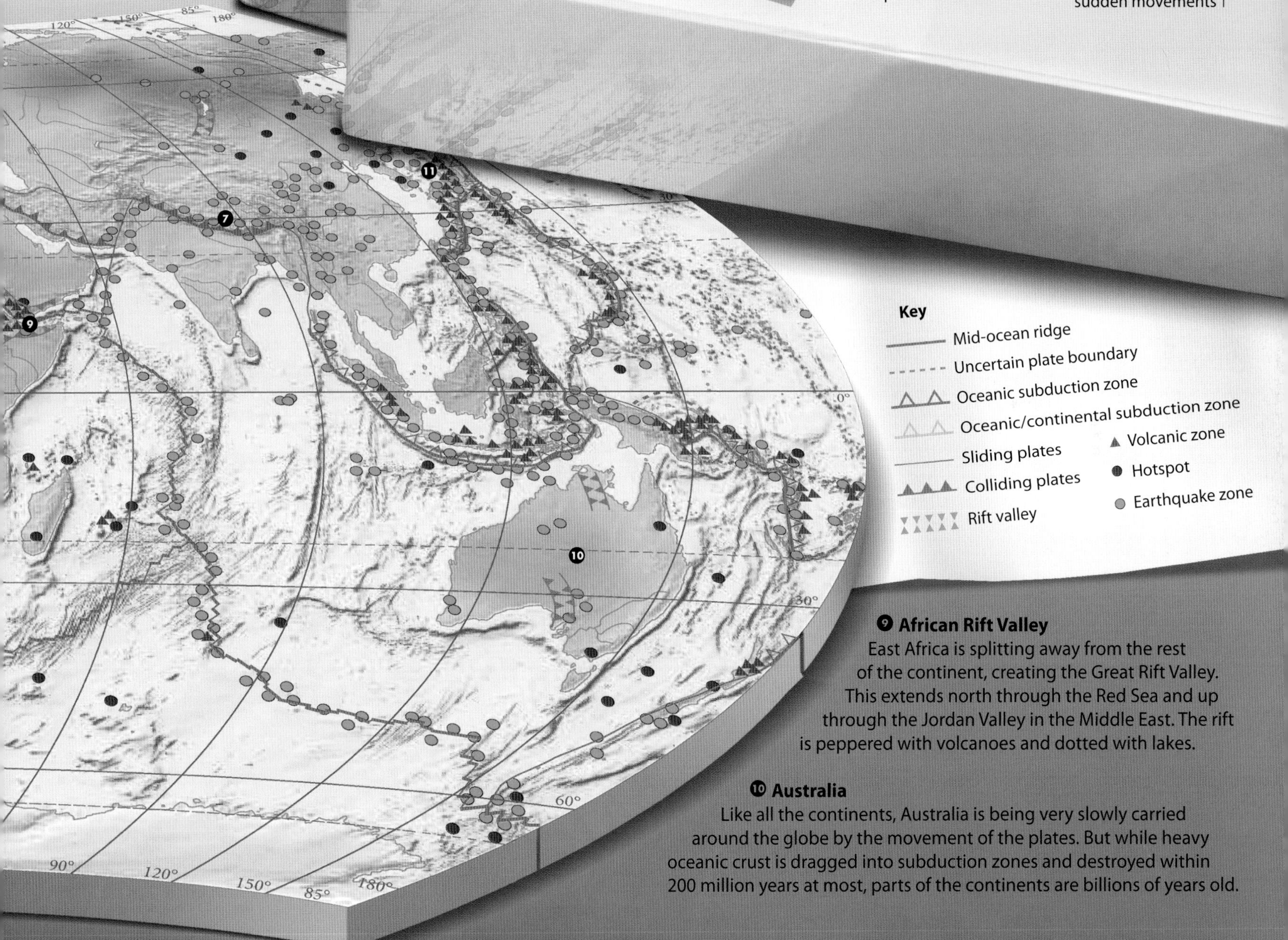

❾ African Rift Valley

East Africa is splitting away from the rest of the continent, creating the Great Rift Valley. This extends north through the Red Sea and up through the Jordan Valley in the Middle East. The rift is peppered with volcanoes and dotted with lakes.

❿ Australia

Like all the continents, Australia is being very slowly carried around the globe by the movement of the plates. But while heavy oceanic crust is dragged into subduction zones and destroyed within 200 million years at most, parts of the continents are billions of years old.

❼ Himalayas

The Indian Ocean floor is moving north towards Asia, carrying India with it. Continents do not slide beneath other continents as ocean floors do. Instead, the collision of India and Asia has created the vast crumple zone of the Himalayas and Tibetan plateau.

❽ Mediterranean

Once an ocean, the Mediterranean has been squeezed into a smaller sea by Africa moving north. This has pushed up the Alps, causes earthquakes in Turkey and Greece, and is responsible for volcanoes such as Vesuvius.

⓫ Japan Trench

Japan is regularly hit by earthquakes, caused mainly by the Pacific plate diving beneath Asia. Where it plunges down, it has formed the Japan Trench – part of a ring of ocean trenches that almost surrounds the Pacific.

CONTINENTAL DRIFT

As early as the 1600s, people noticed that the shapes of South America and Africa fitted together like two sections of a jigsaw. It looked as if they might have split apart to create the Atlantic Ocean, but such "continental drift" seemed impossible. In the 1960s, however, the development of plate tectonic theory showed that it was true. Ever since the continents started to grow from rock erupting from ocean floors, they have been carried around the globe by the mobile plates of Earth's crust. They have joined up, split apart, and crashed together again several times, forming many different arrangements – and they are still moving.

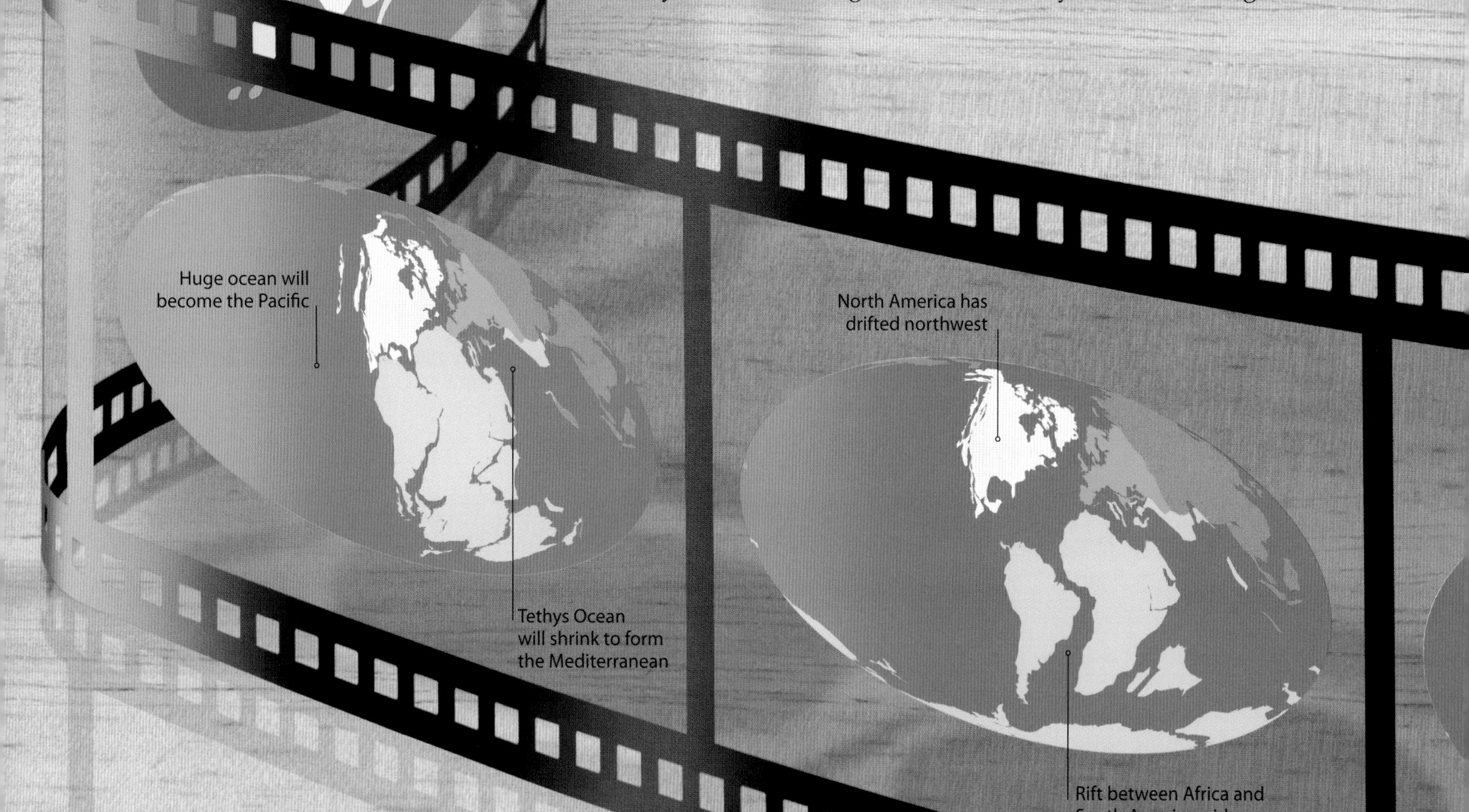

Huge ocean will become the Pacific
Tethys Ocean will shrink to form the Mediterranean
North America has drifted northwest
Rift between Africa and South America widens

▲170 MILLION YEARS AGO
In the Jurassic period, now famous for its dinosaurs, all the southern continents were joined together in a supercontinent known to geologists as Gondwanaland. We know this partly from the way they fit together along the edges of their submerged continental shelves. But the various rocks and rock layers on the coasts also match, and so do the fossils preserved in them. The fossils also give the supercontinent a date.

▲95 MILLION YEARS AGO
By the later age of the dinosaurs, giant rift valleys had split Gondwanaland into the continents we know today, although they were still quite close together. South America parted from Africa, and the mid-Atlantic opened up as North America drifted away towards the northwest. The split isolated animals and plants on their own continents, so they began to evolve in different ways.

▼45 MILLION YEARS AGO

By the early age of mammals, North America and Greenland had split from northern Europe and were moving west, so the Atlantic was getting steadily wider while the Pacific was shrinking. Meanwhile, India was drifting north towards Asia. Australia was isolated, along with the pouched mammals that evolved into the kangaroos, koalas, and other marsupials of today.

▼PRESENT DAY

About 20 million years ago, India collided with Asia and is still ploughing slowly north, pushing up the Himalayas. Some 3.5 million years ago, volcanoes erupting in the Caribbean region created a narrow neck of land linking the Americas, completely altering the pattern of ocean currents. Meanwhile, the northward movement of Africa has almost isolated the Mediterranean.

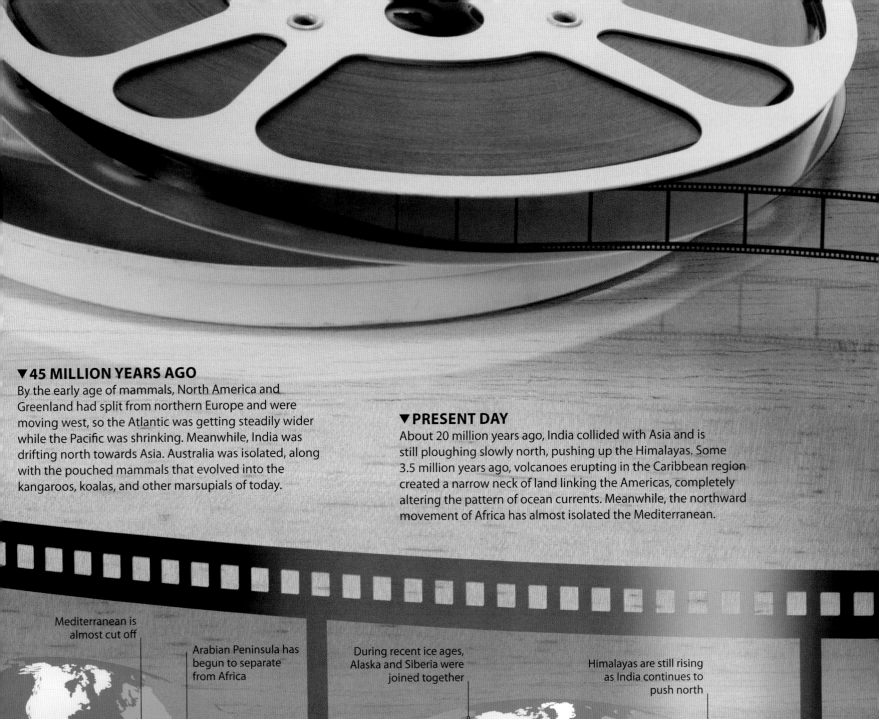

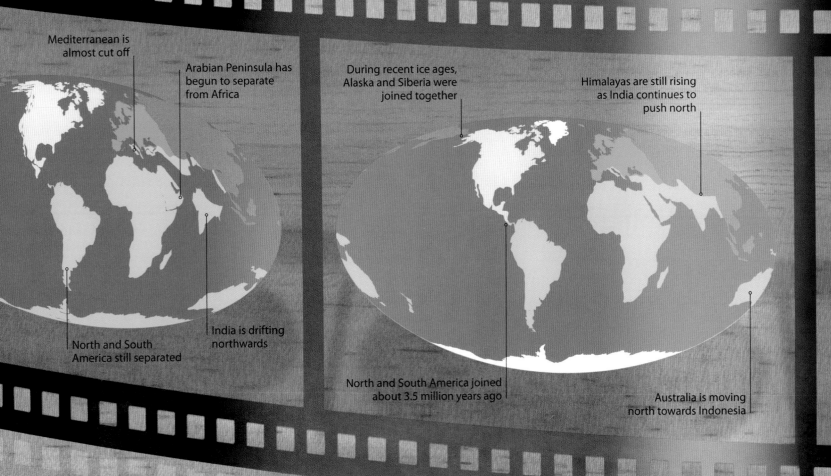

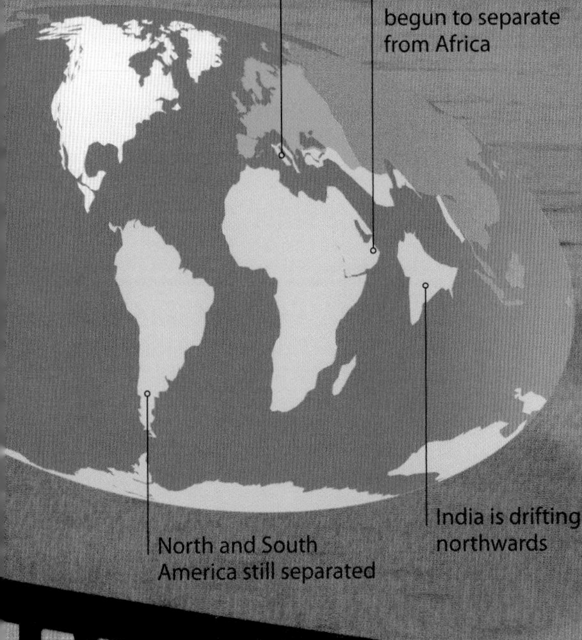
Mediterranean is almost cut off
Arabian Peninsula has begun to separate from Africa
North and South America still separated
India is drifting northwards

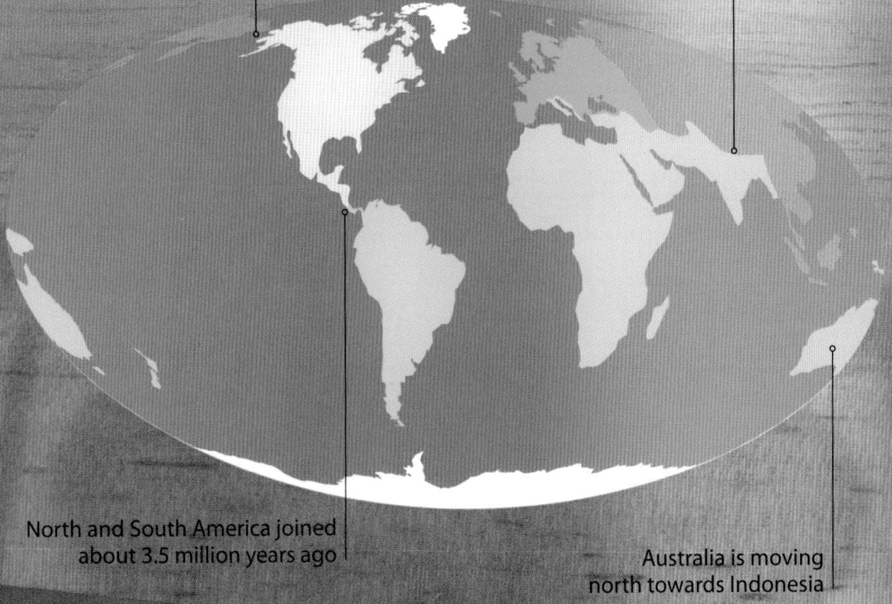
During recent ice ages, Alaska and Siberia were joined together
Himalayas are still rising as India continues to push north
North and South America joined about 3.5 million years ago
Australia is moving north towards Indonesia

MOUNTAINS

Built up by the titanic forces of plate tectonics folding or fracturing Earth's crust, mountains are spectacular evidence of our dynamic planet. The highest, most dramatic mountain ranges, such as the Himalayas, Alps, and Andes, are the youngest, and they are still in the process of being formed. But as fast as mountains are raised up, the forces of erosion start to grind them down, and all mountains are eventually worn away to nothing.

1 RUGGED PEAKS

The spectacular peaks of the Andes are less than 50 million years old, which is young by geological standards. Extending all the way down the western edge of South America, a distance of 7,200 km (4,500 miles), they form the longest mountain range on land. They are still being pushed up, but here in icy Patagonia they have been eroded by glaciers that have carved deep valleys between the peaks.

MOUNTAIN BUILDING

Most mountains are pushed up along the margins of continents, where one tectonic plate is colliding with another. Some, such as the Andes in South America, are forced up by a plate of oceanic crust ploughing beneath the continental fringe. Others, like the Himalayas, are crumple zones created by the collisions of continents. But mountains can also be formed by more complex forces, such as rifting (cracking apart) or molten rock pushing up from below.

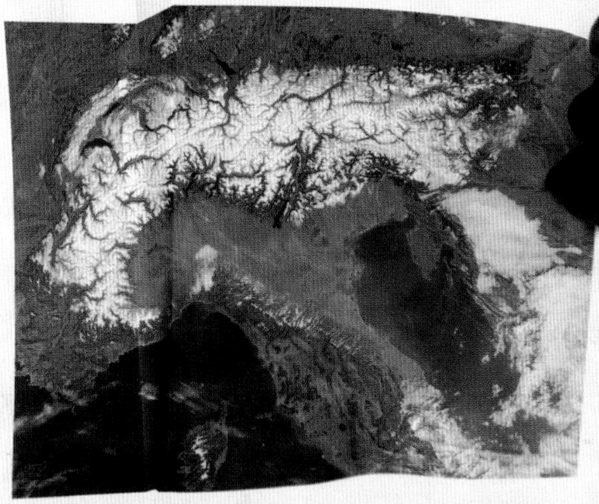

Fold mountains This satellite image of the snow-capped Alps shows the crumple zone created by Italy being pushed by the African plate into the rest of Europe. The process causes massive folding of layered sedimentary rocks that can turn the layers on end or even upside down. It may also raise ancient sea floors into the air, so marine fossils occur on mountain peaks.

Cliffs and plateaus
The steep slopes of the Drakensburg mountains in South Africa were created when a whole landscape was uplifted by molten rock pushing up beneath it. The rock also erupted from volcanoes to create thick lava flows that now form a high plateau, fringed to the east by dramatic cliffs.

❷ ANCIENT RANGES

Many ancient mountain ranges mark geological events in the distant past. The Caledonian mountains of Scotland were formed by a collision of continents more than 400 million years ago, along a tectonic plate boundary that no longer exists. The mountains were once as high as the Himalayas, but they have been worn down to form the heavily eroded landscape that now makes up the Scottish Highlands.

❸ ERODED STUMPS

Eventually all mountains are reduced to rounded stumps by the relentless forces of erosion. The Bungle Bungle range in northwestern Australia was once a high plateau formed from horizontal layers of sandstone. Over some 350 million years, the edge of the plateau has crumbled under the assault of torrential rain, blistering summer heat, and winter frosts to create these layered domes.

❹ MOUNTAIN WILDLIFE

The higher you go, the colder it gets, so being near the top of a high mountain on the equator is almost like being in the Arctic. The plants that live there have to be tough to survive, and at really high altitudes nothing can grow at all. Mountain animals like the snow leopard have thick fur coats to keep out the cold, and must be sure-footed to move confidently through the rugged and often frozen terrain.

❺ THIN AIR

For climbers, every mountain is a challenge. Climbing can involve not only the dangers of ascending steep, icy rock faces, but also the problem of surviving at high altitudes. It can be freezing cold, and the air on the highest peaks is so thin that there is barely enough oxygen to breathe. This makes climbing almost impossible, so many mountaineers are forced to wear breathing equipment.

Barren granite peaks are separated by steep valleys gouged out by ice
The Torres del Paine rise above the steppe in southern Chile
Iron oxide makes the layered sandstone glow rust-red
Suilven in northwest Scotland is the remains of a much bigger peak
2
3

FAULTS AND RIFTS

As plate tectonics squeeze and stretch Earth's crust, the rocks may snap. This causes the fracture lines known as faults. Vertical faults can form where one side of a fault plane has slipped down. Where plate boundaries are diverging, great blocks of crust drop between pairs of vertical faults to create rift valleys. Converging plates can heave one side of a fault upwards, or rock can be pushed sideways along a horizontal fault. Many visible faults are now inactive, but others are moving and causing earthquakes.

❶ VERTICAL FAULTS

Faults that incline vertically are caused by rocks being pulled apart or pushed together. Where layers of sedimentary rock are disrupted in this way, the displacement can be obvious. These sandstones near Canberra, Australia, have been drawn apart, allowing the rocks on the left of each fault to slip down the fault plane. The "bar-code" pattern of the layers allows the displacement to be measured precisely.

1
Fault plane cuts right through the various layers of rock

❷ FAULT PLANES

Most faults are visible only within rocks, but sometimes a fault plane is exposed like a cliff. This sheer precipice near Arkitsa in central Greece has been created by the rock on the far side of the fault being thrust vertically upwards over thousands of years, dwarfing the man at the bottom of the photo. The fault plane itself has vertical grooves etched into it by the relentless movement. These grooves are known as slickensides.

❸ SIDESLIP

If two slabs of Earth's crust slide past each other horizontally, they create faults that can be seen from the air as long lines across the landscape. The paler rock in this aerial view of a fault in Nevada, US, was once a continuous ridge, but it has been pushed to the left at the bottom of the image. The San Andreas Fault in California is another example of this fault type.

❹ RIFT VALLEYS

These steep cliffs are fault planes along one side of the African Rift Valley, a vast feature created by East Africa moving east away from the rest of the continent. This has allowed the central part of the valley – on the left of the picture – to sink into the Earth. On average the valley is 50 km (30 miles) wide, with cliffs marking the fault planes on each side.

Lake Baikal is 636 km (395 miles) long and 50 km (30 miles) wide

❺ RIFT VALLEY LAKES

Many rift valleys are filled with long, very deep lakes. They include Lake Baikal in Russia, which is the deepest lake on Earth and contains a fifth of the world's fresh water. The floor of the rift valley is as much as 1,741 m (5,716 ft) below the lake surface. It is peppered with hot springs that erupt volcanically heated water into the black depths near the lake bed.

❻ MID-OCEAN RIDGES

Immensely long rift valleys have formed where the plates of the Earth's crust are pulling apart on the ocean floors. This is a false-colour sonar image of the East Pacific Rise, showing showing two ridges of mountains (in red) with the rift valley in between. The ridges are created by lava erupting from fissures in the rift valley and heat making the rock of the ocean floor expand upward.

EARTHQUAKES AND TSUNAMIS

Earthquakes are caused by faults giving way under pressure from the movement of Earth's crust. If a fault slips easily, the earthquakes are quite small tremors. But if the rocks on each side of a fault lock together, pressure builds up, distorting the rocks until something snaps, releasing the energy suddenly and causing an earthquake. If this happens underwater, it generates a submarine shock wave that causes a tsunami.

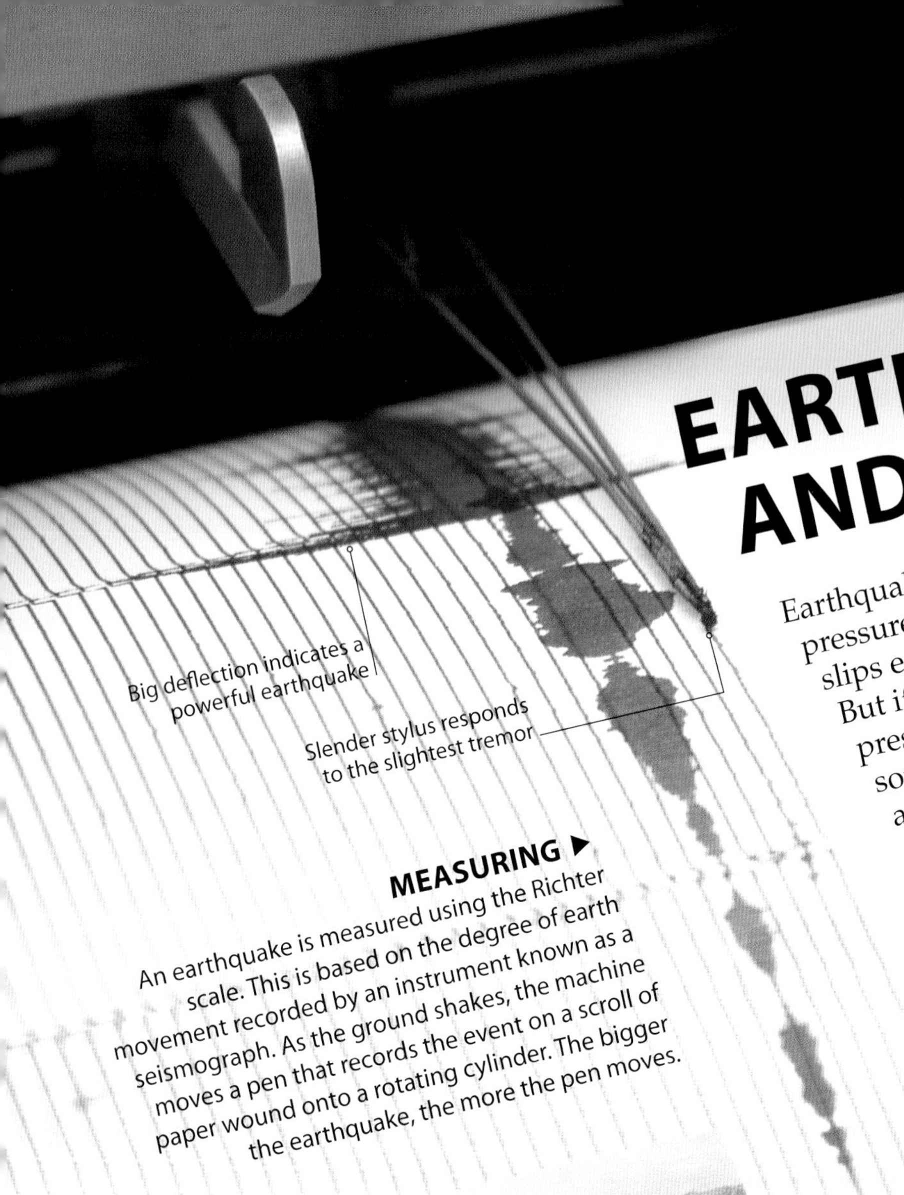

Big deflection indicates a powerful earthquake
Slender stylus responds to the slightest tremor

MEASURING ▶

An earthquake is measured using the Richter scale. This is based on the degree of earth movement recorded by an instrument known as a seismograph. As the ground shakes, the machine moves a pen that records the event on a scroll of paper wound onto a rotating cylinder. The bigger the earthquake, the more the pen moves.

▲GRADUAL SLIP

Many faults slip gently all the time. These include the central part of the San Andreas Fault in California, where the rocks creep past each other at up to 37 mm (1.5 in) a year without causing serious earthquakes. Other parts of the fault are locked, building up the tension that eventually makes something snap.

As plates grind past each other, energy is released
Plates separate and move along fault line
Shockwaves radiate from the earthquake's epicentre

▲SHOCK WAVE

The point where a locked fault snaps is called the epicentre. In this case, the rupture point is below ground on a laterally sliding fault, such as the San Andreas Fault in California. Shock waves radiate from the epicentre in the same way as the shock of an explosion radiates through the air, and can be just as destructive. The further the waves travel, the weaker they get, but they can often be detected on the other side of the world.

◀ GROUNDSHIFT

The fault movement that causes an earthquake is often deep underground, but sometimes it is very obviously on the surface. Here one side of a fault has moved up by well over 1 m (39 in). The strain would have been building up for decades, but when the fault finally gave way, all the movement would have occurred in a few seconds.

EARTHQUAKE CITY ▶

The city of San Francisco lies at the northern end of the San Andreas Fault, and suffers regular earth tremors. The last earthquake struck in 1989, destroying part of the elevated Nimitz Freeway and leading to the deaths of 63 people. But this was relatively mild compared to the massive earthquake that devastated San Francisco in 1906, and it is only a matter of time before another "big one" hits the city.

▲ CATASTROPHE

Earthquakes can have catastrophic effects on cities, especially those built of traditional materials such as bricks. As the ground shakes beneath it, a brick building collapses into a heap of rubble, burying anyone inside. Steel-framed buildings are much stronger, and often remain standing, as seen here in Japan after the Kobe earthquake of 1995.

▲ TSUNAMI

The Asian tsunami of late 2004 was caused by movement of a fault deep in the ocean off Sumatra, where the Indian Ocean floor is grinding beneath Indonesia. The movement built up immense tension that was released in the second most powerful earthquake ever recorded, generating huge waves that devastated this nearby coastline.

VOLCANOES

Volcanoes erupt in places where very hot rock deep below the surface has melted to form liquid magma. This happens where there are rising currents of heat beneath the crust, known as hotspots, and in places where the brittle crust is being pulled apart, reducing the intense pressure that keeps the hot rock solid. It also happens where one slab of crust is being dragged beneath another, along with water which lowers the melting point of the rock. The way the magma is formed affects its nature and how it erupts from volcanoes.

◀ASH CONES

Most volcanoes erupt above the subduction zones where one plate of crust is plunging beneath another. The magma formed in these zones is thick, sticky, and full of gas. It erupts explosively, blasting huge ash clouds high into the sky. The molten rock that erupts from the vent as lava is too viscous to flow far, so it builds up in layers, along with ash falling from the air, to form cone-shaped volcanoes.

MOLTEN RIVERS▶

The magma that forms above hotspots or beneath rifts in the crust is very liquid, almost like water. Any gas can escape easily, so although it can erupt in spectacular "fire fountains" it does not build up enough pressure to cause explosive eruptions. The molten rock that boils to the surface flows in rivers of liquid lava, like this one on Hawaii, that form very broad shield volcanoes.

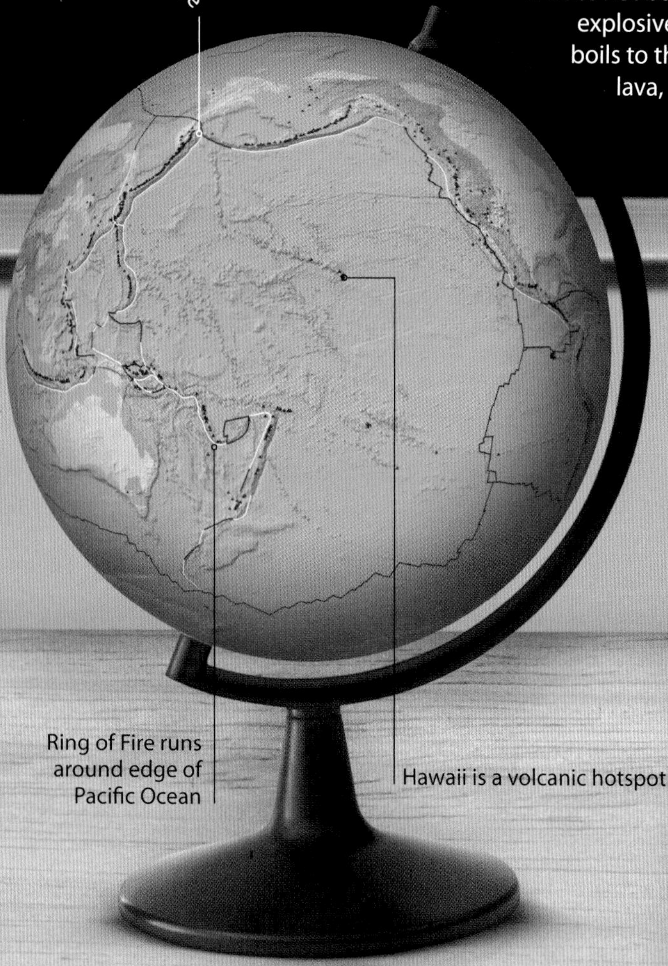
Aleutian Trench is part of the Pacific Ring of Fire
Ring of Fire runs around edge of Pacific Ocean
Hawaii is a volcanic hotspot

Magma chamber fills with molten rock from the base of the crust

▲RING OF FIRE

The Pacific Ocean is surrounded by a ring of more than 450 active volcanoes that have erupted from near deep ocean trenches. The ocean floor in the trenches is being destroyed as plates push together. The volcanoes of this "Ring of Fire" are explosive, erupting sticky lava and clouds of ash. But Hawaii in the middle of the ocean has been formed by hotspot volcanoes that erupt very liquid lava.

▲ANATOMY OF A VOLCANO

A typical volcano has a central crater fed by a magma chamber deep in the crust. The magma chamber forms first, in a place where rock has melted, and the magma melts a path though the rock above until it erupts as lava, gas, and ash. It can also push up through cracks to form secondary vents. The lava and rock debris that erupt from the crater build up to form the cone of the volcano.

▶ VOLCANIC EXPLOSIONS

Thick, viscous lava can block the vent of a volcano, and if gas pressure then builds up, the volcano may explode. A big eruption can also empty the magma chamber, so it collapses to form a vast super-crater or caldera. In 1650 BCE this happened at Santorini, Greece, seen here from space. Sea water pouring into the caldera then caused a cataclysmic explosion that destroyed the civilization on nearby Crete.

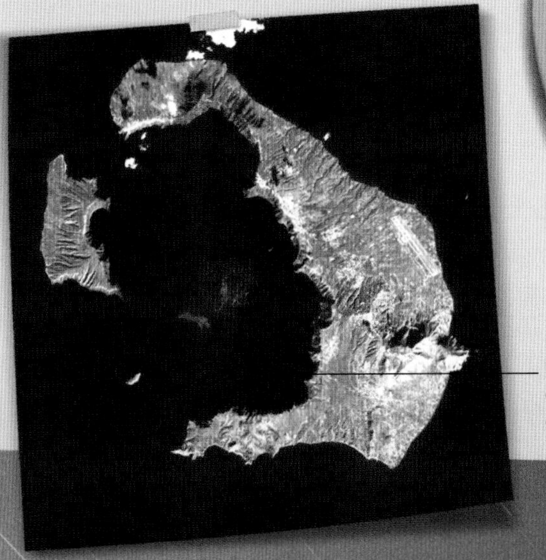

Modern volcano has erupted in the centre of the huge caldera

▲ PYROCLASTIC FLOWS

Some eruptions produce deadly avalanches of red-hot rock and dust known as pyroclastic flows. They surge over the landscape at high speed, and may travel much further than liquid lava. This is a small one, on Arenal in Costa Rica. In 1902, on Martinique in the Caribbean, a pyroclastic flow from Mont Pelée overwhelmed the city of St Pierre, killing 30,000 people in just two minutes.

Liquid lava

Wrinkled surface of pahoehoe lava shows it was very fluid

◀ LAVA

The very liquid lava that flows from hotspot volcanoes like those on Hawaii spreads out and solidifies as sheets of dark basalt. As it cools, movement often wrinkles the skin on the surface to create a rope-like effect known as pahoehoe – a Hawaiian word. More viscous lava tends to break up as it cools, forming blocks that resemble lumps of coal. The stickier the lava, the blockier it is, and the blocks often contain gas bubbles.

Less fluid lava forms tumbled blocks as it cools and solidifies

Blocky lava

VOLCANIC ERUPTIONS

Volcanoes are among the most powerful forces on the planet, and their eruptions can cause almost unimaginable destruction. Strangely, the most active volcanoes are often the least destructive, since they release their energy little by little, in a spectacular but often predictable way. The really dangerous volcanoes are the ones that appear to lie dormant for many years, but are really building up to something big. These are the volcanic eruptions that make history.

❷ KILAUEA

The most active volcano on Earth is Kilauea on Hawaii. It has been erupting continuously since 1983, ejecting huge quantities of gas and molten rock in spectacular fire fountains and rivers of liquid basalt lava. These pour down the flanks of the volcano towards the coast, where they spill into the ocean amid vast clouds of steam. In places the lava has solidified on top to form rocky tubes containing fast-flowing torrents of molten rock.

2

3

❶ MOUNT ETNA

Mount Etna on Sicily is Europe's biggest and most active volcano. It has a history of frequent eruptions dating back 2,500 years. It produces fast-flowing rivers of basalt lava that have destroyed villages and towns, notably in 1669 and 1928. It has also been the site of catastrophic explosions in the distant past.

1

❸ KRAKATAU

One of hundreds of volcanoes that form the islands of Indonesia, Krakatau is notorious for a cataclysmic eruption in 1883 that killed more than 36,000 people. The volcano exploded and then collapsed into a huge oceanic crater or caldera, generating tsunamis that engulfed the coasts of Java and Sumatra. The explosion was heard 4,800 km (3,000 miles) away, and is the loudest sound ever recorded.

❹ MOUNT ST HELENS

In May 1980, a colossal explosion blew the top off Mount St Helens in North America's Cascade mountains. The blast sent a plume of hot ash 24 km (15 miles) high into the sky and flattened 10 million trees. Fortunately, the volcano was being monitored by scientists who could see its flank visibly bulging as the pressure built up. Most of the area was evacuated before the explosion, and only 60 people died.

❺ SURTSEY

Iceland is a part of the Mid-Atlantic Ridge – the spreading volcanic rift that is making the Atlantic Ocean wider each year. Iceland has at least eight active volcanoes, and in 1963 a new volcano erupted from the rift to the south of the island, boiling out of the sea in a cloud of ash and steam. Named Surtsey, it carried on erupting until 1967. It has been dormant ever since, and is being gradually eroded away by the waves.

❻ VESUVIUS

In Roman times, Mount Vesuvius in Italy was thought to be extinct, but in the year 79 CE the volcano erupted violently, spilling deep layers of red-hot ash and debris over the nearby town of Pompeii. Many of the citizens managed to escape before the main eruption, but many more – including this dog – were overwhelmed and killed. The hollow casts left by their bodies were discovered as the city was being excavated in the 1860s.

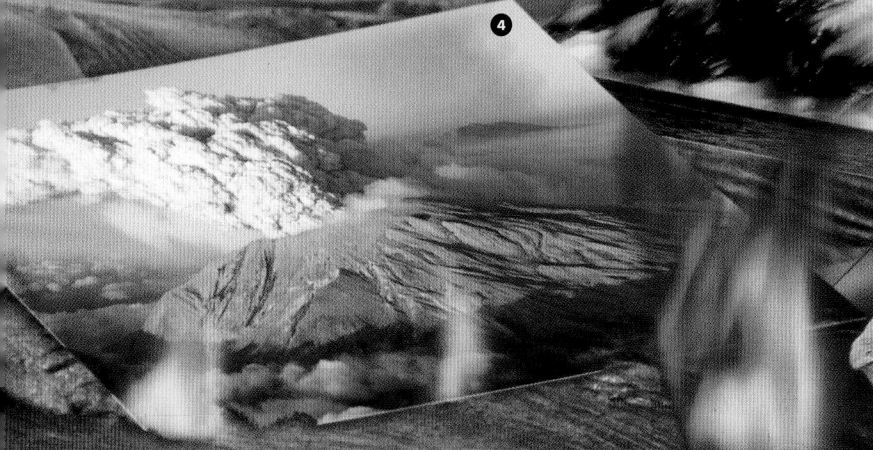

❼ OLYMPUS MONS

Volcanoes are not just found on planet Earth. Olympus Mons is a colossal volcano on Mars. It is 27 km (16.7 miles) high, which is more than twice the height of Mauna Kea, Earth's biggest volcano. It has the same shape as Mauna Kea and seems to have formed in the same way, from a hotspot beneath the crust

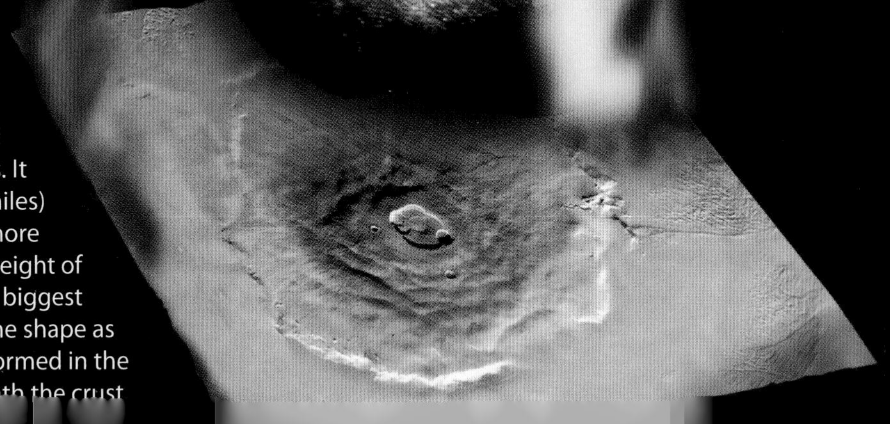

GEYSERS AND HOT SPRINGS

In some volcanic regions, water seeps down through the ground and comes into contact with very hot rock. It usually boils back up to the surface, but in some places the weight of water increases the pressure and stops the hot water turning to steam. Eventually some of the water is pushed up a flue and the pressure drops. This allows all the superheated water to turn to steam at once, blowing the remaining water out of the ground as a geyser.

Mineral terraces retain pools of hot water

▶FLY GEYSER

In 1916, a drilling operation in the Nevada desert, US, struck a source of boiling water, creating an artificial geyser. Decades later, the superheated water found another route to the surface to form a natural geyser, which now has several vents. Unlike most geysers it spouts hot water continuously, building up rocky pinnacles of mineral deposits.

Superheated water bursts up and turns to steam

▼OLD FAITHFUL

The most famous of about 200 geysers in the Yellowstone region of the United States, Old Faithful gets its name from the way it erupts, on average, every 67 minutes. Each eruption sends a jet of steam and hot water to heights of up to 55 m (180 ft). This exhausts its store of water, which takes another 67 minutes to refill and get hot enough to erupt again.

▼BOILING MUD

The hot water that creates geysers can also form hot pools of bubbling liquid mud. The mud pools shown here are at Rotorua in New Zealand, one of the world's most active geyser zones which, like Yellowstone in the United States, is part of a much larger area of simmering volcanic activity. Some 800 years ago Rotorua was the site of a colossal volcanic eruption, but it is now a flourishing tourist resort.

Terraces are built up from soluble calcite

▲EVAPORITE MINERALS

When water is superheated under pressure deep within the Earth, it often dissolves a lot of minerals from the rocks. If the water erupts from geysers or hot springs, evaporation and cooling turn the minerals solid again, and they form evaporites like these at Mammoth Hot Springs in Yellowstone. Every day the water adds some 2,000 kg (4,400 lb) of minerals to these terraces.

▼GEOTHERMAL ENERGY

The hot water that fuels geysers and hot springs can be harnessed as a source of energy. In Iceland and many other parts of the world the superheated water is used to drive electrical power plants. Reykjavik, the capital of Iceland, is heated by this hot water, and the city even has geothermally heated open-air swimming pools.

Up to 250 macaques use the hot pools

▼HOT SPRINGS

At Yamanouchi near Nagano in central Japan, steaming hot springs feed a series of pools high in the snowy mountains. The water stays at about 50°C (122°F), and in the 1960s local Japanese macaques – or snow monkeys – discovered that bathing in the pools was an ideal way of keeping warm in a climate where the winter temperature can drop to a bone-chilling -15°C (5°F].

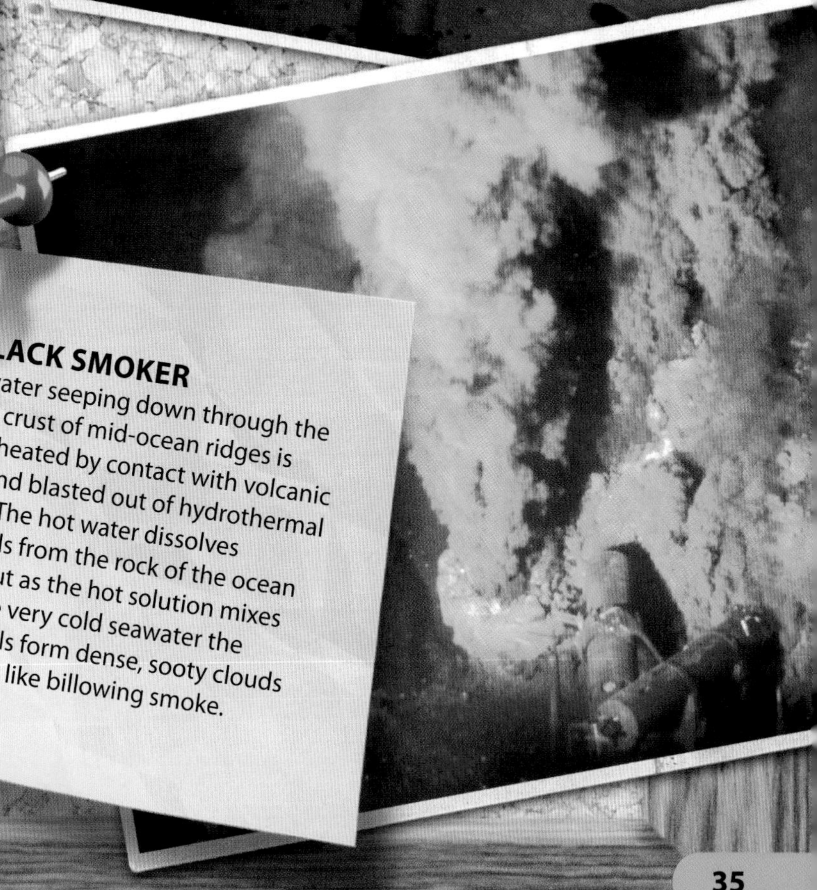

▶BLACK SMOKER

Seawater seeping down through the rifted crust of mid-ocean ridges is superheated by contact with volcanic rock and blasted out of hydrothermal vents. The hot water dissolves minerals from the rock of the ocean floor, but as the hot solution mixes with the very cold seawater the chemicals form dense, sooty clouds that look like billowing smoke.

ROCKY WAVE
At Vermilion Cliffs in Arizona, US, ancient desert dunes that hardened into solid rock have been carved into fantastic shapes by the erosive power of the wind. The rocks are at least 165 million years old.

Rocks and minerals

MINERALS AND GEMSTONES

Minerals are the natural solid substances that form rocks. A few consist of just one element, in which all the atoms are the same. They include diamond, a form of pure carbon. But most of the 4,000 or more known minerals are compounds of two or more elements. Quartz, for example, is a compound of silicon and oxygen. Most minerals can form crystals – natural geometric shapes that reflect the way their atoms are bonded together. The crystals of some minerals are cut and polished into valuable gems.

Halite can be tinted by impurities
Quartz can form big, six-sided, pyramidal crystals
1
2
3
Olivine is named for its olive colour
Graphite
Rough diamond looks like glass
4
Diamond
5
6
Sulphur crystals form as sulphurous water evaporates
Calcite crystals may be transparent or opaque

❶ HALITE

Often known as rock salt, halite is the same mineral as the salt used in cooking – a compound of sodium and chlorine. Halite deposits found deep underground were created by the evaporation of salt water in ancient oceans. It forms cubic crystals that can often be found in coarse-ground table salt, and is colourless when pure.

❷ QUARTZ

The most abundant mineral on Earth's surface, quartz is one of the main ingredients of granite and similar hard rocks that have formed from molten magma. When these rocks are broken down by erosion, the tough quartz crystals tend to survive as sand grains, and these are used to make glass. Various coloured forms of quartz, such as purple amethyst, are valuable gemstones.

❸ OLIVINE

Like quartz, olivine is a mineral based on silica – the compound of silicon and oxygen that is the basis of most rocks – but it also contains iron and magnesium. It is more abundant than quartz, but mostly below the crust because it is the main ingredient of the peridotite rock that forms much of the planet's deep mantle. Olivine crystals are usually green, as seen here.

❹ DIAMOND AND GRAPHITE

Although they are both pure carbon, diamond and graphite are physically quite different. Diamond is the hardest of all minerals and a valuable gemstone, while graphite is the soft, streaky mineral used to make pencils. The difference is due to the way diamond has a very strong atomic structure, while the atoms of graphite are arranged in layers.

❺ SULPHUR

Most frequently found as deposits around volcanic craters and hot springs, pure sulphur is a soft, usually bright yellow mineral. It consists of just one type of atom, but it combines with other elements such as iron and oxygen to form compounds such as pyrite and sulphur dioxide. It is an important ingredient of many artificial chemicals.

❻ CALCITE

Another of the most common minerals, calcite is the main ingredient of limestones. These are usually formed from the shells or skeletons of marine organisms, which absorb the mineral from seawater. Calcite is easily dissolved by slightly acidic rainwater, but recrystallizes in a variety of forms.

❼ BERYL

The main source of beryllium, one of the lightest metals, beryl is better known for its big prismatic crystals. These are cut into gemstones that have different names depending on their colour, such as deep green emerald and pale blue-green aquamarine. Some beryl crystals are very big – an aquamarine found in Brazil in 1910 weighed 110.5 kg (243 lb).

❿ FELDSPAR

Big, colourful feldspar crystals are a conspicuous part of many types of granite, and can often be seen in the polished granite slabs used in architecture. The crystals often show a feature called twinning, where the crystal structure is symmetrical with a clear centreline. Feldspar can contain a variety of elements depending on how it formed, but it always contains aluminium and silicon.

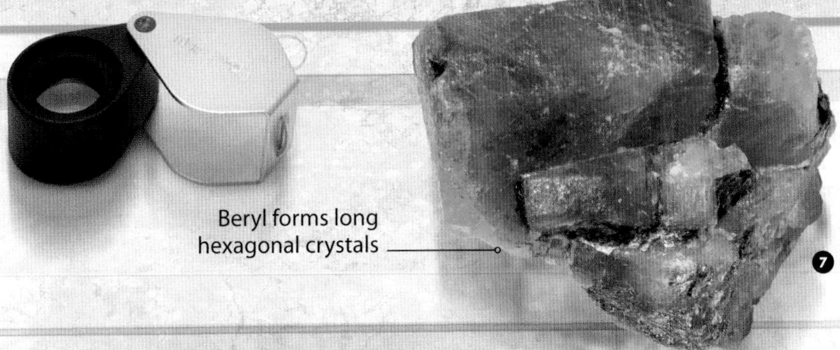
Beryl forms long hexagonal crystals
7

Mica crystals can be split into thinner sheets
11

❽ ZIRCON

Similar to diamonds and often used as gemstones, zircon crystals are extremely hard and resistant to erosion. As a result, they survive when other minerals are destroyed. Some Australian zircon crystals have been radiometrically dated to 4.2 billion years ago, which is almost as old as Earth and older than any other known substance on the planet.

Zircon is is often purplish brown
8

⓫ MICA

A major ingredient of granite and similar rocks, mica has an unusually complex chemical make-up and forms strange flat, flaky crystals with six sides. These can be astonishingly big – one crystal found in eastern Russia had an area of 5 sq m (54 sq ft). Mica has a high melting point, and thin, transparent sheets of it are sometimes used as furnace windows.

Pyroxene often occurs in massive form, without obvious crystals
9

Pink feldspar is also called orthoclase
10

Talc is usually non-crystalline
12

❾ PYROXENE

One of the most important rock-forming minerals, pyroxene is a major ingredient of ocean-floor rocks such as basalt. It can contain a variety of metallic elements such as iron, magnesium, or titanium, but always in combination with silicon and oxygen. One form, jadeite, is very strong and was once used to make polished axe blades.

⓬ TALC

The softest mineral, easily scratched by a fingernail, talc is sometimes known as soapstone because of its soapy feel. It is used for decorative carvings and ground into talcum powder, but its main use is in the manufacture of heat-resistant ceramics such as cookware, and in papermaking.

Lightweight drinks cans are made of aluminium alloy
Sphalerite is a compound of zinc, iron, and sulphur
Many wristwatches have cases made of tough titanium
1
2
Car battery
Galena is a very heavy mineral
Garnierite can be up to 40 per cent nickel, but is quite rare
Iron is derived from iron oxide, which is the same as rust
4
5
6
Most copper is refined from ores such as chalcopyrite
Pure gold may occur embedded in minerals such as quartz
Cinnabar is a very heavy, deep red compound of mercury and sulphur
8
9
10
Refined mercury melts at -39°C (-38°F), so it rarely occurs in solid form

METALS

Apart from artificial alloys, all metals are elements – substances that contain just one type of atom. Some, such as gold and silver, are naturally found in this pure "native" form, but most metals occur as more complex minerals known as ores. Iron, for example, is usually obtained from compounds of iron and oxygen called iron oxides. Once purified, metals have the tough, workable nature that makes them such useful materials. They also conduct heat and electricity well, making them vital to modern technology.

3
Tin is alloyed with lead to make solder – vital to all electric circuits
7
Native silver occurs in branching or wiry form in mineral veins
11

❶ **Aluminium** Very light, aluminium conducts electricity well and does not corrode easily. It is rather soft in pure form, so it is combined with other metals to make tougher alloys for use where light weight is vital, as in aircraft. Aluminium is obtained from a complex but abundant ore called bauxite.

❷ **Zinc** Usually obtained from an ore called sphalerite, this white metal is widely used as a rust-proof coating for steel – a plating process known as galvanizing. It is also alloyed with copper to make brass, the shiny yellow metal that is widely used to make door handles and decorative metalwork.

❸ **Titanium** Like aluminium, this is a very lightweight metal – but it is harder and much stronger. It is also much rarer, so it is usually combined with other metals to make the tough, yet light alloys used in aircraft and spacecraft. Its main ore is a compound of oxygen and titanium called rutile.

❹ **Lead** Very heavy, and with a low melting point, lead is also very soft and easy to work. It has been used to make all kinds of things, from Roman water pipes to modern lead-acid car batteries. The main ore is a compound of lead and sulphur called galena.

❺ **Nickel** This metal probably forms about a fifth of Earth's inner core, the rest being iron. At the surface, it occurs in the form of complex ores such as garnierite. Iron and nickel are combined to make strong, corrosion-proof stainless steel, one of the most useful alloys.

❻ **Iron** Forming most of Earth's core and very common in rocks and soils, iron is the most abundant metal on the planet. It is a very important material because of its hardness, even though it is brittle and corrodes badly. Iron is refined into steel, which is springy and easier to work.

❼ **Tin** About 4,000 years ago, early metal-workers discovered that mixing a small amount of molten tin with molten copper made a much stronger alloy, bronze. They obtained the tin by heating ores such as greenish cassiterite to about 1,000°C (1,800°F) in a charcoal furnace.

❽ **Copper** This was one of the first metals to be used by humankind, from about 7,000 years ago. This is because, like gold, it can be found in its native form. An excellent conductor of electricity, it is widely used in the form of copper wire.

❾ **Gold** Since gold does not easily combine with any other element, it is usually found as gleaming nuggets or grains. This also means that it does not tarnish, a fact that – combined with its rarity – has always made it valuable. Although very heavy, it can be beaten into very thin sheets.

❿ **Mercury** The only metal that is liquid at room temperature, mercury is obtained from a colourful ore called cinnabar. The metal is best known for its use in medical thermometers, but it is also used to make batteries, electronic components, and the silvery backing of glass mirrors.

⓫ **Silver** Like gold, silver is a rare metal that is soft, easy to work, and found in its native form – all qualities that have made it highly valued for thousands of years. Unlike gold, it tarnishes, but it is very attractive when polished.

IGNEOUS ROCKS

Igneous rocks form from molten mixtures of minerals that erupt from deep within the Earth as magma or volcanic lava. As the minerals cool, they form interlocking crystals, giving the resulting rocks their strength. Some minerals are heavier than others, or melt at higher temperatures, so they tend to get left behind when the molten rock wells up. This means that an igneous rock is rarely the same as its parent rock, and usually lighter. The process has created a wide variety of rocks from the same raw material.

❶ PERIDOTITE

This is the rock that forms much of the deep mantle beneath the crust, and therefore 80 per cent of the planet. It is rare on the surface, occurring in places where major earth movements have squeezed it up from beneath the ocean floor. It is very heavy and mainly consists of dark green olivine, rich in magnesium and iron.

❷ BASALT

Dark, dense basalt forms the bedrock of the ocean floors. It erupts from the spreading rifts of mid-ocean ridges, and also from hotspot volcanoes like those on Hawaii. It is created by partial melting of peridotite in the mantle, to form a very fluid lava that contains far less of the heavy, greenish olivine that is such an important ingredient of peridotite. This makes basalt lighter, too.

❸ ANDESITE

Named after the Andes of South America, where it is abundant, andesite is solidified volcanic lava that has erupted from deep below the mountains. Here, basalt ocean floor is being dragged beneath the continent and is melting. The molten rock that rises to the surface contains fewer heavy minerals than basalt, so andesite is a lighter rock. It is one of the main rocks that form continents.

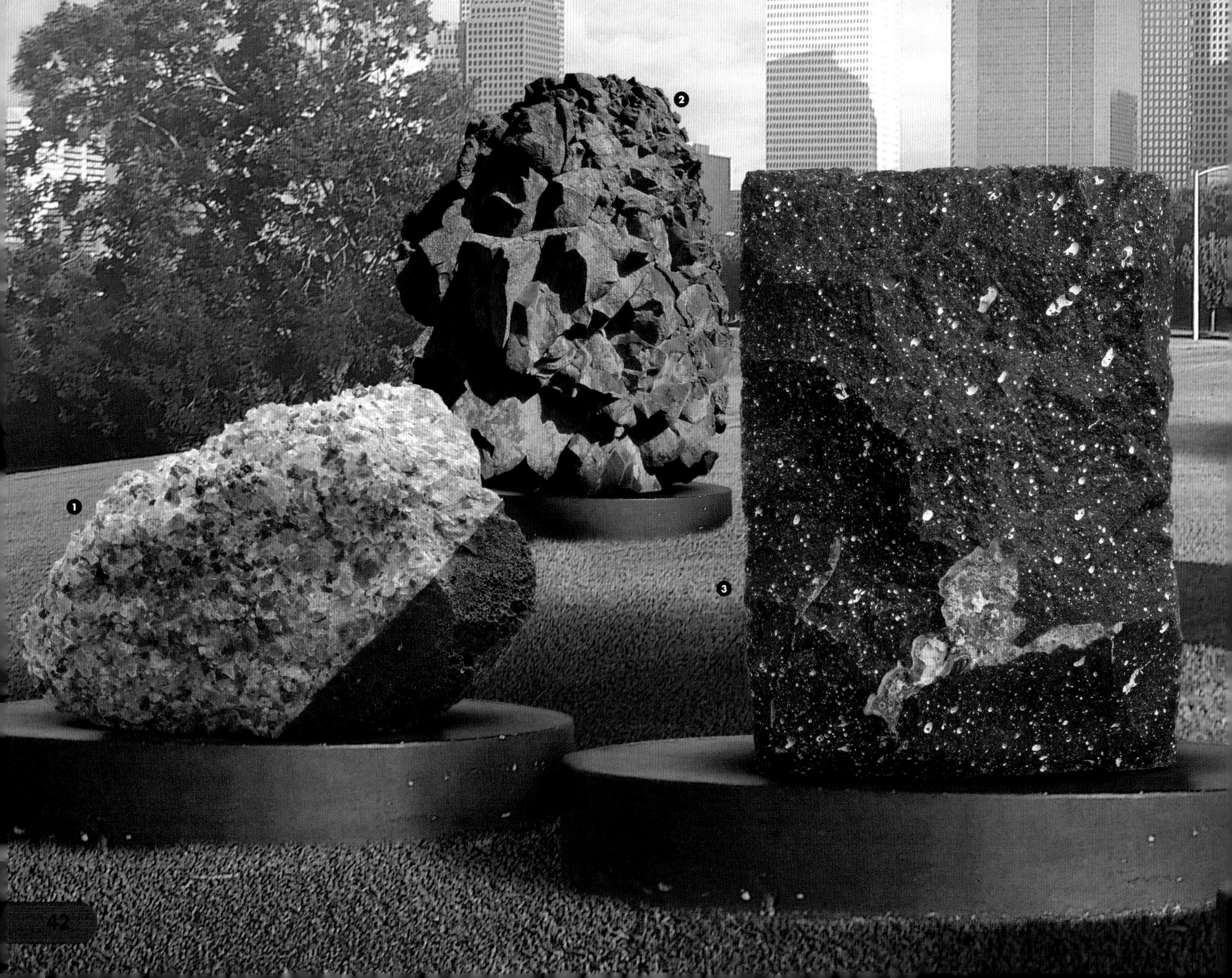

❹ GRANITE

All rocks contain silica – the substance that we use to make glass. This can form relatively light minerals that melt at much lower temperatures than the heavy minerals in rocks like basalt. As the rocks beneath continents are heated, the silicate minerals may form sticky magma that rises and then cools, turning into relatively light but very hard granite. It is mostly pale feldspar and quartz, with very little dark, heavy material.

❺ RHYOLITE

The magma that becomes granite usually cools deep in the crust. This takes a very long time, allowing big crystals to grow and form the granite. But if the magma reaches the surface it erupts as very viscous lava that cools quickly into fine-grained rhyolite. The only difference between the two rocks is their crystal size. In the same way, basalt that cools deep in the crust forms a coarse-grained rock called gabbro.

❼ PUMICE

The lava erupted from volcanoes often contains a lot of gas. The gas usually boils out of very liquid basalt lava quite easily, but has more difficulty escaping from much stickier silica-rich lava such as rhyolite. If the rock then solidifies with the gas bubbles still inside, it forms pumice. This has much the same structure as plastic foam, and is so light that it floats on water.

❻ OBSIDIAN

Obsidian is volcanic lava that has cooled too fast for crystals to form. It can be created from any type of lava, but usually has the same mineral composition as rhyolite or granite. When it breaks it has a rippling fracture pattern like that of flint or glass, and equally sharp edges, so like flint it was used to make stone tools in the past. Always very dark, it has also been used as a gemstone.

Rhyolite crystals are too small to be seen with the naked eye
Bubbles of volcanic gas form a frothy lava that turns into pumice
4
5
6
7

IGNEOUS INTRUSIONS

As molten rock forms deep in the crust, it forces its way up through cracks or as big molten masses. The viscous magma that forms granite usually starts solidifying deep below the surface to create massive igneous intrusions called batholiths. Over millions of years, the rock above may wear away to expose these as granite mountains. More fluid types of lava tend to harden in cracks to form dykes, or force their way between rock layers to create sills. Lava can also harden in the core of an extinct volcano, to be exposed by erosion as a volcanic plug.

▼GRANITE BATHOLITHS

The rounded mass of Sugar Loaf Mountain in Rio de Janeiro, Brazil, is just part of a huge granite batholith that lies beneath the city. Originally formed deep in the crust, the granite is much harder than the surrounding rocks, which is why it has survived the erosion that has worn those other rocks away. A similar batholith forms the mountains of the Sierra Nevada in California, US.

Hard igneous intrusion forms a rocky wall
Granite of Sugar Loaf Mountain is 800 million years old

◀ DYKES

If molten rock forces its way up through vertical cracks, it forms slabs of igneous rock called dykes. Since they cool much more quickly than big igneous intrusions, the rock has much smaller crystals and is very fine-grained. In places, such dykes form rings around ancient volcanic craters, having formed in circular cracks created by the collapse of the volcano.

▼ FLOOD BASALTS

The Deccan Traps are sheets of basalt more than 2 km (1.2 miles) thick that cover 500,000 sq km (190,000 sq miles) of central India. They are igneous extrusions rather than intrusions, because they were formed by enormous outpourings of molten basalt that solidified in the layers visible in these cliffs. They erupted some 65 million years ago, at exactly the same time as the dinosaurs became extinct, and the two events may be connected.

▶ VOLCANIC PLUGS

The magma chambers that lie beneath volcanoes can harden in the same way as granite batholiths when the volcanoes are extinct. If the softer rock above then wears away, the hardened magma is revealed as a volcanic plug. The Devil's Tower in Wyoming, US, formed like this. As it cooled, the rock shrank and fractured into the vertical columns that give it such a dramatic appearance.

Long cooling cracks form many-sided columns
Cliffs expose layers of basalt

SILLS ▶

If molten rock intrudes between two layers of sedimentary rock, the result is a sill. It may form at any angle, depending on the slope of the rock layers. The Whin Sill in Britain is a sheet of coarse basalt some 30 m (100 ft) thick that lies at a slight angle. This exposes its edge, which has vertical joints like those of the Devil's Tower. The Romans used it as the basis for Hadrian's Wall, marking the northern frontier of their empire.

◀DISSOLVING LIMESTONE
Rainwater dissolves carbon dioxide from the air to become weak carbonic acid. This attacks most rocks, but particularly limestones. The water enlarges cracks to create flat, fissured (grooved) limestone pavements and caves. In the Chinese Guilin Hills, vast amounts of limestone have been dissolved completely, leaving these isolated pinnacles.

WEATHERING AND EROSION

As soon as solid rock is exposed to the air, it starts being attacked by the weather. It is baked by the sun, shattered by frost, and dissolved by rainwater, which is naturally slightly acid. Meanwhile it may be scoured by wind-blown sand, and by rock fragments carried by flowing water and ice. By degrees, the weathered rock is worn away – a process known as erosion. This affects all exposed rock, however it was formed, although hard rock is more resistant and often survives when softer rock has been eroded away.

▼PLANT POWER
Living things play a big part in breaking down rocks. The roots of trees like these can penetrate cracks in rocks and force them apart. The lichens that grow on rocks produce acids that help dissolve the minerals. Microorganisms living in the soil and even within some rocks also contribute to rock decay, turning their minerals into other forms.

WADIS AND CANYONS▼
Rare but violent rainstorms in deserts cause flash floods that pour over the bare rock in torrents, carving gullies known as wadis, arroyos, or slot canyons. The water is loaded with sand, stones, and boulders that, over thousands of years, erode the rock into fantastic shapes like these at Antelope Canyon in the United States.

▲EXFOLIATION
Rocks such as granite are formed deep underground under extreme heat and pressure. When they are exposed to the air, they cool and shrink as the pressure is released. This can make layers of rock split away like onion skin – a process called exfoliation that is accelerated by hot days and cold nights.

◄FROST-SHATTERING
In cold climates and at high altitudes, water seeping into cracks and crevices freezes at night, expanding as it turns to ice. This exerts enormous pressure on the rock, pushing it apart. Repeated freezing and thawing can shatter the rock, creating drifts of rubble known as scree that build steep slopes at the foot of the frost-shattered cliffs.

MESAS AND BUTTES ▼
Monument Valley in the western United States is a landscape of isolated plateaus and pinnacles called mesas and buttes. They were created over millions of years by desert flash floods pouring over barren land that was being pushed up by earth movements. Most of the surface was eroded away, leaving these towering "monuments".

Sheer cliffs of this mesa (plateau) reveal horizontal rock layers

▲SAND-BLASTING
In desert zones, where there are few plants to bind the soil together, the wind picks up sand grains and hurls them at exposed rocks. The sand enlarges any fissures, but may also smooth the rock surface into swooping curves like these at Coyote Buttes in the United States. The curved lines mark ancient rock layers.

◄BREAKING WAVES
On exposed coasts, big waves smash into the rock and penetrate any cracks, exerting tremendous hydraulic pressure that can blow the rock apart. Rocky debris picked up by the waves completes the demolition job. As these mushroom-shaped Pacific islands show, all the active erosion happens at wave level, undercutting the rock and eventually causing it to collapse into the sea.

TRANSPORT AND DEPOSITION

The debris eroded from exposed rock is swept away by flowing water and wind, either by rolling and bumping it along or, if the particles are small enough, carrying them along in suspension. As the flow of water in a river slows down, it drops the heavier particles but keeps moving the lighter ones. This usually means that the particles are deposited in order of size. The lightest grains of silt and mud end up in sheltered places where the flow is slowest.

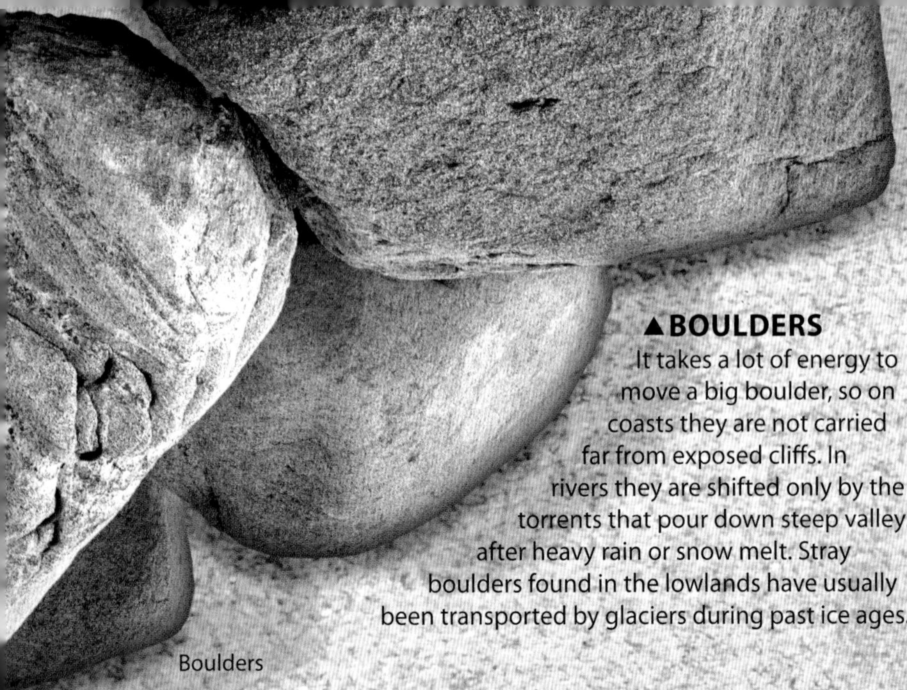

▲BOULDERS
It takes a lot of energy to move a big boulder, so on coasts they are not carried far from exposed cliffs. In rivers they are shifted only by the torrents that pour down steep valleys after heavy rain or snow melt. Stray boulders found in the lowlands have usually been transported by glaciers during past ice ages.

▲COBBLES
Over the years, boulders break up into smaller, lighter stones that can be bounced around by water currents and carried much further. The rolling and tumbling caused by the flowing water knocks the corners off the stones to create rounded cobbles and even smaller pieces of shingle.

▶GRAVEL BEDS
Many upland rivers swell to torrents when the snow melts in spring. The rushing water transports masses of small stones, then drops them in quieter stretches as gravel beds. These are also found in lowland areas that experienced torrents of meltwater during ice ages.

▲SANDY BEACHES
Exposed rocky headlands on coasts are often interspersed with bays containing sandy beaches. The sand is all that is left of solid rock that has been shattered by the waves. Currents sweep the sand into the sheltered bays and then drop it because the water is not moving so vigorously.

◀WIND-BLOWN DUST

Strong winds can pick up fine dust and carry it over great distances before dumping it to form beds of fine-grained sediment called loess. The most famous are in northern China, where thick deposits of yellow loess form the basis of fertile farmland. But it erodes easily, and the Yellow River is named for the heavy load of loess that it carries into the Yellow Sea.

▲SAND DUNES

The wind can build dry sand into immense dunes, both on coasts and in deserts. It bounces the sand grains up the windward slope of each dune so they roll over the crest, and by degrees the dune creeps downwind. On coasts, dunes stabilize as they move inland, but new ones keep forming. Desert dunes may keep moving for thousands of years, forming vast "sand seas" in regions such as Arabia.

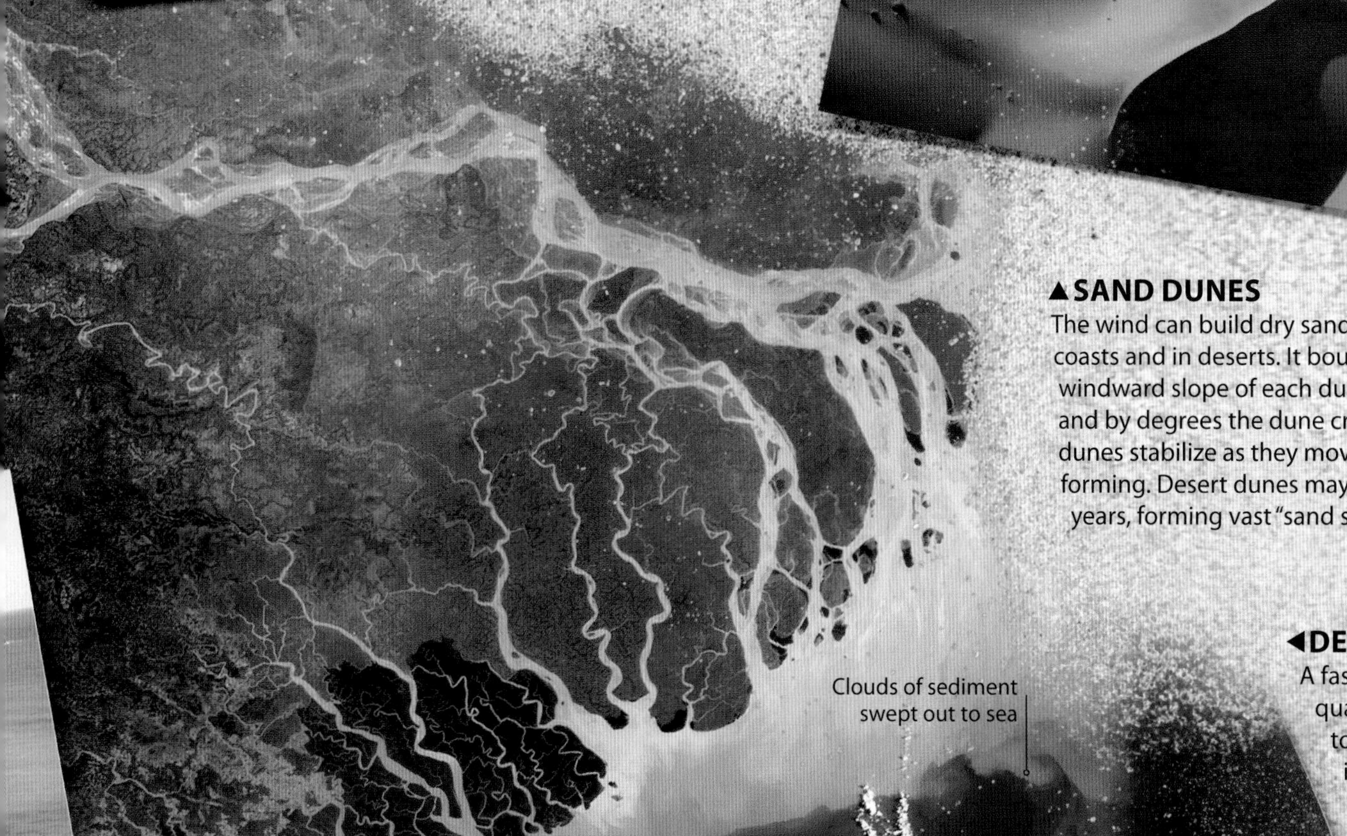

◀DELTAS AND FANS

A fast-flowing river can carry huge quantities of sediment right down to the sea. Here the river loses its energy, so the sediment falls to the sea bed and creates a deep submarine fan, so heavy that its weight can distort Earth's crust. Meanwhile the river mouth migrates seawards over the top of the fan to form a low-lying delta with many channels, as seen in this satellite view of the Ganges Delta in Bangladesh.

◀MUDDY ESTUARIES

When slow-flowing rivers approach the coast, any fine particles suspended in the water settle to form thick layers of mud in the tidal lower reaches. This is partly because rising tides stop the river flow, but salt water also makes the mud particles clump together and become heavier, making them sink. The mudflats are exposed at low tide, when the sea water drains away.

Clay is on the borderline between a soft sediment and a true rock
Shale beds have been tilted by earth movements
1
2
3
4
5
Layers indicate different episodes of evaporation
Rusty colour of this sandstone is due to iron oxide

1 CLAY

Clay is the softest of rocks, created from tiny flakes of minerals released by the weathering of hard rocks such as granite. The flakes combine with at least 17 per cent water. In this condition clay feels dry and brittle, but if it absorbs more water it becomes sticky. Heating clay in a kiln drives off the water and turns it into a stony form.

2 SHALE

Clay particles that settle in deep, still water form layers of mud. Over time the weight of more sediment drives out the water, turning the mud to shale. This is a relatively soft rock that splits easily along the boundaries between the original layers. Scientists can expose fossils in shale by prising the layers apart with a chisel.

3 CONGLOMERATE

Most sedimentary rocks are made of small rock fragments or mineral grains, but conglomerate consists of big pebbles that have been cemented together. The rounded pebbles were once transported by water, and they are often the remains of an ancient beach. A similar rock, breccia, is made of sharp-edged stones once carried by ice.

4 EVAPORITES

These rocks are formed by the evaporation of water that contains a lot of dissolved minerals. As the water vapour is driven off, the minerals stay behind. Evaporating seawater, for example, can leave thick salt deposits, which may then be buried and compressed into rock salt.

5 SANDSTONES

Some of the most recognizable sedimentary rocks are sandstones, which are made of cemented sand grains. Some were formed underwater. Others are fossilized desert sand dunes, and are built up from sand grains that were rounded and "frosted" by wind erosion in the distant past. Some sandstones crumble easily into separate grains but others, such as the sarsen stones of Stonehenge in Britain, are very hard.

SEDIMENTARY ROCKS

Sediments carried by water or wind may build up in deep layers, either on land or more commonly on the sea bed. As more material is added, its weight compresses the lower layers. Over millions of years minerals dissolved in seawater or groundwater cement the compressed grains of sediment together to form sedimentary rocks. Most of these are made of rock debris, but typical limestones consist of the skeletons and shells of marine organisms, while coal is made of the remains of long-dead plants.

Sandstone is made up of grains of hard quartz
Limestone often has a jointed, blocky look
6
7
8

❻ LIMESTONE

Marine organisms absorb dissolved chalky minerals from seawater and use them to build their skeletons and shells. When they die the chalky, calcareous material survives decay and builds up in layers on the sea bed. Over time, the layers may be compressed into chalk or limestone, which often contains visible shell fragments.

❼ FLINT

Chalk is a soft white limestone made of the calcareous skeletons of countless microscopic marine organisms that lived roughly 100 million years ago in a shallow tropical sea. It often contains nodules of hard black flint, which probably formed from the glassy skeletons of other organisms such as sponges. Flint is very like glass, fracturing to produce razor-sharp edges, and was widely used by early humans to make stone tools.

❽ COAL

If plant remains accumulate in waterlogged, airless conditions, they turn into peat. If the peat is buried deep beneath more sediments, it can be compacted and heated to form coal – a black, shiny rock that can be burnt as fuel. The oldest, hardest coal, formed from plants that lived some 300 million years ago, is almost pure carbon.

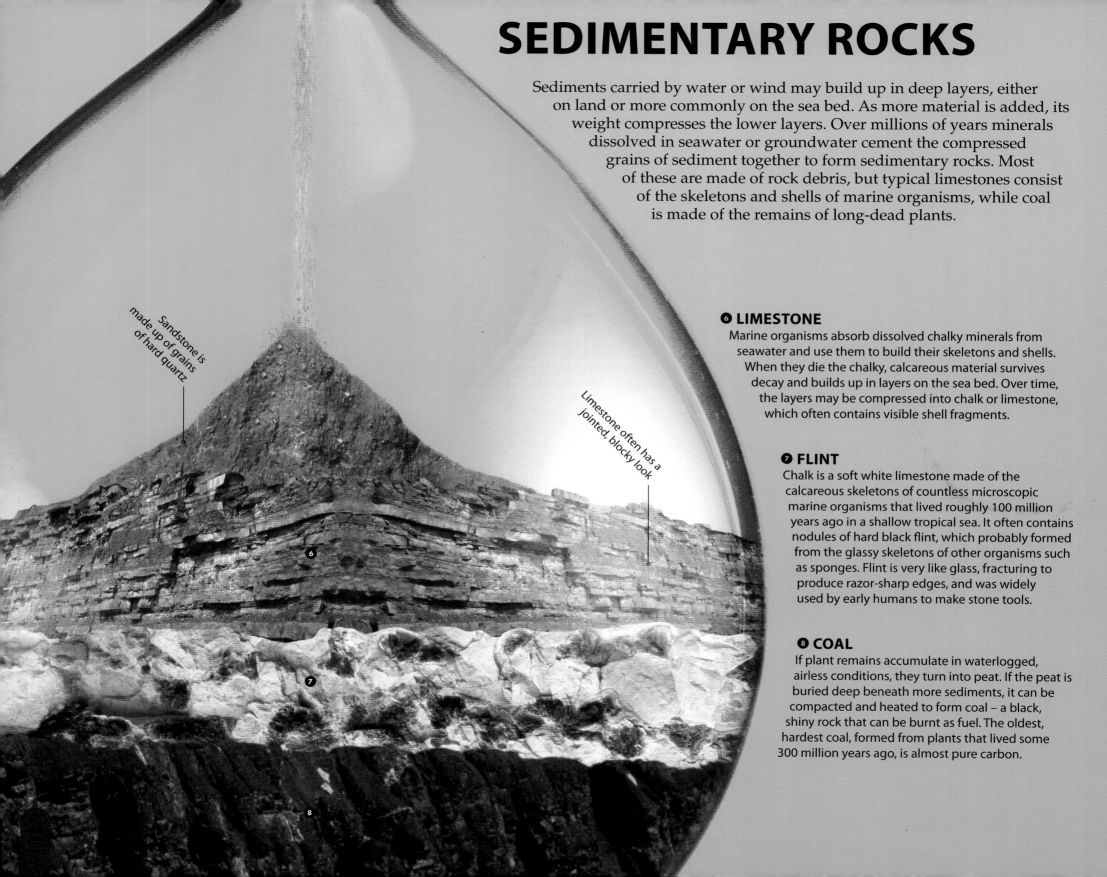

FOSSILS

If the remains of living organisms are buried by sediments that turn into rock, they can be preserved as fossils. A fossil may be any once-living thing, or even its impression, that survives the normal processes of decay. But most fossils are formed by minerals seeping into the organic material and turning it to stone. This usually happens to hard shells or bones, but sometimes even soft tissues are preserved, giving us vital information about life in the distant past.

❷ DISCOVERY

The finest fossils have been buried for millions of years, and are discovered only when they are partly exposed by erosion of the surrounding rock. They may be revealed by coastal cliff falls or heavy rain. Experts return frequently to good sites. Once they find a fossil, they start removing the rock around it.

❶ FOSSILIZATION

Most living things are destroyed after they die, but a very few may be smothered by something that preserves them. Insects and spiders drowned in sticky tree sap millions of years ago are perfectly preserved in the hardened sap, known as amber. Sea shells and dinosaur bones may be soaked in water containing minerals that slowly fossilize them. Even a footprint in mud may be preserved if it is buried and the mud turns to rock.

Only the hard shell of this ancient sea creature is preserved as stony fossil

Spider in amber is perfectly preserved down to every tiny detail of its body

❸ EXTRACTION

Small fossils are often easy to remove, especially if the surrounding rock is quite soft. Bigger fossils such as dinosaur bones are more awkward, because they are heavy and often fragile. Excavators cover them with protective plaster before digging them out. They then add more plaster so that the fossils can be transported safely to a laboratory.

❹ PRESERVATION

Fossils rarely come out of the ground in perfect condition. They are usually surrounded by a rocky "matrix", which has to be chipped away using tools ranging from rock chisels to dentist's drills. When the bones are exposed, they are preserved, often with a varnish, to stop them falling apart. Scientists can then work out how they once fitted together.

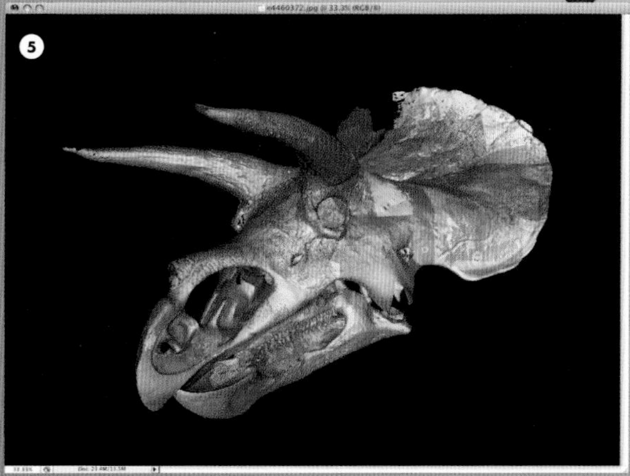

6 FOSSILS AND EVOLUTION

Fossils show that, although extinct animals are not exactly like those that live today, they are similar. This provided the first evidence that living things evolve into new forms. The course of evolution can often be traced through fossils – but since many organisms, such as birds, are rarely found as fossils, we still have a lot to learn.

5 INTERPRETATION

Most fossils are just bones, or even fragments of bones. Scientists can use medical scanners to probe the fossils for fine details, but it is very hard to know what the animals really looked like, or how they lived. Some clues may survive, such as imprints of feathers or scales, and experts can use these to create reconstructions of the living animals.

Dinosaur claw

Trilobite

ROCK STRATA

Sedimentary rocks are usually laid down as layers of soft sediment, such as mud on a lake bed. The oldest layers lie at the bottom, so if they are compressed into rock, the oldest rock layers, or strata, are also the lowest. However, Earth movements can fold and even overturn the strata, so geologists need other ways of working out the ages of rocks. The nature and sequence of the strata can also reveal a great deal about climates and events in the distant past.

▼HORIZONTAL STRATA

When soft sediments are turned into rock without being disturbed, they become horizontal strata. The lowest strata are the oldest. All these rocks date from the Cretaceous period of the age of dinosaurs. The older brown and red strata are described as lower Cretaceous, while the younger white chalk is upper Cretaceous.

▼FOSSIL EVIDENCE

Rocks can now be dated using a technique known as radiometric dating. Before radiometric dating was developed, rocks were dated relatively by their position in layers of strata. Rocks can also be dated by any fossils they contain, since living things keep changing over time. Some of these fossils are big bones, but most are sea shells and other remains of sea creatures.

▼DUNE BEDDING

Sediments that settle in water nearly always form horizontal layers. But a sand dune builds up as a series of inclined layers as wind-blown sand settles on the lee, or sheltered, side of the dune. If the dune becomes sandstone, the "dune bedding" is preserved in the rock. This reveals that the rock formed in a desert, even though its current location may have a wet climate.

Sand laid down on the slope of an ancient dune

▼BENDING AND FOLDING

If rock strata are bent rapidly by a dramatic earthquake, they snap. But steady pressure over long periods, or at high temperatures, can bend and fold the rock. The strata may seem to be simply tilted. This is because you can see only part of a very big fold. Sometimes the folding is tight enough to create visible ridges and troughs, known as anticlines and synclines, or even complete overfolds that turn the strata upside down.

▼FAULT PLANES

If rock strata snap, the result is a fault plane, like the one this climber has her feet on. Strata can snap due to extreme or sudden pressure, but more frequently they snap due to tension pulling the rocks apart. One side of the fault drops relative to the other – or is pushed up by pressure – and the rock strata become offset. By matching the layers, you can often see how they used to join up, and how far they have moved.

▼UNCONFORMITIES

Ancient, distorted strata are often ground flat by erosion. If more rock layers are then laid down on the smooth, horizontal surface, this creates an effect known to geologists as an unconformity. It becomes visible only if both groups of strata are revealed on a cliff face. Unconformity is evidence of dramatic change, such as a mountain range being eroded away and submerged beneath the sea.

Rocks above this unconformity are much younger than those below it
Folded strata are evidence of massive Earth movement
Climbers often use fault planes to secure a firm footing

SCHIST

Relatively soft metamorphic rocks such as slate are created by modest pressure and heat. If these forces are more intense, they create rocks called schists. Schists contain bigger crystals, such as glittering mica and deep red garnet. All the crystals are aligned in sheets, as they are in slate.

GNEISS

Very high temperatures and pressures form the hardest metamorphic rocks, known as gneisses. These granite-like rocks have clear pale and dark bands, which show how they formed. Gneisses include the oldest rocks on Earth, found in Greenland and Canada. These formed some 4 billion years ago – although the rocks that they were created from must have been even older.

Marble can be scratched by steel

MARBLE

One of the most familiar metamorphic rocks, marble is an altered form of limestone. Some types of marble have been baked, and contain intact fossils of sea shells. Others, like these, have been created by intense pressure, which has squeezed the minerals into layers. Marble is mostly relatively soft calcite, so it is easy to carve and highly valued for sculpture.

Minerals form coloured bands

Magnifying glass

Loupe

Rock hammer

SLATE

If mudrock or shale is heated and squeezed by the forces that build mountains, new minerals form in layers that are flattened by the pressure. The result is slate, a rock that can be easily split into thin sheets, and is often used for roofing. Slate is an example of regional metamorphism – a change in rock type that affects very large areas.

METAMORPHIC ROCKS

The forces that distort, snap, or melt rocks can also change their physical nature. Extreme pressure can make the rock harder and align its crystals in distinct bands, as when shale is turned into slate. Heat can cause partial melting followed by recrystallization into new minerals. These may include gemstones, such as the garnet in some schists, or veins of precious metals. Metamorphic processes are often triggered by intrusions of molten magma that distort and bake the surrounding rock.

QUARTZITE
If sandstone is heated enough, the quartz crystals that form the sand grains become welded together by more quartz. This creates a very hard, brittle rock called quartzite. Many mountain peaks survive erosion because they are capped with a pale, glittering layer of tough quartzite.

ECLOGITE
Most metamorphic rock is formed from sedimentary rocks, but under extreme conditions of heat and pressure even very hard igneous rocks can be turned into new forms. Deep in the crust, granite may be transformed into a type of gneiss, while darker, heavier gabbro may become eclogite. The very heavy rock that forms much of Earth's mantle, peridotite, may be baked and squeezed into greenish serpentinite.

HORNFELS
A rock that is baked by a nearby intrusion of molten magma such as granite becomes harder and is often spotted with the crystals of new minerals. Known as a hornfels, the rock loses all its original features. These features survive in rock that is further from the heat source.

exposed rock eroded and carried away
VOLCANIC LAVA
VOLCANIC LAVA
Much of the rock that erupts from continental volcanoes forms broad deposits of lava and ash. The deposits build up the continents and may survive for many millions of years, but some of the rock is broken down by erosion and carried into the oceans. Vast amounts of volcanic ash billow up into the air and fall in the sea.
rocks lifted up
magma rises
IGNEOUS INTRUSIONS
Sticky, silica-rich magma forms deep in continental crust and pushes slowly upward to solidify underground as granite intrusions. Eventually these may be exposed as the rock above is worn away. The granite is attacked by rainwater and reduced to sand and clay, which are carried to the ocean.
IGNEOUS INTRUSIONS
pressure transforms rock
magma solidifies
MAGMA
Although the rock beneath Earth's crust is very hot, it is normally kept in a solid state by intense pressure. However, rifting of the crust can reduce the pressure, and water carried down by sinking oceanic crust lowers the rock's melting point. This turns some of it into the magma that fuels volcanoes or bubbles up as granite intrusions.
rock buried deeper
MAGMA
melting metamorphic rock
solid metamorphic rock

ROCK CYCLE

Over millions of years, rocks are transformed from one form to another. Mountains are worn down by erosion, and the debris is carried into the sea to form sedimentary rocks. These may be pushed up into more mountains by the movement of tectonic plates, or carried deep into Earth, where they are transformed into metamorphic rocks or melted. The molten rock pushes up and cools to form igneous rocks that are eroded to create more sediments.

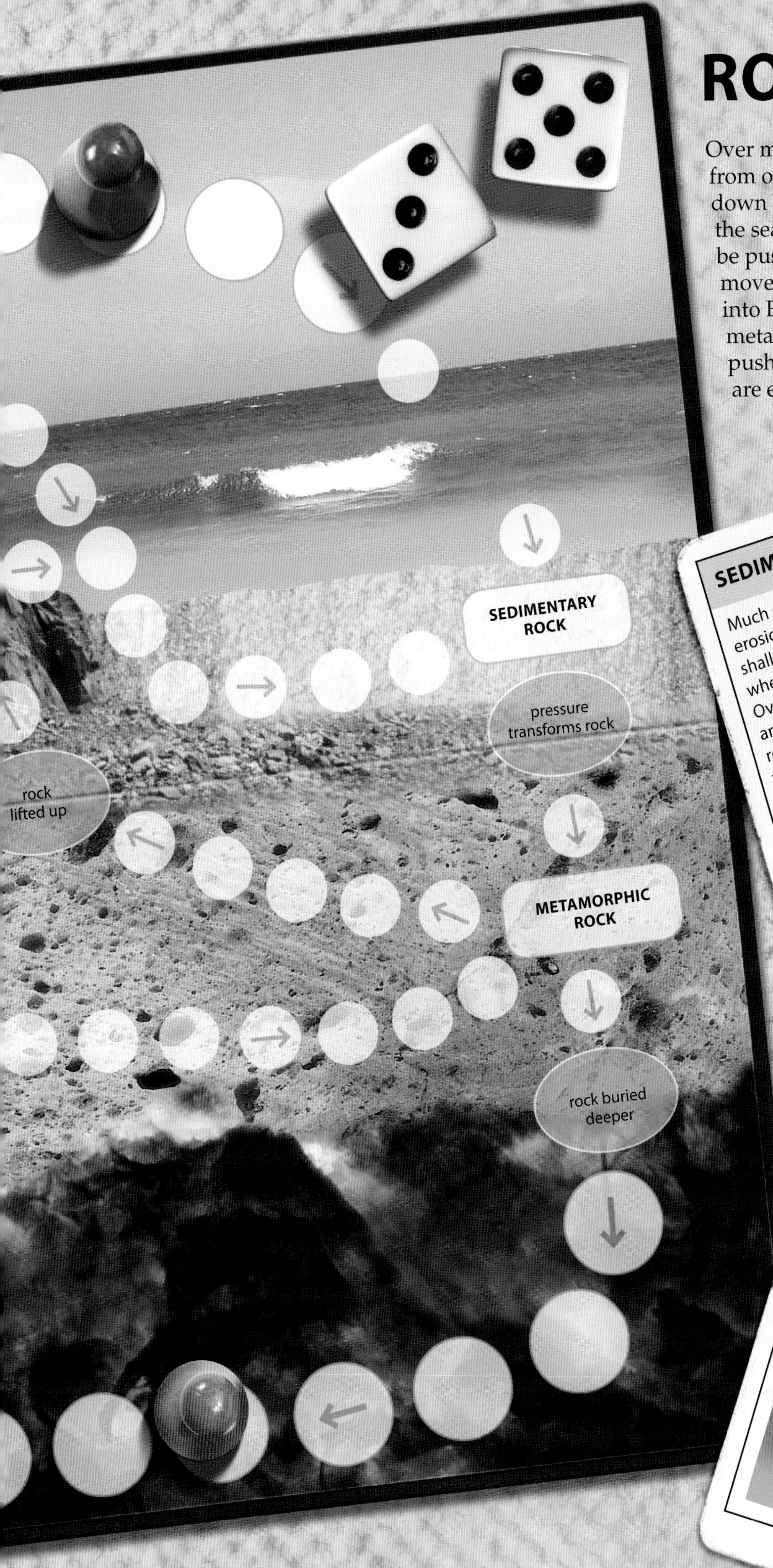
SEDIMENTARY ROCK
pressure transforms rock
rock lifted up
METAMORPHIC ROCK
rock buried deeper

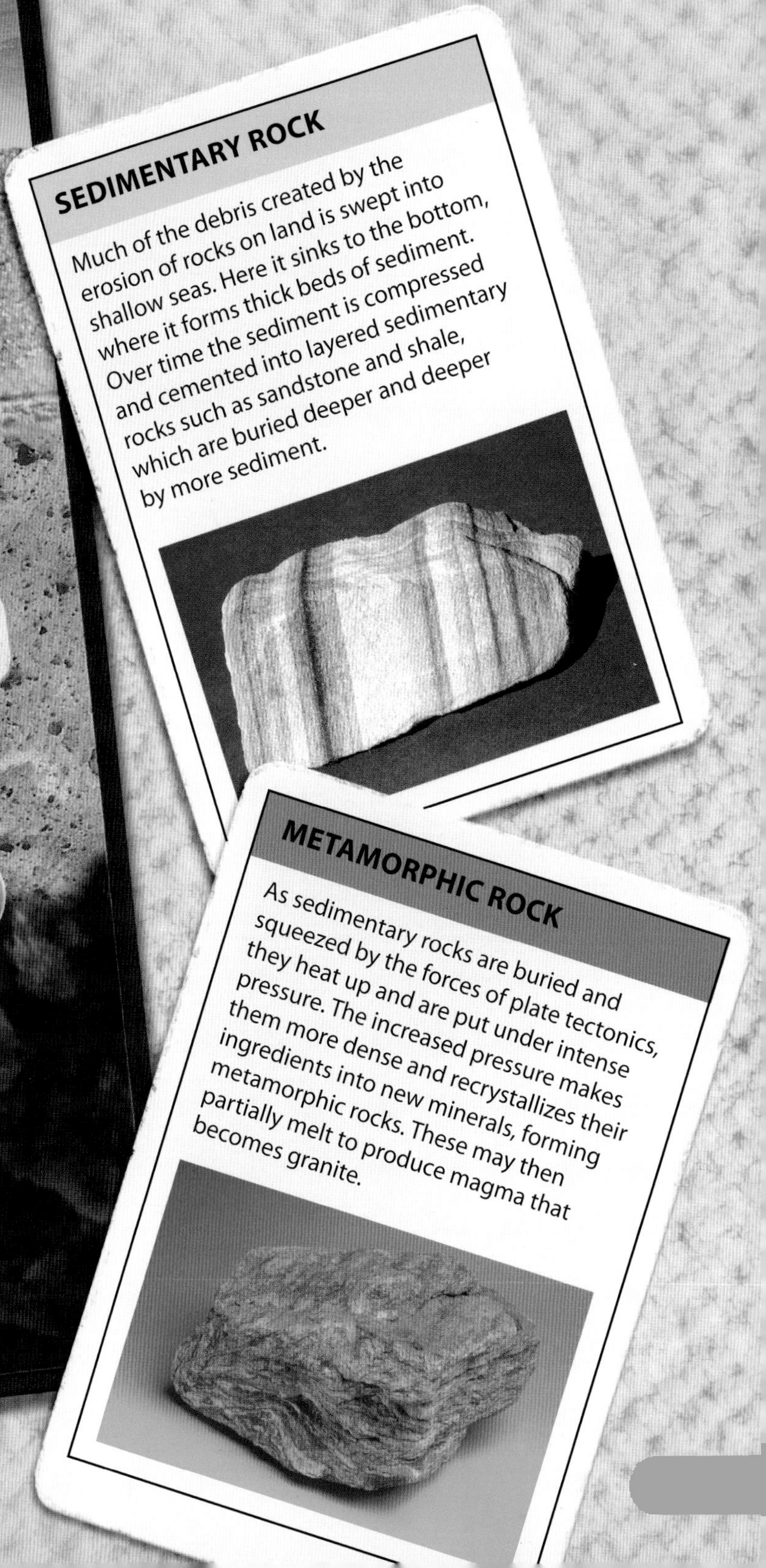
SEDIMENTARY ROCK
Much of the debris created by the erosion of rocks on land is swept into shallow seas. Here it sinks to the bottom, where it forms thick beds of sediment. Over time the sediment is compressed and cemented into layered sedimentary rocks such as sandstone and shale, which are buried deeper and deeper by more sediment.
METAMORPHIC ROCK
As sedimentary rocks are buried and squeezed by the forces of plate tectonics, they heat up and are put under intense pressure. The increased pressure makes them more dense and recrystallizes their ingredients into new minerals, forming metamorphic rocks. These may then partially melt to produce magma that becomes granite.

SOILS

Soils are essential to most plants, because they supply the substances that plants use as nutrients. They consist of rock that has broken up into mineral fragments and become mixed with humus – a "compost" created from decaying plant and animal remains by countless soil organisms. The activity of these soil organisms is affected by the rock type, climate, and vegetation, and this in turn creates many different types of soil with varying degrees of fertility.

Dark, fertile topsoil forms a deep layer above mineral subsoil

❸ GRASSLAND SOIL

Centuries of grass growth and decay on prairies and steppes creates a deep, brown, fertile soil containing a lot of organic matter. It is neither acid nor alkaline, which is ideal for the microbes that break down organic matter into plant nutrients. It also suits the earthworms that churn up the soil, keeping it well mixed. Most grassland soils are now used for growing crops because they are very fertile.

Soil is shallow, and is mainly clay and rock fragments

❶ YOUNG SOILS

Many soils develop from solid rock that is being broken down by weathering. This clay soil is being created from a soft mudstone, which is also being split and crumbled by plant roots pushing down through cracks to find water. The soil above the rock is too young to have distinct layers, but over time a fertile topsoil will form near the surface.

Dark plant material lies on a pale, washed-out layer of sand

❷ TEMPERATE ACID SOIL

Rain washing through sand or gravel dissolves alkaline plant nutrients and carries them to a lower level. This creates distinct layers of soil, with those near the top being too acidic and infertile for most plants. Those that can thrive, such as pine and heather, take over and create conifer woodlands, heaths, and moorlands.

4
5
6
Woodland soil has distinct layers, but is more fertile than acid soil
Plant remains build up and gradually turn into dark peat
Volcanic soil on Hawaii is red with iron

5 PEATY SOILS

These soils begin life as waterlogged masses of half-decayed vegetation on peat bogs and fens. Bog peat is fed by rainwater and is very acidic, mainly due to the growth of sphagnum moss, which acidifies the water. Fen peat is waterlogged by neutral groundwater, and if it is drained it dries out to create very fertile soil. It has little mineral content, which means that it is light and easily blown away by the wind.

4 WOODLAND SOIL

The soils that form under deciduous trees, such as oak or maple, get a regular input of organic matter from the leaves that fall each year with the approach of winter. The leaves contain acids that dissolve some of the minerals in the upper layers, carrying them down to lower levels. However, microbes and worms still flourish, and the soil is naturally fertile.

6 VOLCANIC SOILS

The rock that erupts from volcanoes is rich in the minerals that plants need, so soils that develop from cooled volcanic ash are often very fertile. The basalt that erupts from some volcanoes also contains a lot of iron. A volcanic soil may include big lumps of solidified lava that have been blown from the crater, and sometimes there are layers of pale ash marking recent eruptions.

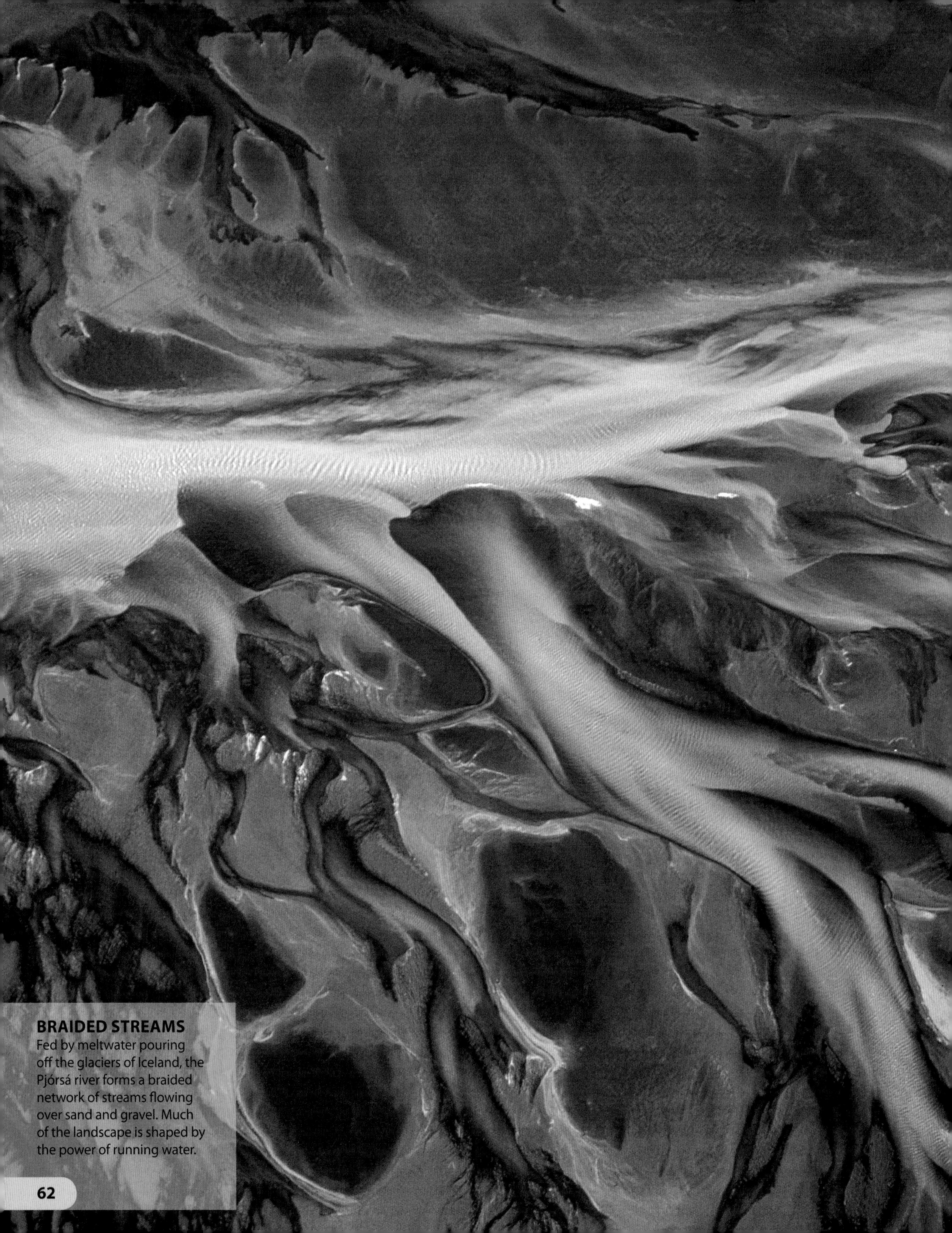

BRAIDED STREAMS
Fed by meltwater pouring off the glaciers of Iceland, the Þjórsá river forms a braided network of streams flowing over sand and gravel. Much of the landscape is shaped by the power of running water.

Water and weather

WATER AND ICE

The feature of planet Earth that makes it so special is liquid water – the substance that is vital to life as we know it. As a simple compound of hydrogen and oxygen, water is probably common throughout the Universe, but mainly in the form of solid ice or gaseous water vapour. Both occur throughout the Solar System, but liquid water is rare, mainly because the other planets are either too hot or too cold. Earth is unique in the Solar System in having temperatures that allow all three forms of water to exist, sometimes in the same place at the same time.

▼ATOMS AND MOLECULES

Water is a mass of molecules, each with two hydrogen atoms and one oxygen atom. This explains its chemical formula, H_2O. The molecules of liquid water are loosely bound by electronic forces, enabling them to move in relation to each other. When water freezes, the molecules become locked together, and when it evaporates they burst apart.

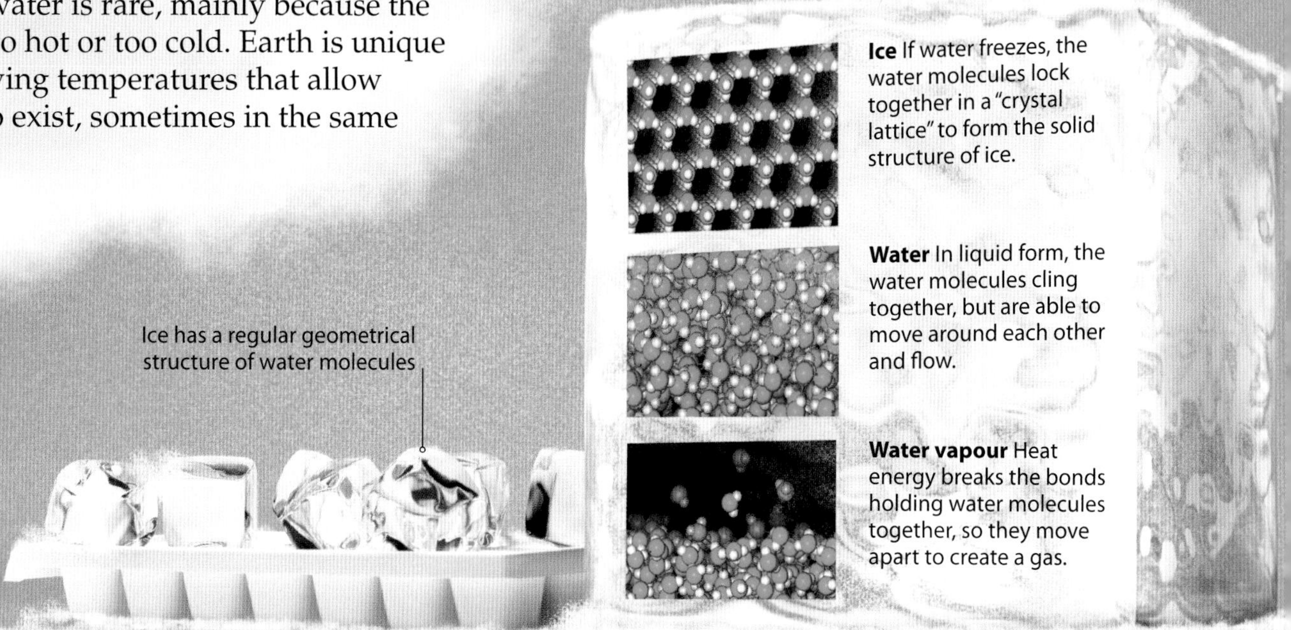

Ice If water freezes, the water molecules lock together in a "crystal lattice" to form the solid structure of ice.

Water In liquid form, the water molecules cling together, but are able to move around each other and flow.

Water vapour Heat energy breaks the bonds holding water molecules together, so they move apart to create a gas.

Ice has a regular geometrical structure of water molecules

◄WATER IN SPACE

Water is constantly careering around the Solar System in the form of comets – "dirty snowballs" of ice, dust, and rock fragments. It also occurs on other planets, but mainly as water vapour or, as in this crater near the north pole of Mars, as ice. However, liquid water may exist beneath the icy surface of Europa, one of the moons of Jupiter – and where there is water, there may be life.

Ice forms a thin crust on the sand dunes of this crater floor on Mars

▼LATENT HEAT
When water evaporates, its molecules absorb energy. This makes them moves faster, so they burst apart to form water vapour. This energy is called latent heat. If the vapour condenses into clouds, latent heat is released, warming the air and making it rise, building the clouds higher. This helps fuel thunderstorms and hurricanes, and indeed the whole weather machine of our planet.

▼WATER ON EARTH
Most of the water on Earth is salty seawater. Only 3 per cent is fresh water, and most of that is either frozen or lying deep underground. Of the rest, two-thirds is contained in freshwater lakes and wetlands, with far less in rivers. Almost 10 per cent of the fresh water that is neither frozen nor buried is in the form of atmospheric water vapour or clouds.

▼FLOATING ICE
When water freezes, the molecules become locked into a structure in which they are further apart than they are in cold water. This means that ice is less dense than liquid water, so it floats. Water is the only substance that behaves like this. This is vitally important to life on Earth, for if water sank when it froze, the ocean depths would probably freeze solid.

▼WATER AND LIFE
The electronic forces that make water molecules cling together also make them cling to the atoms of other substances such as salts, pulling them apart so they dissolve. This makes water an ideal medium for the chemical reactions that are the basis of life. Living cells like these bacteria are basically envelopes of water, containing dissolved chemicals which the organisms use to fuel their activities and build their tissues.

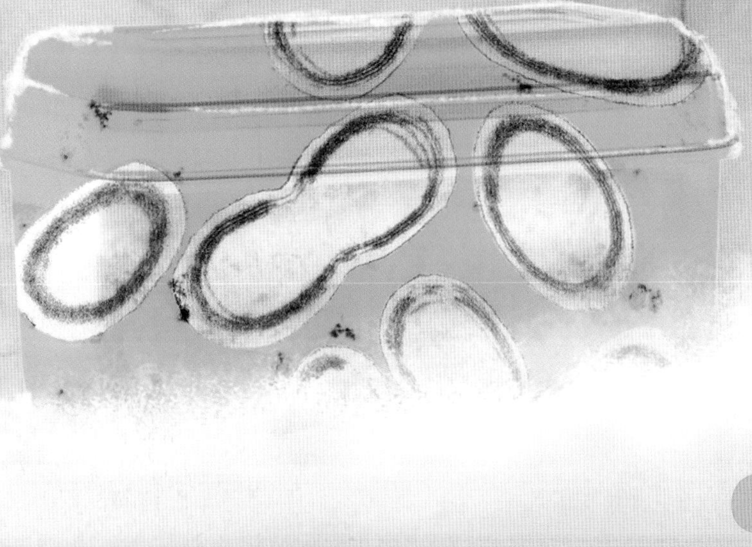

WATER CYCLE

Water vapour evaporating from the oceans forms clouds that are carried over the land by wind. More clouds build up from water vapour rising off the land. Eventually, rain and snow fall, and the water that seeps into the ground drains into streams and rivers that flow back to the ocean. The process turns salty seawater into fresh water, which then picks up minerals from the land and carries them back to the sea. Some parts of this cycle take just a few days or weeks, while others take hundreds or even thousands of years to run their course.

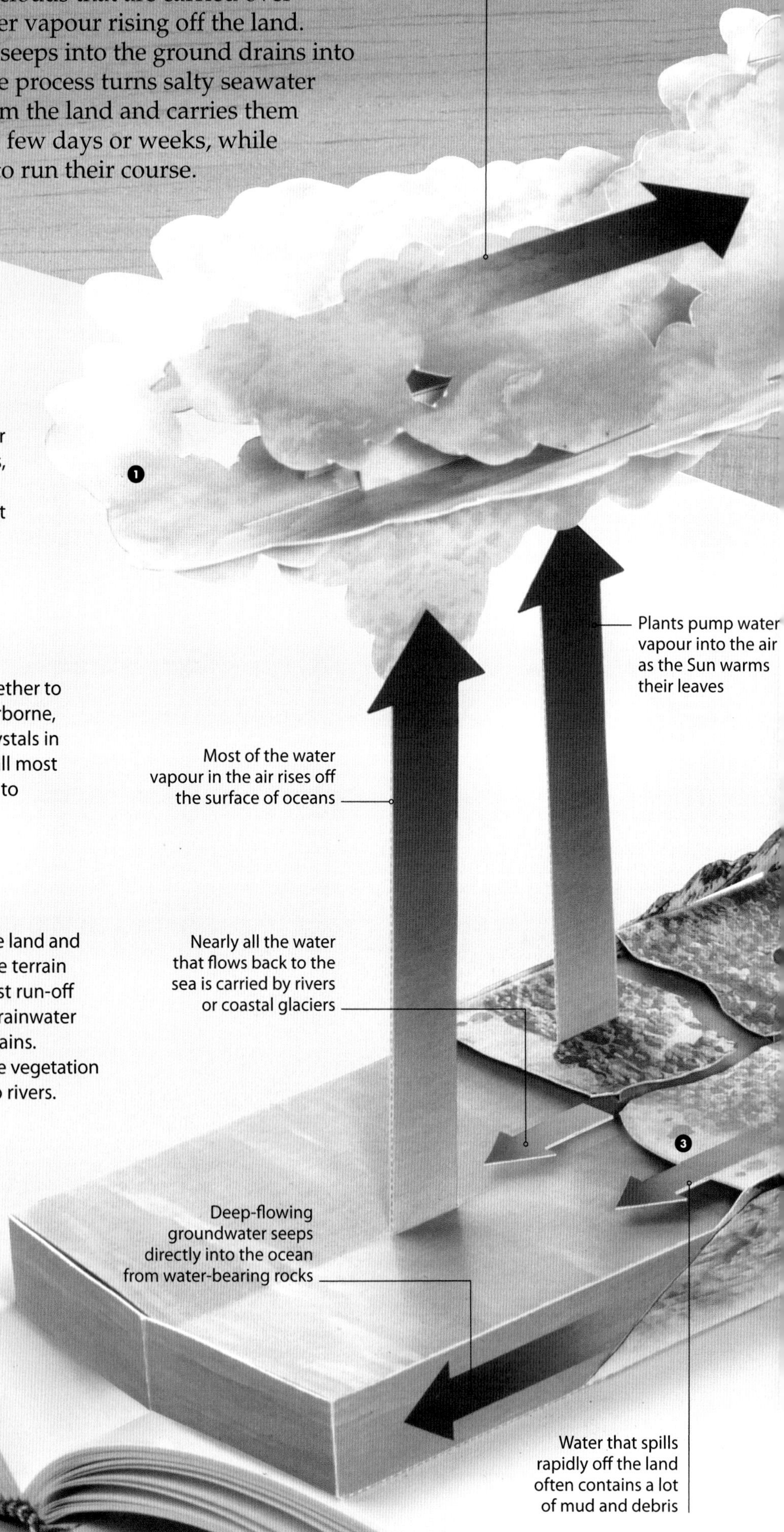
Clouds are blown on the wind, so they form in one place and spill rain in another
1
Plants pump water vapour into the air as the Sun warms their leaves
Most of the water vapour in the air rises off the surface of oceans
Nearly all the water that flows back to the sea is carried by rivers or coastal glaciers
3
Deep-flowing groundwater seeps directly into the ocean from water-bearing rocks
Water that spills rapidly off the land often contains a lot of mud and debris

❶ WATER VAPOUR

As the ocean surface is warmed by the Sun, water molecules absorb energy. This makes them break free from the liquid water and rise into the air as pure water vapour, leaving any impurities, such as salt, behind. The same thing happens to the water in lakes, rivers, and vegetation. Water vapour is an invisible gas, but as it rises it expands and cools, losing energy and turning into the tiny droplets of liquid water that form clouds.

❷ RAIN AND SNOW

Air currents within clouds make the tiny cloud droplets join together to form bigger, heavier drops. When these get too heavy to stay airborne, they fall as rain. The same process makes the microscopic ice crystals in colder clouds link together as snowflakes. Both rain and snow fall most heavily over high ground, which forces moist, moving air to rise to cooler altitudes and form more clouds.

❸ SURFACE WATER

Some of the water that falls as rain flows straight off the land and back to the sea, especially in coastal regions where the terrain consists of hard rock with steep slopes. This type of fast run-off is also common in urban areas, where concrete stops rainwater soaking into the ground and channels it into storm drains. Deforestation can have a similar effect, by removing the vegetation that traps water and stops it spilling straight into rivers.

As moist air passes over high ground, most of the moisture turns to rain and snow
Many mountain peaks are capped with snow that may have fallen long ago but has never melted
Porous rocks soak up water like vast mineral sponges and retain it for centuries
Groundwater flows very slowly, except in polar regions where it is often frozen solid
Lakes and wetlands return water vapour to the air in the same way as the oceans
2
6
5
7
4

❹ CREEPING GROUNDWATER

A lot of rainfall is soaked up by the soil, and seeps down into porous rocks, sand, and gravel. The upper limit of this saturated zone is called the water table, and if you dig down to this level, the water fills the bottom of the hole to form a well. This groundwater tends to creep very slowly downhill in broad sheets, through layers of porous rock called aquifers. In some places, the water may emerge from springs to join streams and rivers.

❺ LOCKED UP IN ICE

In polar regions, or at high altitudes, the climate may be too cold for the summer Sun to melt all the snow that falls. The snow then builds up over the years, compacting under its own weight to form deep layers of ice. On Greenland and Antarctica, vast ice sheets have locked up water in this way for many thousands of years. However, some of this ice flows downhill in glaciers, and eventually melts and rejoins the water cycle.

❻ VOLCANIC WATER

A very long-term part of the water cycle involves water that is carried below Earth's crust. This water is contained by ocean-floor rocks that are being dragged into the subduction zones marked by deep ocean trenches. The water lowers the melting point of the hot rock beneath the crust so that the rock melts and erupts from volcanoes, along with water vapour. This transfers water from the oceans to the atmosphere over timescales of millions of years, and also lubricates the whole process of plate tectonics.

❼ FOSSIL WATER

Sometimes, groundwater collects in porous rock that is then sealed beneath a layer of waterproof rock. Unable to escape, the water may be permanently removed from the water cycle. One of the biggest of these "fossil water" reservoirs lies beneath the eastern Sahara, with an estimated volume of 150,000 cubic km (3,600 cubic miles). In places, wind erosion has stripped away the capping rock to expose the water-bearing rock and form oases.

RIVERS

As water drains off the land it flows into a network of streams that join together to form bigger and bigger rivers. Rivers shape the landscape by eroding valleys and, by degrees, wearing down mountain ranges. They carry the eroded debris from the uplands to the lowlands, and so tend to level out the land. They also transport plant nutrients that make most lowlands so fertile. In general rivers have a fast, turbulent upper course in the uplands, a tranquil middle course in the lowlands, and a tidal lower course as they flow across coastal plains into the sea.

◄ SPRINGS
Many rivers can be traced back to a source that bursts out of the ground as a spring. The spring is fed by groundwater that seeps downwards until it reaches a layer of waterproof rock. The water flows over the top of this layer. If the rock outcrops on the slope of a hill, the water spills out above it as a spring. It is usually crystal clear, but may contain dissolved minerals.

► MOUNTAIN STREAMS
As it tumbles down the steep slopes, a mountain stream flows very fast, with many waterfalls and rapids. Seasonal torrents caused by heavy rain or snow melt can shift big boulders, as well as great volumes of gravel and sand eroded from the mountain. The water is clear, cold, and rich in dissolved oxygen.

► YOUNG RIVERS
As it flows down through the uplands, a young river lays down a bed of gravel. Most of the gravel is bounced downstream by fast-flowing water during times of spate (heavy flow) such as the spring thaw. The river often follows several channels across the gravel to create a complex "braided stream". Eventually all the channels join up to create one broad, shallow river flanked by gravel banks.

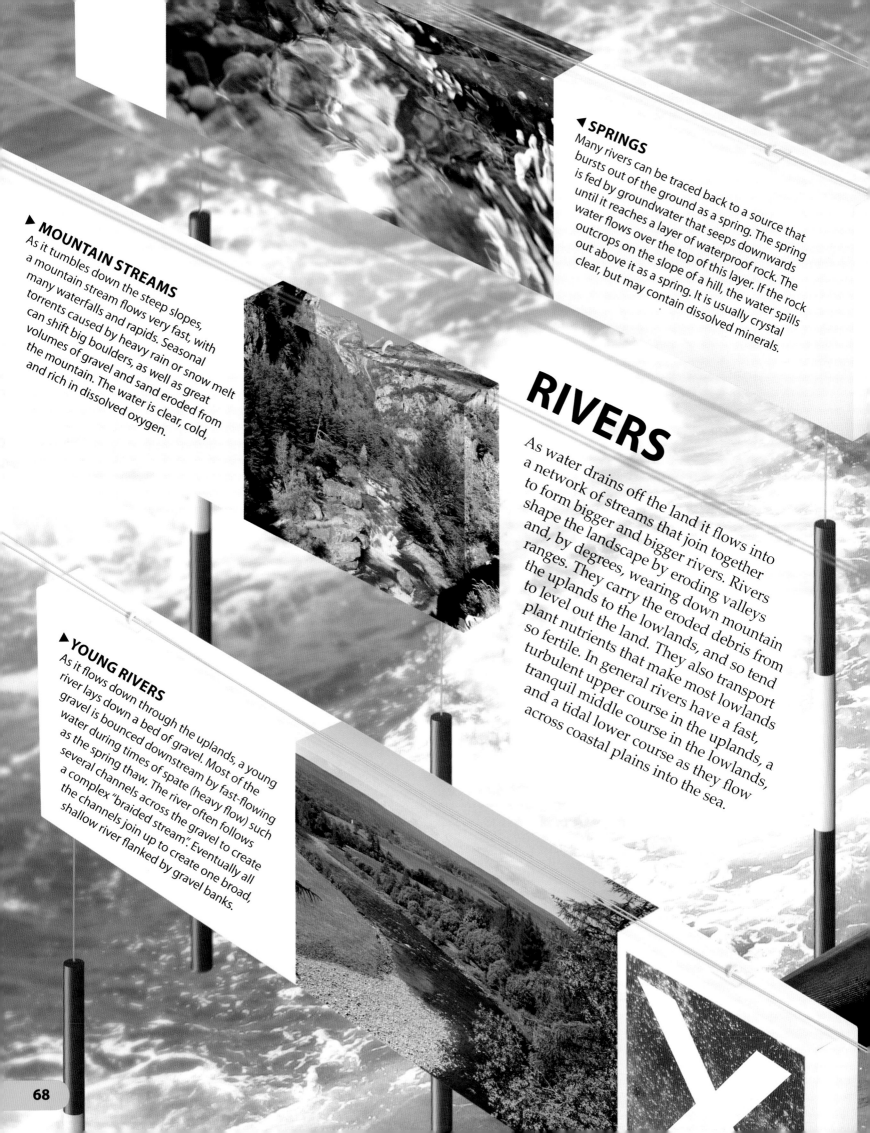

FLOODPLAINS

Rivers slow down as they reach the lowlands, and this makes them drop lighter particles of sand and mud. If they are not artificially confined, they tend to overflow their banks in winter or during the wet season and flood the surrounding landscape. The floodwaters drop fine sediment to create broad floodplains of nutrient-rich silt and organic material, and over the centuries this develops into a fertile soil.

MEANDERS

A river often winds across its floodplain in a series of loops called meanders. The river flows more strongly around the outside of the bend, cutting away the bank. It flows more slowly on the inside of the bend, where it deposits sediment. This exaggerates the meanders, making them wider. Some meanders become so extreme that the river takes a short cut, leaving an isolated oxbow lake.

ESTUARIES AND DELTAS

Most rivers flow to the sea. When the fresh water encounters salty seawater in the tidal lower course, the salt makes fine mud particles in the water settle to form the broad tidal mudflats of an estuary. Where the flow is faster, it carries coarser sediment out to sea to build up a delta with many radiating channels, as shown in this satellite image of the River Lena in Siberia.

RIVER VALLEYS AND GORGES

The fast-flowing water of upland rivers carries rocks, stones, and sand that erode watercourses into V-shaped valleys. These join up to create patterns of tributaries that form a drainage basin, or river catchment. Most river valleys get broader as the river gets bigger, but rivers flowing through limestone may disappear into underground systems that then collapse, creating limestone gorges. Earth movements can also push the land up slowly as the river keeps cutting down, and this can carve even deeper gorges.

❶ BRANCHING PATTERNS
This satellite view of the snow-capped western Himalayas shows how the valleys of small rivers join up to create bigger rivers that flow into the lowlands. Eventually these join up too, forming vast rivers like the Indus and Ganges. The pattern of valleys resembles the trunk, branches, and slender twigs of a tree.

❷ UPLAND VALLEY
Torrents of debris-laden water pouring off mountains after heavy rain or snow-melt cut deep, steep-sided valleys into the mountain slopes. The water flows too fast to drop any fine sediment, so the valley is etched right down to the bedrock in a narrow V-shape. Its course zigzags between ridges of harder rock.

❸ MATURE VALLEY

As a river flows out of mountains and hills across flatter land, it flows more slowly. This makes it drop a lot of the rocky debris that it carries out of the uplands, filling up the bottom of its valley. So instead of being confined by a deep V-shaped valley, a mature river flows over a broad plain built up from deep layers of sediment. It may change its course regularly, and the valley often has traces of old river channels.

❹ WATERFALLS

Mountain streams often tumble over precipices to create waterfalls, but they are less common on mature rivers. In places, however, a rift in a capping layer of hard rock allows a big river to plunge into a gorge that has been eroded in the softer rock below. In Zambia, southern Africa, the mighty Zambezi river plunges 108 m (355 ft) over Victoria Falls, known locally as Mosi-oa-Tuya, or "the smoke that thunders".

❺ UPLIFT CANYON

The titanic forces that push up mountains can raise the beds of rivers, forcing them to erode deeper valleys. In Arizona, US, massive uplift of the landscape has made the Colorado river cut down through more than 1.8 km (1 mile) of rock to create a gorge 350 km (220 miles) long and up to 29 km (18 miles) wide – the Grand Canyon. In the process it has revealed rock strata dating back nearly 2 billion years.

❻ LIMESTONE GORGE

Limestone is mostly calcite, a mineral that is dissolved by naturally slightly acid rainwater. This encourages the water to seep down through joints and fissures in the rock and flow through underground cave systems. The caves may eventually get so large that their ceilings collapse, and the river ends up flowing through a spectacular steep-sided gorge, like this one in Provence, southern France.

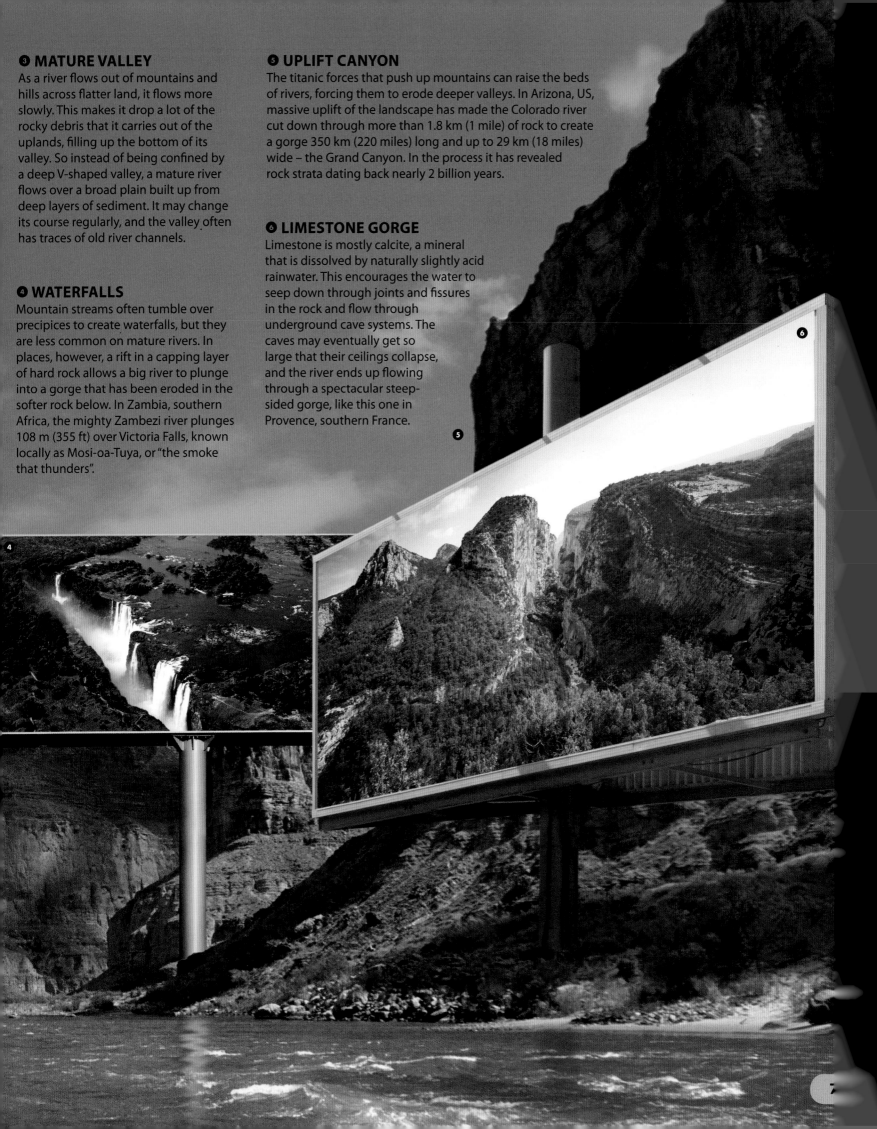

GLACIERS AND ICEBERGS

In the polar regions and on high mountains, freezing temperatures stop snow melting away. As more snow falls on top, it builds up in deep layers that, over centuries, are compressed into solid ice. This tends to creep downhill as glaciers, and where these reach the sea the ice breaks away to form floating icebergs. In the coldest regions, the same process creates immensely thick ice sheets. The East Antarctic ice sheet forms a huge dome up to 4.5 km (2.8 miles) thick, and its weight has depressed the continent more than 1 km (0.6 miles) into Earth's crust.

❶ CIRQUE GLACIER

High in the mountains, snow collects in rocky basins and is compacted into ice. Eventually this overflows each basin and heads downhill as a glacier. Meanwhile, the moving ice freezes onto the mountain, plucking rock away to form vertical rock walls and deepen the basin. The result is a bowl-shaped cirque, which typically acts as the source of a valley glacier.

❷ VALLEY GLACIER

Ice flows down valleys extremely slowly – too slowly to be seen as movement. In the process, it deforms to flow around bends, and may even flow uphill over a hump of hard rock. But mostly the ice grinds the rock away. This often forms dark lines of shattered rock on the glacier surface, like these on the Kennicott Glacier in the Wrangell Mountains of Alaska.

❸ GLACIER SNOUT

Most mountain glaciers terminate on the lower slopes of the mountains, at the point where the warmer climate makes the ice melt as quickly as it is moving downhill. This is the snout of the glacier, which stays in the same place unless the climate changes. Meltwater pouring from tunnels and caves in the ice flows away in outwash streams or rivers.

❹ MORAINE

A glacier moves a lot of rock downhill, both embedded within the ice and in long piles, called moraines, that are carried on its surface. It acts rather like a conveyor belt, dumping all the debris near its snout as a terminal moraine – a pile of angular rock fragments mixed with fine "rock flour" created by the grinding action of the ice. A lot of the finer rocky material is swept away by water from outwash streams.

❺ TIDEWATER GLACIER

In the polar regions, southeastern Alaska and southern New Zealand, glaciers flow all the way to the coast and out to sea. Here, the floating snout of the Hubbard Glacier flows into the Gulf of Alaska. Great chunks of ice break away from these glaciers and float away as icebergs, while much of the rubble carried by the ice is dumped on the sea floor.

❻ ICEBERG

The icebergs that break away from tidewater glaciers float with at least 90 per cent of their mass underwater, depending on the weight of rock they carry. Many drift long distances before melting, and those that drift south from Greenland into the North Atlantic are very dangerous to shipping – notoriously causing the sinking of the *Titanic* in 1912.

❼ ADVANCE AND RETREAT

Climate change is making glaciers behave in strange ways. Many are retreating as higher temperatures make them melt back to higher altitudes, leaving empty valleys and fjords. But melting can also make a glacier flow faster and advance, because extra meltwater beneath the ice stops it sticking to the rock. This increases the number of icebergs that spill into the ocean, raising sea levels.

1
2
3
5
6
7

ICE AGES

Earth has gone through several phases when the climate has cooled, mainly because of regular variations in its orbit around the Sun. Each of these phases, known as ice ages, has included warm and cold periods. We are now living in the warm period of an ice age. During the last cold period, which ended about 12,000 years ago, glaciers and permafrost extended across much of northern Eurasia and North America, reshaping the landscape. The Southern Hemisphere was less affected because it has little land in cooler latitudes – except for Antarctica, which is still frozen.

❶ GLACIATED VALLEYS

The deep U-shaped valleys found in many mountain landscapes in the north were gouged out by ice-age glaciers. The ice ground away the rock to create the steep valley walls, and scooped hollows in the valley floors, which now contain lakes. Many mountain peaks were reduced to narrow ridges and pinnacles by ice ripping away their flanks to form rounded cirques.

❷ FJORDS

During the last ice age, so much water was locked up as continental ice that the sea level fell by more than 100 m (330 ft). Glaciers eroded deep valleys as they flowed to the coast. When the ice melted, the seas filled up again, reaching their present level about 6,000 years ago. Water flooded coastal valleys to create the steep-sided fjords of regions such as Scandinavia, and southern New Zealand.

Glacial valley, Norway
❶
Moving ice once filled this valley
Groove shows direction of ice flow
Ice-scoured rock, Canada
❸
❷
Fjord is 400 m (1,300 ft) deep
Milford Sound, New Zealand

3 ICE-SCOURED ROCKS

Sheets of moving ice grinding across northern regions such as Canada and Scandinavia scraped away soil and soft rock to reveal ancient, hard rocks below. Some rocks show graphic evidence of this, with long grooves scored into their surface by boulders embedded in the ice. These landscapes are dotted with hundreds of lakes, which fill hollows gouged out by the ice.

4 GLACIAL DEBRIS

As the ice melted and retreated, it left heaps of rubble known as moraines, and broad expanses of soft clay mixed with rock fragments, known as boulder clay or till. It also dumped any big rocks that it was carrying. The most striking of these "glacial erratics" are quite different from the surrounding bedrock, because the ice has carried them from areas with different geology.

5 ANCIENT TUNDRA

In the tundra that surrounds ice sheets, groundwater freezes solid to form permafrost. During the ice ages, permafrost covered vast areas not buried beneath ice. The freezing soil created strange patterns in the ground. Where big lumps of underground ice have melted away, the ground has subsided to form "kettle holes" that are now filled with water.

6 GLACIAL REBOUND

The colossal weight of the ice-age ice sheets distorted Earth's crust downwards. In the 12,000 years since they melted, the crust has been steadily rising at the rate of up to 1 cm (0.4 in) a year. This "glacial rebound" effect has raised many former beaches well above the waves. Some 1,000-year-old Viking harbours in Scandinavia are now 10 m (33 ft) above sea level.

Glacial erratic, *UK*
Sandstone rock sits on limestone
4
Rhossili Bay, *UK*
6
Raised beach was once at sea level
Tundra is frozen but not glaciated
5
Ellesmere Island, *Canada*

LAKES

Lakes are large pools of standing water that form on land. The water may collect in hollows left by melting glaciers, in the folds and rifts created by earth movements, or even in volcanic craters. Most contain fresh water, which flows into the lake at one end and out at the other. In hot climates the water may evaporate from the surface rather than flow out, and this causes a build-up of dissolved minerals that makes the lake very salty. Lakes are slowly silted up by sediment, which is carried into them by rivers and settles on the lake floors. Over time, this can turn a lake into a swamp, and eventually make it vanish altogether.

❶ UPLAND LAKE

Lakes in upland regions with hard rocks usually contain pure, cold water with few of the mineral nutrients needed to support aquatic life. As a result there are relatively few drifting organisms – plankton – and the water is extremely clear. Lake Tahoe, which has formed in a rift in the mountains of the western United States, has so little plankton that its deep blue waters are as clear as glass.

❷ LOWLAND LAKE

The water that flows into lowland lakes is usually rich in plant nutrients dissolved from the surrounding soil and soft rocks. These support a lot of plankton, making the water relatively cloudy. Such lakes teem with life of all kinds, including aquatic plants, but these grow so fast that the lake becomes choked with vegetation and eventually turns into a swamp.

❸ SALT LAKE

Nearly all "fresh water" contains salts of some kind, dissolved from rocks and soils. As water evaporates from lakes it leaves these salts behind, and in a hot desert climate this can create a salt lake. The waters of the Great Salt Lake in Utah, US, are five times as salty as the sea, and the margins of the lake, seen here, are encrusted with glittering white salt crystals.

❹ SODA LAKE

Typical salt lakes are rich in sodium chloride, or table salt. But some lakes contain other salts. Many lakes in Africa's Rift Valley, such as Lake Nakuru, contain strong solutions of sodium carbonate, or soda. Despite this, the lake water supports a dense population of specialized life, including microscopic algae and shrimp-like copepods, which are eaten by vast flocks of flamingos.

❺ GLACIAL LAKE

Most of the world's lakes were formed by ice-age glaciers. The moving ice scooped hollows in the rock, or dumped thick moraines of rocky debris in valleys that now act as natural dams, holding back the lake water. Similar lakes are being formed today by active glaciers like this one in southern Norway. Meltwater flowing from the glacier in the background is rich in mineral sediment, which gives the lake its greenish blue colour.

❻ CRATER LAKE

The craters of extinct or dormant volcanoes often contain near-circular crater lakes. They fill with pure rainwater, but, if there is any volcanic activity, the water may become acidified by gases such as sulphur dioxide and carbon dioxide. The water of this crater lake in eastern Siberia is unusually acidic, enabling it to dissolve the minerals that have turned it a milky blue.

▲SINKHOLES
Much of the water that forms cave systems seeps into narrow cracks in the rock and apparently vanishes underground. In places, however, a concentrated flow of water enlarges a joint into a vertical shaft, forming a waterfall that plunges into a black void. These sinkholes may be hundreds of metres deep, and often open out into caverns containing underground rivers and lakes.

▲POTHOLES
The narrow passages that link bigger caves are known in some limestone regions as potholes. Their walls are often visibly scoured and polished by the torrents of water that flow through them after heavy rain, and many are full of water all the time. This does not stop determined cavers, who use specially modified diving equipment to pass through flooded passages that may lead to unexplored cave networks.

▲CAVERNS
As caves get broader, their roofs may collapse through lack of support. This may turn a cave near the surface into a rocky gorge open to the sky, but deeper underground the rock falls away, leaving the natural arch of a cavern. Some of these caverns are colossal – the Sarawak chamber in the Gunung Mulu caves of Borneo is at least 700 m (2,300 ft) long, more than 300 m (1,000 ft) wide, and 100 m (330 ft) high.

CAVES AND UNDERGROUND RIVERS

The power of the sea can carve caves into many kinds of coastal rock, but underground cave systems are nearly always the result of groundwater seeping down through limestone. The alkaline limestone is slowly dissolved by acids that are naturally present in rainwater and soils. As the rock dissolves, joints and fissures become enlarged into vertical sinkholes and narrow, winding passages that lead to underground streams and rivers. Some of these cave networks extend for great distances underground, and may carry away all the water so that there are no streams or rivers on the rocky, often half-barren surface.

▲MEXICAN CENOTES

The Yucatan peninsula in Mexico is an ancient, uplifted coral reef. Since coral rock is a form of limestone it is affected by rainwater in the same way as other limestone landscapes. Tropical rain has eroded a complex cave network that swallows up all the surface water, but it is accessible through sinkholes and collapsed caverns called cenotes. Many of these contain beautiful, yet eerie underground lakes, which were sacred water sources for the ancient Mayan civilization.

▲STALACTITES AND STALAGMITES

As slightly acidic water seeps through limestone, it dissolves the rock and becomes a weak solution of the mineral calcite. If this then drips into a cave system, exposure to air changes its chemistry and makes the calcite crystallize. Over many years, the crystals build up to form hanging stalactites, or rise from the cave floor as stalagmites. The same process can create other features, such as the curtains of calcite known as flowstones.

▼UNDERGROUND RIVERS

The water that pours into limestone cave systems tends to keep draining downwards through joints in the rock. It may abandon one string of caves to flow through another lower down, leaving the older caves high and dry. But sometimes it reaches a layer of impermeable rock and cannot sink any further. Here, it forms a broad underground river that flows through a passage until it emerges from a hillside like a gigantic spring – a fully formed river flowing straight out of the ground.

OCEANS AND SEAS

Oceans and shallow seas cover more than two-thirds of the planet, to an average depth of 3.8 km (2.4 miles). The Pacific Ocean alone covers nearly half the globe. The oceans contain about 1,330 million cubic km (320 million cubic miles) of salty seawater, which accounts for 97 per cent of the water on Earth. Most of this water forms a dark, cold realm deep below the surface, where life is scarce, but the shallow, sunlit waters of coastal seas are some of the world's richest wildlife habitats.

❶ VOLCANIC ORIGINS

Most of the water in the oceans probably erupted as water vapour from massive volcanoes some 4 billion years ago. The vapour formed part of the early atmosphere, but, as the planet's surface cooled, it condensed into rain that poured down for millions of years to fill the oceans. Some water may also have arrived from space in the form of icy comets, which crashed into Earth and vaporized on impact.

❷ SALT WATER

Seawater became salty very slowly, as continents built up from volcanic islands erupting from the ocean floor. As fast as these appeared, they were eroded by heavy rain, which carried mineral salts into the ocean. The main salt is sodium chloride, or table salt, which can be obtained from seawater by evaporating it in coastal salt pans like these.

❸ BLUE TWILIGHT

Sunlight consists of all the colours of the rainbow, but where it shines into deep water the various colours are progressively filtered out, starting with red and yellow. Soon only blue light is left. Below 200 m (660 ft) there is just dim blue twilight, and by 1,000 m (3,300 ft), this fades into darkness. Since the oceans are on average 3,800 m (12,460 ft) deep, most ocean water is pitch black.

❹ HEAT SINK

Water can soak up a lot of heat energy without getting noticeably warmer, which is why the sea is cooler than the land in summer. It cools down as slowly as it warms up, so the sea lapping this snowy beach in winter is warmer than the land. This effect gives coastal regions relatively mild climates, with fewer summer heatwaves or winter frosts.

❺ OCEAN LAYERS

The dark ocean depths are uniformly cold, even in the tropics. This is because the sun-warmed water at the surface expands and becomes less dense, so it floats on top of the colder water like oil on a puddle. These layers are permanent in open tropical oceans, but in cooler regions the layers tend to become mixed in winter.

Only blue light penetrates far below the ocean surface

The salt content of the oceans has now stabilized

Vocanoes like these on Java still erupt a lot of water vapour

❻ CRYSTAL DESERT

The permanent layer of warm surface water in open tropical oceans is usually crystal clear. This is because the layering effect stops nutrients reaching the sunlit surface and fuelling the growth of plankton that makes the water cloudy. As plankton is the basis of the oceanic food chain, there is very little food to support ocean life. So these clear blue oceans are little more than marine deserts.

5
Surface waters are much warmer than the ocean depths

WAVES, CURRENTS, AND TIDES

Oceanic winds whip up waves and drive surface currents that swirl around oceans in vast circulating "gyres". Surface currents are linked to deepwater currents driven by the sinking of cool, salty water towards the ocean floor, especially in the North Atlantic and around Antarctica. Between them these currents carry ocean water all around the world, redistributing heat and the dissolved nutrients that support oceanic life. Meanwhile the gravity of the Moon causes the tides that rise and fall daily, shifting large volumes of water in tidal streams that flow much faster than ocean currents.

❶ SURFACE CURRENTS

Oceanic winds tend to blow towards the west in the tropics, and towards the east in the mid-latitudes further north and south. They drag the surface waters of the oceans with them, creating huge clockwise current gyres in the northern hemisphere, and anticlockwise gyres in the southern hemisphere. As they swirl around the oceans, these currents carry warm water towards the poles and cold water into the tropics.

❷ CALM ZONES

Oceanic winds and surface currents swirl around regions where the seas are calm and the winds are very light. The calm zone at the heart of the North Atlantic is known as the Sargasso Sea, famous for its floating seaweed, which is concentrated in the area by the circulating currents. These also heap up the water slightly, so the sea level at the centre of the Sargasso Sea is roughly one metre (39 in) higher than the level of the surrounding ocean.

❸ THE GULF STREAM

One of the fastest-flowing ocean currents, the Gulf Stream carries warm tropical water across the Atlantic Ocean from the Gulf of Mexico towards northern Europe. This helps keep Europe relatively warm, and the climate of the Atlantic coast of Scotland is mild enough for tropical palm trees to grow. Conversely, the Humboldt Current that flows up the western coast of South America from the fringes of Antarctica carries cold water to the tropics, allowing penguins to live on the equatorial Galápagos Islands.

❹ WAVES

Winds blowing over the oceans create ripples that grow into waves. These get bigger the longer the wind acts upon them, so the highest waves are those that have been blown by strong, steady winds across broad oceans. The largest reliably recorded wave was 30 m (98 ft) high, seen in the North Atlantic in 1995. Such huge waves transfer vast amounts of energy, but the water within each wave does not move forward with it until the wave breaks, and its crest topples onto the shore.

❺ TIDAL RISE AND FALL

Ocean water around the globe is dragged into a slight oval by the gravity of the Moon, creating two "tidal bulges". As Earth spins, most coastal regions move in and out of these tidal bulges so the water level rises and falls, usually twice a day. These tides vary with the nature of the coast. Some places such as the Mediterranean are almost tideless, while the Bay of Fundy in eastern Canada, seen here, has a huge tidal range of up to 16 m (52 ft) between low and high tide.

❻ WHIRLPOOLS AND RACES

As the tide rises, it pushes seawater up river estuaries and along coasts. When the tide falls again, the water ebbs away and the flow reverses. Normally these tidal streams are not very obvious. But where they flow around headlands or through narrow straits, they can be concentrated into fast-moving, turbulent tidal races and even giant whirlpools, like this one in the Gulf of Corryvreckan off the west coast of Scotland. These build up to their full fury at mid-tide, then die away altogether as the tide turns.

❼ LUNAR CYCLES

The tides vary with the phases of the Moon. Twice a month, at full moon and new moon, the difference between high and low tide is much greater than at half moon. This is because the Moon is aligned with the Sun, and their gravities combine to create extra-large tidal effects known as spring tides. At half moon, the gravity of the Sun offsets that of the Moon, reducing its influence and causing far smaller tides, called neap tides. As a result, the tidal range at any point on the coast changes from day to day.

ATMOSPHERE

Earth is covered by a mantle of air that is roughly 78 per cent nitrogen and 21 per cent oxygen. The rest consists of small amounts of carbon dioxide, methane, ozone, and water vapour, plus other gases including argon, helium, and neon. Eighty per cent of the air is concentrated in the troposphere, the lowest layer of the atmosphere. It acts as a sunscreen by day and retains heat at night. A layer of ozone, a form of oxygen, in the stratosphere also protects all life from dangerous ultraviolet radiation.

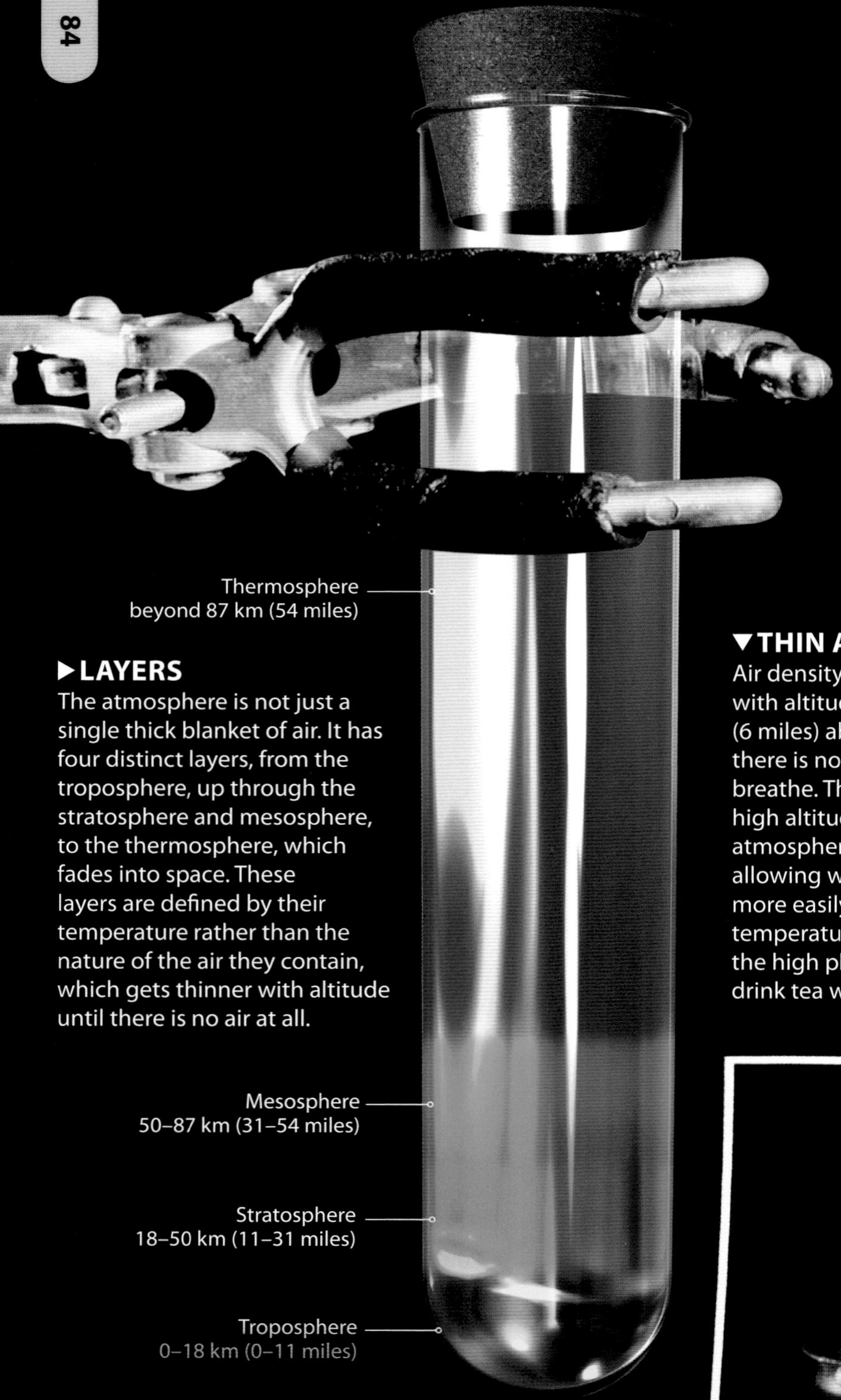

Thermosphere beyond 87 km (54 miles)

Mesosphere 50–87 km (31–54 miles)

Stratosphere 18–50 km (11–31 miles)

Troposphere 0–18 km (0–11 miles)

▶ LAYERS
The atmosphere is not just a single thick blanket of air. It has four distinct layers, from the troposphere, up through the stratosphere and mesosphere, to the thermosphere, which fades into space. These layers are defined by their temperature rather than the nature of the air they contain, which gets thinner with altitude until there is no air at all.

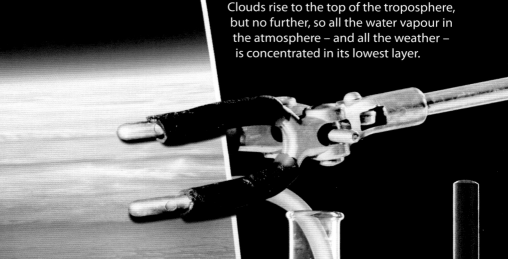

▼ THIN AIR
Air density decreases with altitude, so just 10 km (6 miles) above sea level, there is not enough air to breathe. The thin air at high altitudes reduces atmospheric pressure, allowing water to evaporate more easily and boil at a lower temperature. People living on the high plateau of Tibet can drink tea while it is still boiling.

▼ FRAGILE ENVELOPE
Seen from space, the atmosphere forms a shallow, glowing blue halo around the planet. The outer atmospheric layers are invisible, because the air in them is so thin. Clouds rise to the top of the troposphere, but no further, so all the water vapour in the atmosphere – and all the weather – is concentrated in its lowest layer.

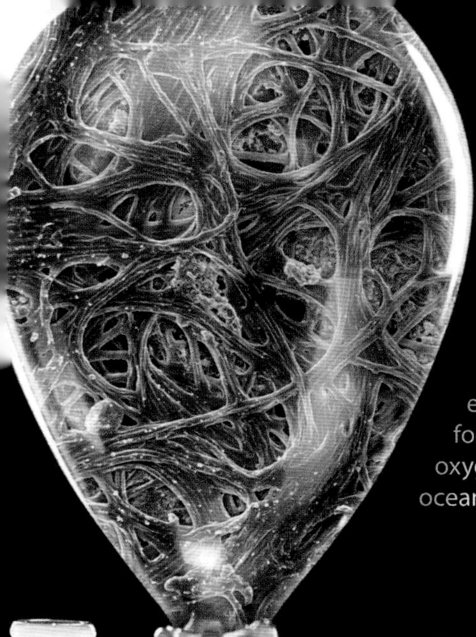

◀OXYGEN

Almost all living organisms depend on oxygen for survival, yet it was not part of Earth's original atmosphere. It was created by organisms called cyanobacteria in the distant past, when bacteria were the only form of life. They were the first living things to use solar energy to turn carbon dioxide and water into food – the process of photosynthesis that releases oxygen. Similar organisms still live today in the oceans and a few shallow coastal lagoons.

▲CLIMATE CHANGE

The greenhouse effect is vital to life on Earth. But we are adding more carbon dioxide and other "greenhouse gases" to the atmosphere – mainly by burning coal, oil, and gas, but also by felling and burning forests. This makes the atmosphere retain more heat, raising the average air temperature, warming the oceans, and melting polar ice. This could have serious consequences for all life on the planet.

▼GREENHOUSE EFFECT

Most of the Sun's rays can pass right through the atmosphere, allowing their energy to warm Earth. The warmed planet radiates heat back into space, but some of this is absorbed by carbon dioxide and a few other gases in the atmosphere. This warms the air, meaning that it retains the heat. This effect keeps the average temperature on Earth roughly 30°C (86°F) higher than it is on the Moon, which has no atmosphere. If heat were not retained in this way, life could not exist.

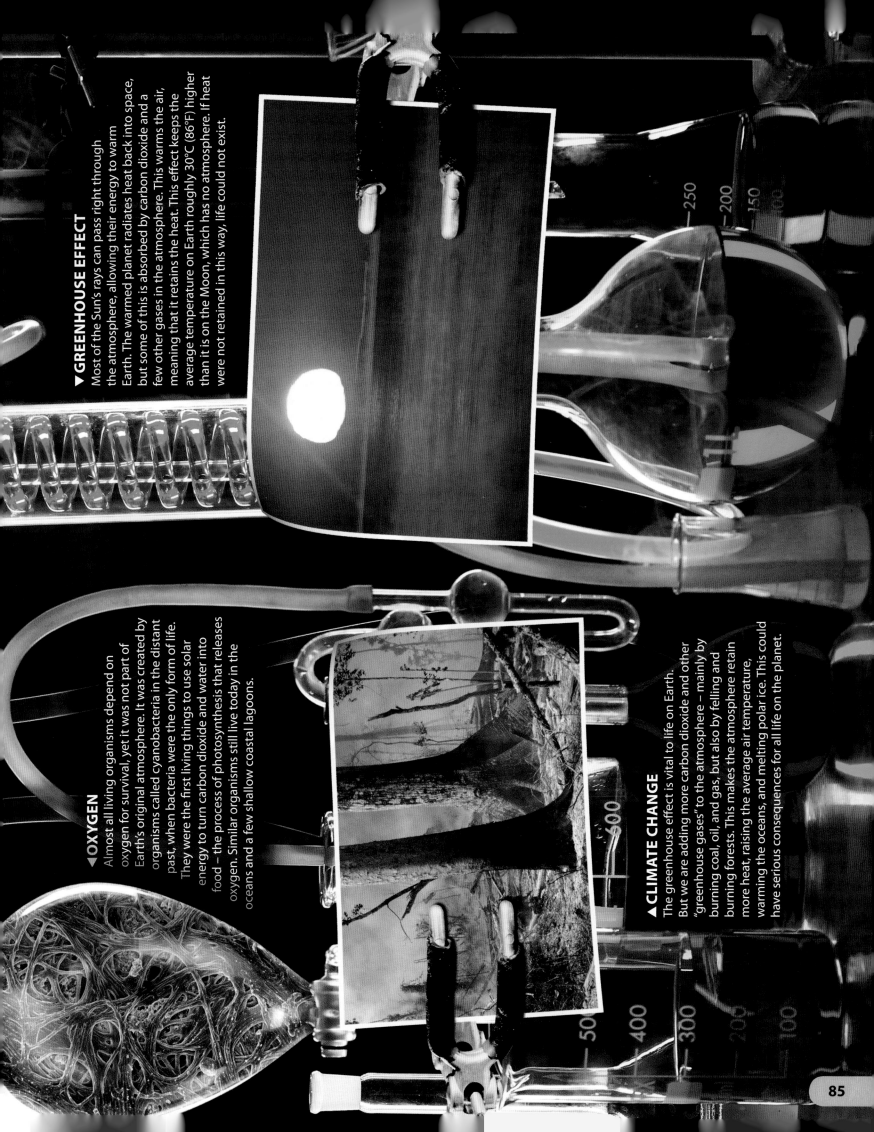

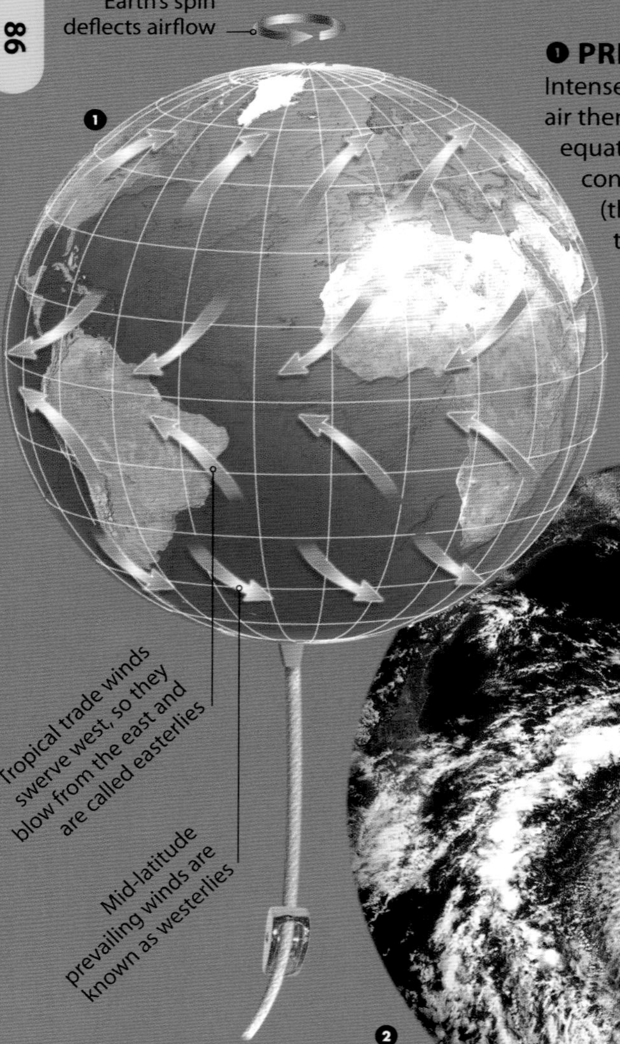

Earth's spin deflects airflow

Tropical trade winds swerve west, so they blow from the east and are called easterlies

Mid-latitude prevailing winds are known as westerlies

1 PREVAILING WINDS

Intense heat in the tropics makes air rise near the equator. The air then sinks in the subtropics and flows back towards the equator as surface winds. This air circulation is known as a convection cell. The winds are deflected by Earth's spin (the Coriolis effect) and swerve towards the west as the trade winds. In regions midway between the poles and the equator, winds are deflected to the east. Since these blow from the west they are called westerlies and include the "Roaring Forties" of the Southern Ocean.

Satellite view of a southern tropical cyclone reveals clouds spiralling clockwise

2 HIGHS AND LOWS

As warm air rises, the upward movement reduces the weight of air to create a low-pressure zone. The rising air draws in more air, which swirls inward and upward in a spiral known as a cyclone, shown in the circling clouds that form as moist air rises and cools. South of the equator the air spirals clockwise, as shown here, while in the north it spirals anticlockwise. Cool, descending air creates cloudless high-pressure anticyclones that spiral in the opposite direction.

Rain falls in a broad column over Montana, US

Thermometers record variations in daily temperatures

6

WEATHER

The weather is powered by the energy radiated by the Sun. Its heat generates convection currents in the lower atmosphere that cause global prevailing winds, and carry moisture and heat around the world. Rising warm, moist air forms low-pressure systems that bring clouds, rain, and snow. These are separated by areas of cooler, sinking air, creating high-pressure conditions that suppress cloud formation, bringing clear skies and sunshine. Air flows from high to low pressure as local winds, often in different directions from prevailing winds, and sometimes with the violence of storms.

3 CLOUD FORMATION

When air rises, it expands and cools. Any invisible water vapour that it contains cools too, and condenses into the countless tiny water droplets – or ice crystals – that form clouds. The condensation process releases energy as heat, making the air warmer. This makes it rise even further, building up more cloud. The cloud may keep building until there is no water vapour left.

4 RAIN

Warm air rising inside clouds pushes cooler air aside. This cooler air sinks and swirls in to replace the rising air. The air currents hurl the cloud droplets around so they collide and form bigger droplets. When these get too heavy to be supported by the rising air, they fall as rain. The strong rising air currents in big clouds can support a greater weight of water, so the rain is heavier when it finally falls.

5 SNOW

At high altitude or in winter, the air can be cold enough for rising water vapour to freeze into microscopic airborne ice crystals. These form as six-sided plates or prisms, but if they are tossed around by air currents inside big clouds they stick together to form snowflakes. Every snowflake has a different arrangement of crystals, so each one is unique.

6 WEATHER FORECASTING

Weather forecasters gather data on atmospheric pressure, temperature, and rainfall using satellites, weather balloons, automatic weather stations, and simple instruments such as these thermometers. Forecasters feed all the figures into a computer program, and this works out how the weather is likely to change.

CLOUDS

There are ten basic types of clouds. Their names are combinations of the Latin words cirrus (curl), stratus (layer), cumulus (heap), and nimbus (rain). Low-level clouds have bases that lie below 2,000 m (6,560 ft). Medium-level clouds, which normally have names beginning with the word alto-, occur at 2,000–6,000 m (6,560–19,680 ft). High-level clouds, with names that begin with cirro-, occur above this. Colossal cumulonimbus storm clouds rise through all the levels, and may be up to 16 km (10 miles) high.

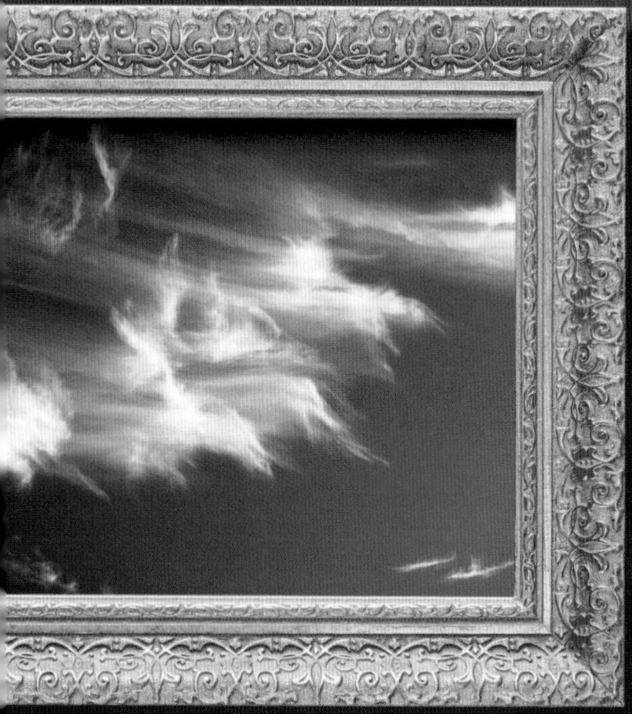

▲ CIRRUS
This basic high-level cloud is formed from tiny ice crystals. Winds sweep the crystals into wispy, curling shapes, so cirrus cloud usually shows the wind direction at high altitude. Although cirrus usually forms in blue skies, it often indicates the approach of rain or snow. It can also be created artificially from the condensation trails of aircraft.

◄ALTOSTRATUS
Mid-level cloud that blends into broad sheets, as in the distance here, is called altostratus. The highest parts are made of ice crystals, but the lower parts are composed of water droplets. Altostratus often starts as a thin layer that allows the Sun to shine through, as here. It then becomes gradually thicker, marking the arrival of a cyclone or depression that will bring wet or snowy weather.

◄NIMBOSTRATUS
Dark, threatening nimbostratus is a thick layer of mid-level or low-level raincloud that blocks out the Sun. It often follows after thinner, mid-level altostratus clouds as a cyclone or depression moves overhead and the weather gets steadily worse. It usually produces persistent rain or snow, which can be heavy but is rarely as torrential as the rain produced during thunderstorms.

▶ALTOCUMULUS

Fleets of small, puffy clouds that drift across the sky at mid-level are called altocumulus. This type of cloud usually develops in a layer of moist air where the air currents are moving in shallow waves. The clouds form at the cooler wave peaks. They can also form patterns of long, parallel cloud bands that either cover the sky or have clear blue sky between them.

▲CIRROSTRATUS

A continuous sheet of high-altitude cloud, as at the top of this picture, is described as cirrostratus. It can turn the sky white by day and red at sunset, but is so thin that the Sun, or even the Moon, is clearly visible through it. If cirrostratus is forming from wispy cirrus clouds, it usually means that bad weather is on the way. But if the cloud is breaking up, it generally means that the weather is going to improve.

◀STRATUS

Any cloud that forms a continuous sheet or layer is known as stratus. It usually forms at low level, turning the whole sky a dreary grey, but may form a little higher, as in this photograph taken at sunset. Stratus often forms when moist air is carried over a cold surface such as the sea, cooling the water vapour so it condenses into cloud. The same process also causes fog.

◀CUMULONIMBUS

The biggest clouds are those that produce torrential rain, lightning, and hail. Seen in the background here, a cumulonimbus cloud has its base near the ground but builds up to the highest level where it often spreads out like a mushroom because it cannot rise any higher. These clouds contain violent upcurrents that toss raindrops and ice crystals up and down until they finally fall as heavy rain and hail.

▶CUMULUS

The fluffy clouds that form in blue summer skies are known as cumulus clouds. They form when warm, moist air rises to a height where the temperature is low enough for water vapour to condense into droplets. As the air rises, cooler air descends around each cloud, and this stops it spreading sideways. Cumulus can grow into more threatening forms, but the type shown here never leads to rain.

EXTREME WEATHER

Intense solar heating can cause very high evaporation rates that make warm, moist air rise unusually fast. This builds up huge cumulonimbus clouds that cause thunderstorms and hail, and creates conditions of extremely low pressure. Air swirls into the low-pressure zone, creating a deep depression with very strong winds. In tropical oceans, intense heating generates hurricanes. In extreme cases the updrafts can give rise to the destructive vortex of a tornado.

▶ HAILSTORMS

The giant cumulonimbus clouds that cause thunderstorms are built up by powerful air currents with vertical speeds of 160 kph (100 mph) or more. Ice crystals hurled around by the turbulent air pick up water that freezes onto them, and if they are tossed up and down enough this builds up layer after layer of ice to form hailstones. If the air currents are strong enough, they can create huge – and very dangerous – hailstones like these.

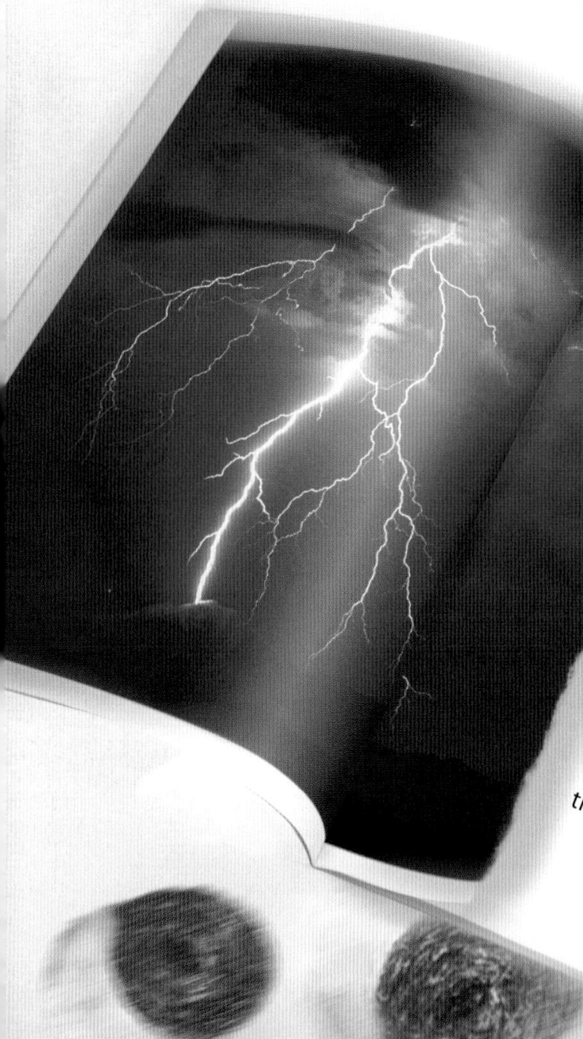

◀ LIGHTNING

As the air currents inside a storm cloud throw ice crystals around, friction between the crystals generates static electricity. It charges up the cloud like a giant battery, with the positive charge at the top and the negative charge at the bottom. If the voltage reaches about one million volts, it is discharged as a giant spark of lightning. This heats the air along its path to such a high temperature that it expands explosively, causing the shockwave that we call thunder.

▶ TORNADOES

These terrifying events are caused by air swirling into the base of a very vigorous storm cloud and spiralling upwards. The updraughts are powerful enough to rip houses apart, and the winds around such tornadoes are the most powerful ever recorded, reaching at least 512 kph (318 mph) on one occasion.

▼ HURRICANES

In tropical oceans, summer warmth makes vast quantities of water turn to water vapour. This rises to form extremely big storm clouds, which circulate around an area of very low air pressure. The clouds spiral inwards, with the windspeed building up to 300 kph (185 mph) or more as the spiral tightens – yet the eye of the storm is calm and clear.

▲ WATERSPOUTS

Tornadoes can develop over seas and large lakes, especially in the tropics and subtropics. The powerful upcurrents spiralling up into the cloud draw water up with them, so they are known as waterspouts. They are usually less violent than tornadoes, but a waterspout is strong enough to easily capsize a boat. It is most destructive when it collapses and dumps its heavy load of water.

Updraught can reach 240 kph (150 mph)
Narrow funnel cloud extends down to ground level

▲ STORM SURGE

During a hurricane, the converging winds and extremely low air pressure over the ocean build up a hump of water or "storm surge". This can sweep over the land like a tsunami and causes massive devastation. A storm surge almost destroyed New Orleans in the US in 2005, and killed at least 150,000 people in Burma (Myanmar) in 2008.

CLIMATES

The climate of any region is basically its average weather – its temperatures, rainfall, and winds – and how this varies from season to season. It is defined by a combination of a region's distance from the equator, its altitude above sea level, and how near it is to an ocean. The climate is one of the key influences on the character of the landscape – whether it is green and lush, barren and dusty, or frozen for part or all of the year. So, although the climate itself is defined by statistics, its effects are usually very obvious.

❶ SOLAR ENERGY
Sunlight is most intense in the tropics, where it strikes Earth directly, and least intense in the polar regions, where it is dispersed. Earth spins on a tilted axis, so the regions facing the Sun most directly change throughout the year, creating the seasons. These become more extreme towards the polar regions, where there is almost constant daylight in summer and constant darkness and extreme cold in winter.

❷ TROPICAL
In the tropics, the intense heat during the day makes vast amounts of water evaporate from the oceans, building up a virtually permanent belt of storm clouds around the world. These spill torrential rain on the land, often almost every day. The rain supports the tropical rainforests, which help make their own climate by pumping more moisture into the air.

❸ SUBTROPICAL
The moist air that rises in the tropics flows away to north and south at high altitude. By the time it reaches the subtropics it has cooled and lost all its water vapour. It starts to sink, creating broad high-pressure zones, but as it sinks it heats up, absorbs any moisture in the land below, and carries it away, creating subtropical deserts such as the Sahara or the arid interior of Australia.

❹ MONSOONS
Northern Asia gets very cold in winter, so it cools the air above and makes it sink. The air flows south towards the Indian Ocean, where it rises again. So in winter India is swept by dry continental air, and there are months of drought. But in summer the continent heats up. This warms the air so it rises and draws moist air from the ocean, causing torrential rain. The seasonal reversal is called a monsoon.

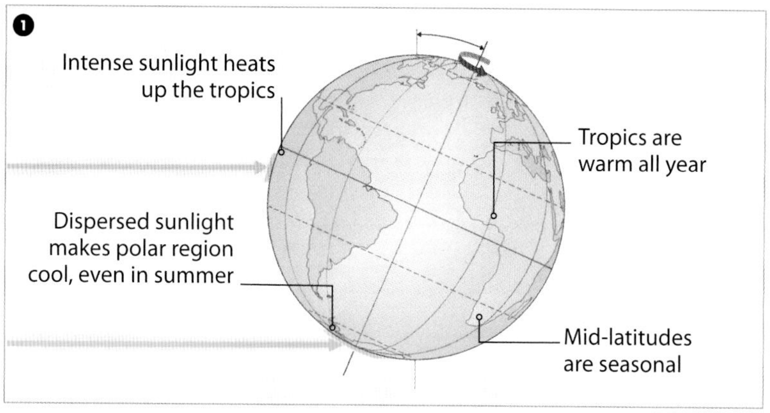

❶
Intense sunlight heats up the tropics
Tropics are warm all year
Dispersed sunlight makes polar region cool, even in summer
Mid-latitudes are seasonal

Solar energy and seasons

❸

Libyan desert

❺

Mediterranean shrubland, France

❷
MENU
OK
SCENE

5 DRY SHRUBLANDS

Around the Mediterranean, and in similar regions such as parts of California and Australia, hot dry summers are followed by mild wet winters. This suits evergreen shrubs with small, leathery leaves, such as wild olive and sagebrush, which lie dormant in summer and grow in the winter. Many are adapted to survive frequent fires, and some even need a fire to make them release their seeds.

6 MARITIME

In the temperate regions, weather systems move east from the oceans over the land. This means that the western fringes of the continents – places such as Ireland – have mild, often damp maritime climates, with forests and lush grass. By the time the air reaches the continental heartlands it has lost most of its moisture, so the forests are replaced by dry grassland and even deserts.

7 POLAR FRINGES

The Arctic ice is surrounded by treeless, barren-looking tundra that eventually gives way to a vast belt of evergreen forest. The winters are extremely cold, especially in continental regions that are a long way from oceans. In the tundra this creates permanently frozen ground, or permafrost. The summers are cool, but warm enough to melt the winter snow and allow tough, cold-adapted plants to grow.

8 POLAR DESERTS

Very little snow falls over polar regions, owing to cold air sinking over the poles and preventing cloud formation. These regions are, in fact, cold deserts. Over most of Greenland and Antarctica the summers are not warm enough to melt the snow, which builds up over centuries to create permanent ice sheets. Plants cannot grow in such conditions, and there is very little life at all.

Monsoon rains, India

Coastline, Republic of Ireland

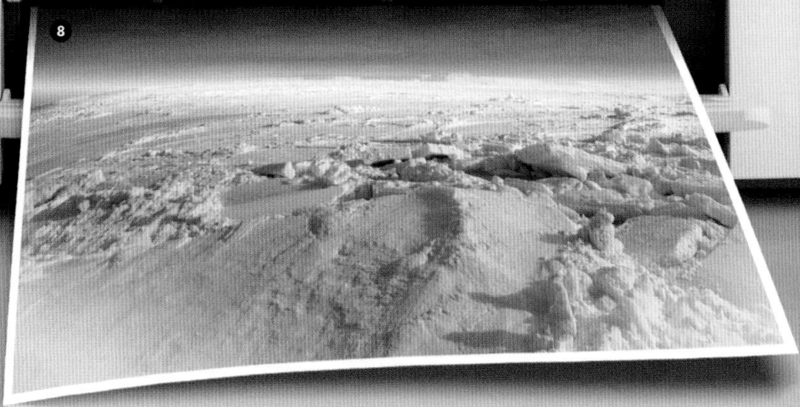

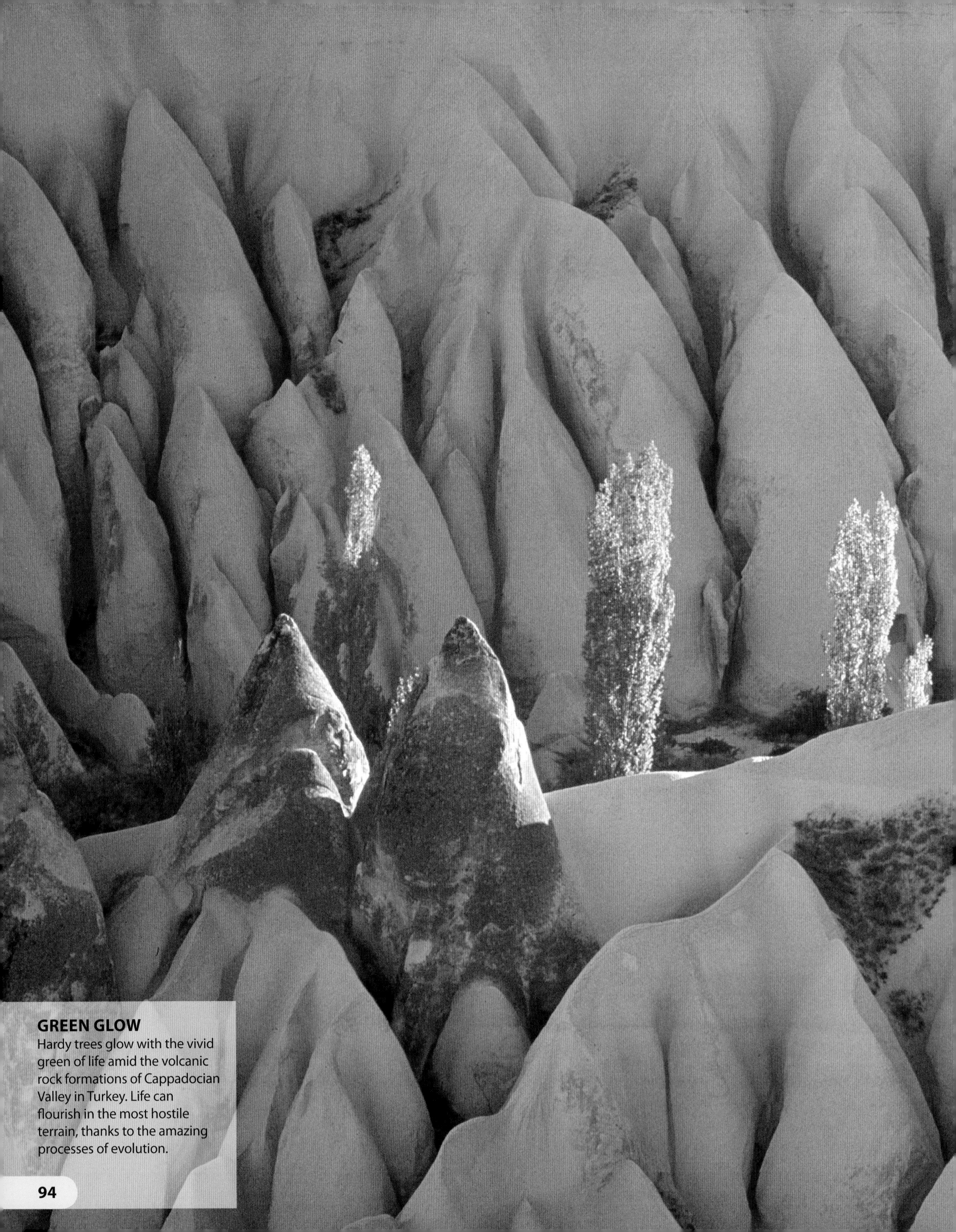

GREEN GLOW
Hardy trees glow with the vivid green of life amid the volcanic rock formations of Cappadocian Valley in Turkey. Life can flourish in the most hostile terrain, thanks to the amazing processes of evolution.

Life zones

STORY OF LIFE

No one really knows how life began. Some people suggest that the seeds of life might have been delivered to Earth in some of the many frozen, watery comets that crashed into the planet early in its history. This may be possible, but any organic material that arrived in this way must have been formed somewhere, by a process that assembled simple chemicals into the extremely complex molecules that are vital to even the most primitive life forms. Most scientists believe that this happened here on Earth, roughly 3.8 billion years ago, within 800 million years of the formation of the planet.

❶ FORMATION OF EARTH
When Earth formed out of a mass of gas and dust some 4.6 billion years ago, it was a biologically dead planet. But its cooling rocks contained all the elements that are vital to the chemistry of living organisms. Its gravity and position in the Solar System also enabled it to retain an atmosphere and oceans of liquid water – both essential conditions for the evolution of life.

❷ ORGANIC MOLECULES
All life depends on the carbon-based molecules that form complex organic materials such as proteins. Living organisms make their own proteins, using coded instructions contained in the spiral molecules of DNA (deoxyribonucleic acid) inherited from their parents. But the very first organic molecules must have been formed by a purely chemical reaction, possibly triggered by the electrical energy of lightning.

❸ LIVING CELLS
The DNA molecule can reproduce itself by splitting in two and adding raw chemicals to each half. To do this – and to make proteins – it needs a reliable supply of chemical nutrients. Key to the evolution of life was the development of the cell – a microscopic package containing water and vital nutrients, as well as DNA and other organic molecules. The first such cells were bacteria, the simplest of all life forms.

❹ ENERGY FROM LIGHT
Life needs energy. Some 3.8 billion years ago, the first bacteria relied on the energy locked up in chemicals. Similar organisms still survive in hot springs. More than a billion years later, bacteria evolved a way to absorb the energy of sunlight, and use it to turn carbon dioxide and water into sugar and oxygen. By this process, called photosynthesis, these cyanobacteria created all the oxygen in the atmosphere.

❺ SUPERCELLS
Bacteria are simple "prokaryotic" cells – tiny bags of chemicals and organic molecules. Approximately 2.5 billion years ago, a more complex type of cell evolved, with structures specialized for different tasks. These include a nucleus that contains the cell's DNA and controls other structures such as those that turn food into energy. Such "eukaryotic" cells are more diverse than bacteria and include a huge variety of single-celled organisms such as planktonic diatoms.

❻ CELL COLONIES
All the earliest living things were single-celled organisms, like most microbes today. Over time, however, some joined together to form colonies like *Volvox* – a modern freshwater organism that is made up of more than 500 eukaryotic cells linked in a sphere. By about 2.2 billion years ago, similar colonies included specialized cells that relied on the others for vital support. Such colonies were becoming the first multi-celled organisms.

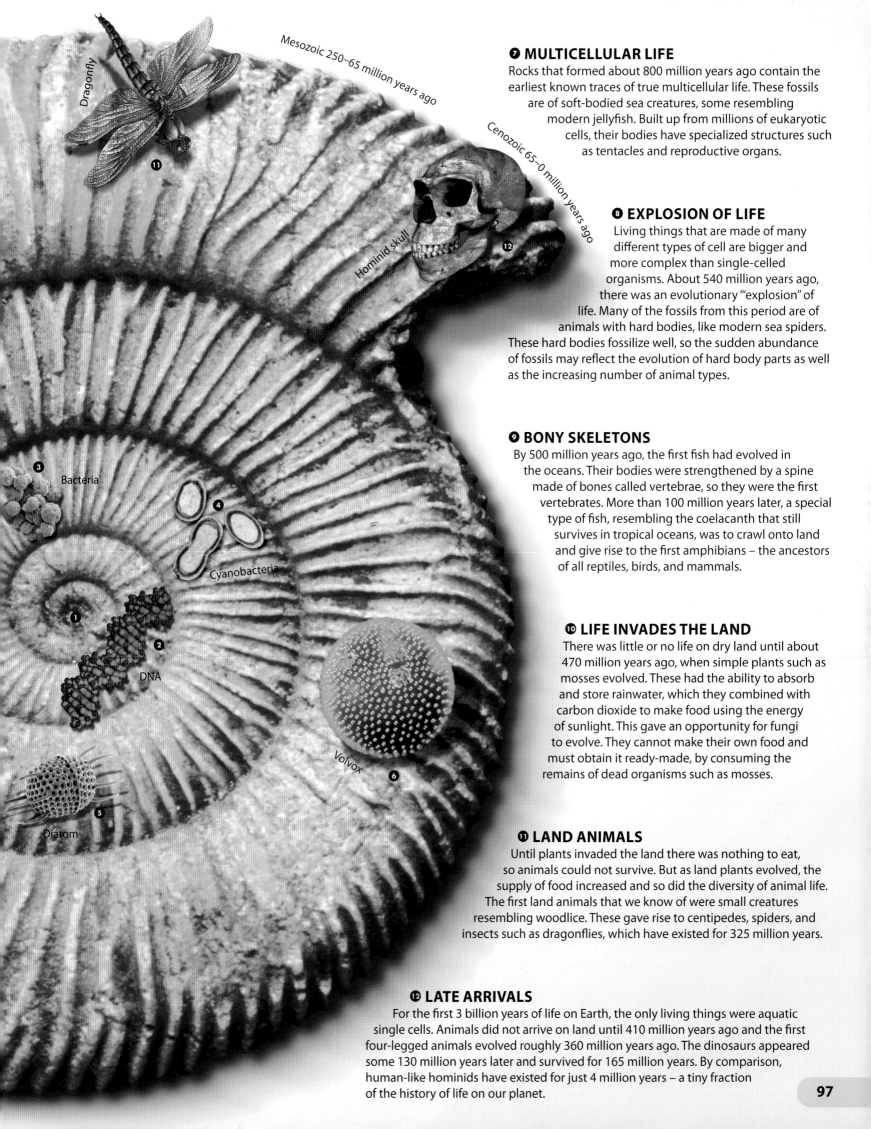

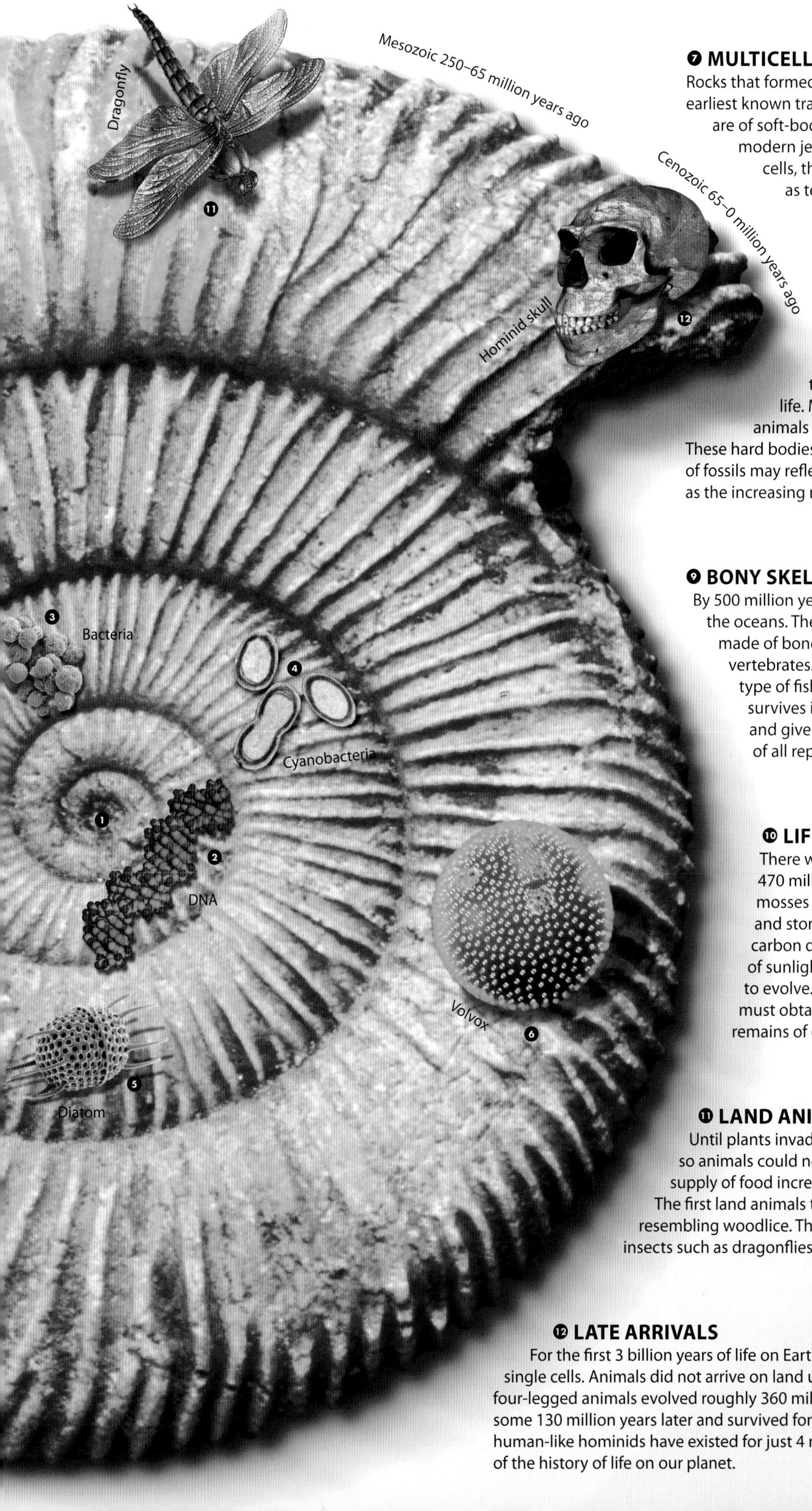

7 MULTICELLULAR LIFE

Rocks that formed about 800 million years ago contain the earliest known traces of true multicellular life. These fossils are of soft-bodied sea creatures, some resembling modern jellyfish. Built up from millions of eukaryotic cells, their bodies have specialized structures such as tentacles and reproductive organs.

8 EXPLOSION OF LIFE

Living things that are made of many different types of cell are bigger and more complex than single-celled organisms. About 540 million years ago, there was an evolutionary "explosion" of life. Many of the fossils from this period are of animals with hard bodies, like modern sea spiders. These hard bodies fossilize well, so the sudden abundance of fossils may reflect the evolution of hard body parts as well as the increasing number of animal types.

9 BONY SKELETONS

By 500 million years ago, the first fish had evolved in the oceans. Their bodies were strengthened by a spine made of bones called vertebrae, so they were the first vertebrates. More than 100 million years later, a special type of fish, resembling the coelacanth that still survives in tropical oceans, was to crawl onto land and give rise to the first amphibians – the ancestors of all reptiles, birds, and mammals.

10 LIFE INVADES THE LAND

There was little or no life on dry land until about 470 million years ago, when simple plants such as mosses evolved. These had the ability to absorb and store rainwater, which they combined with carbon dioxide to make food using the energy of sunlight. This gave an opportunity for fungi to evolve. They cannot make their own food and must obtain it ready-made, by consuming the remains of dead organisms such as mosses.

11 LAND ANIMALS

Until plants invaded the land there was nothing to eat, so animals could not survive. But as land plants evolved, the supply of food increased and so did the diversity of animal life. The first land animals that we know of were small creatures resembling woodlice. These gave rise to centipedes, spiders, and insects such as dragonflies, which have existed for 325 million years.

12 LATE ARRIVALS

For the first 3 billion years of life on Earth, the only living things were aquatic single cells. Animals did not arrive on land until 410 million years ago and the first four-legged animals evolved roughly 360 million years ago. The dinosaurs appeared some 130 million years later and survived for 165 million years. By comparison, human-like hominids have existed for just 4 million years – a tiny fraction of the history of life on our planet.

BIODIVERSITY

The last 800 million years have seen a spectacular diversification of life in all its forms. The single-celled organisms that dominated life for the previous 3 billion years have been joined by fungi, plants, and animals which, together with bacteria and the mainly single-celled protists, make up the five kingdoms of life. While millions of species have evolved, millions more have suffered extinction, in an endless process that is constantly transforming the nature of life on Earth.

◀PLANTS
Nearly all plants use energy from the Sun to turn carbon dioxide and water into food using a process called photosynthesis. This creates the food that is vital to other forms of life on land. The first plants were low-growing mosses, later joined by ferns and cycads, and the conifers and flowering plants that include many trees.

▼FUNGI
Unlike a plant, a fungus cannot make its own food and must consume it in ready-made form, just like an animal. Microscopic yeasts are single-celled, but most fungi are multi-celled, with networks of thread-like stems that may produce the spore-bearing structures we call mushrooms. Some fungi contain food-making algae, forming tough, compound organisms called lichens.

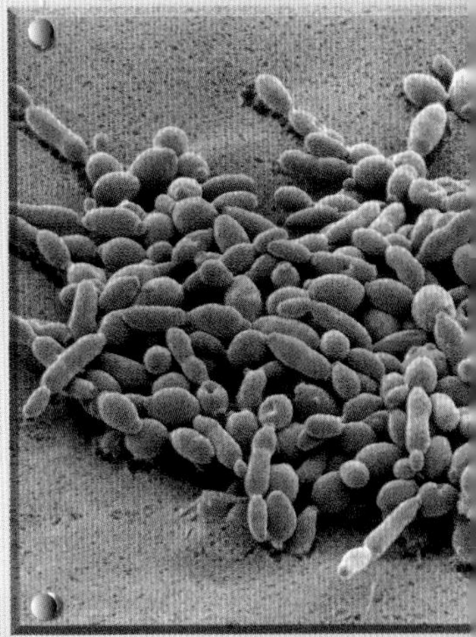

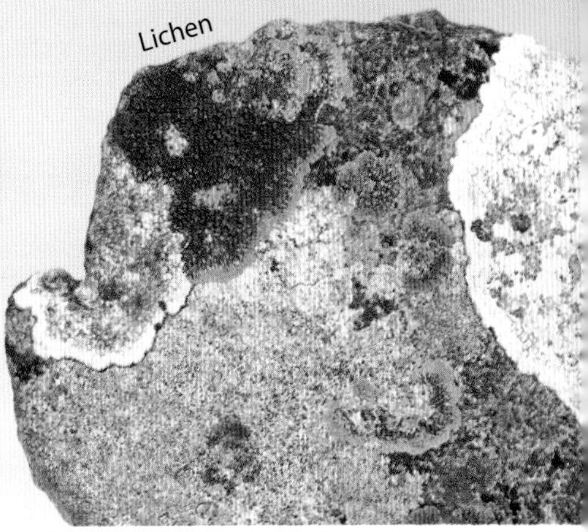

▲ANIMAL LIFE – ON LAND
As animals became adapted to life on land, they had to evolve ways of stopping their bodies from drying out. Some retained a connection with water for breeding, but others developed ways of breeding that did not involve water. Some animals, such as snails, land crabs, and frogs, are still tied to moist places. Others, such as insects, reptiles, mammals, and birds, have been able to colonize every viable habitat on dry land.

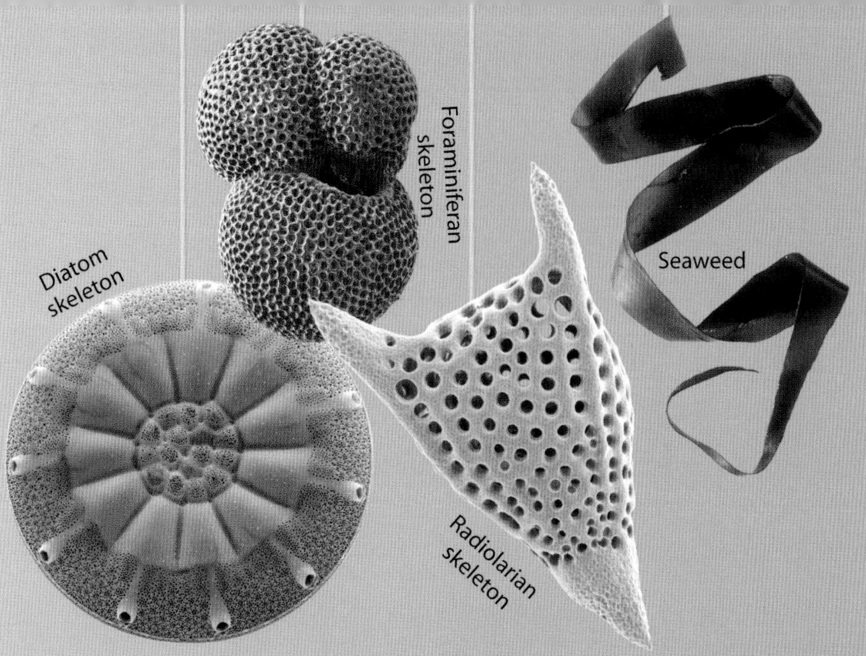

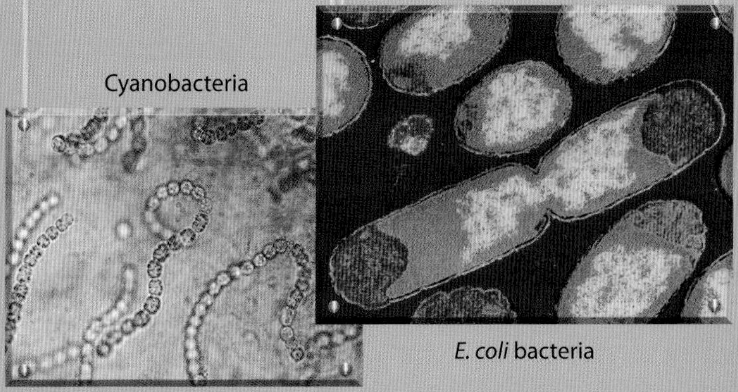

E. coli bacteria

▲ BACTERIA

The simplest of all life-forms, bacteria consist of a single "prokaryotic" cell, which has a much simpler structure than the eukaryotic cells of protists and multi-celled organisms. Despite this, some forms – cyanobacteria – use photosynthesis to make food, releasing oxygen in the process. In the distant past, this produced the oxygen that made animal life possible.

▲ PROTISTS

Most protists are microscopic organisms, each consisting of a single "eukaryotic" cell. Some, such as diatoms and algae, make food in the same way as plants. Others, such as foraminiferans and radiolarians, are consumers that behave as animals. All these drift in oceans as plankton. Seaweeds are multicelled algae, which can grow very much bigger.

▶ ANIMAL LIFE – IN WATER

All animals are multicelled organisms that get their nutrients from food produced by other living things. They also need oxygen to turn some of these nutrients into energy. The first animals evolved in water, and most still live in aquatic habitats. They range from sponges, which are little more than colonies of cells, to highly active vertebrates such as fish.

OCEAN LIFE

Most of the life on Earth lives in the surface zone of the oceans. Here, sunlight provides the energy for plankton and seaweeds to produce food by photosynthesis, and this supports the animals. The deep oceans are too dark for photosynthesis, so animals survive by eating debris drifting down from above, or by eating each other. In general, energy passes up the food chain from microscopic plankton to the most powerful hunters.

1 Phytoplankton These microscopic single-celled protists turn raw chemicals into the organic tissue that other organisms rely on for food. They thrive only in nutrient-rich water, especially around coasts and in polar oceans.

2 Zooplankton Swarms of mainly tiny animals drift with the phytoplankton, eating it and preying upon each other. They include adult animals such as copepods, and the larvae of creatures such as crabs and molluscs that change their way of life when they mature.

3 Herring Shoals of small to medium-sized fish, such as anchovy and herring, feed on the plankton, using their gill rakers to strain the small organisms from the water. These shoals can build up to immense sizes in plankton-rich seas.

4 Seabirds Fish shoals are attacked from the air by squadrons of seabirds, such as gannets. These birds plunge headlong into the water to seize the fish in their long bills. They spend most of their time hunting at sea, but breed in vast coastal colonies.

5 Tuna The shoals of fish that target plankton swarms attract bigger, predatory fish, such as salmon and tuna. These also form shoals, but are more mobile, crossing oceans in search of prey. Tuna are fast swimmers and travel very long distances.

6 Sharks Hunters such as tuna are hunted in turn by bigger predators such as marlin, swordfish, and oceanic sharks. The tiger shark is one of the most powerful and dangerous, with sharp teeth that can slice straight through a turtle shell.

7 Filter-feeding giant The biggest animals in the sea are giant sharks and whales that feed by straining small animals from the water. The basking shark may grow to more than 12 m (40 ft) long.

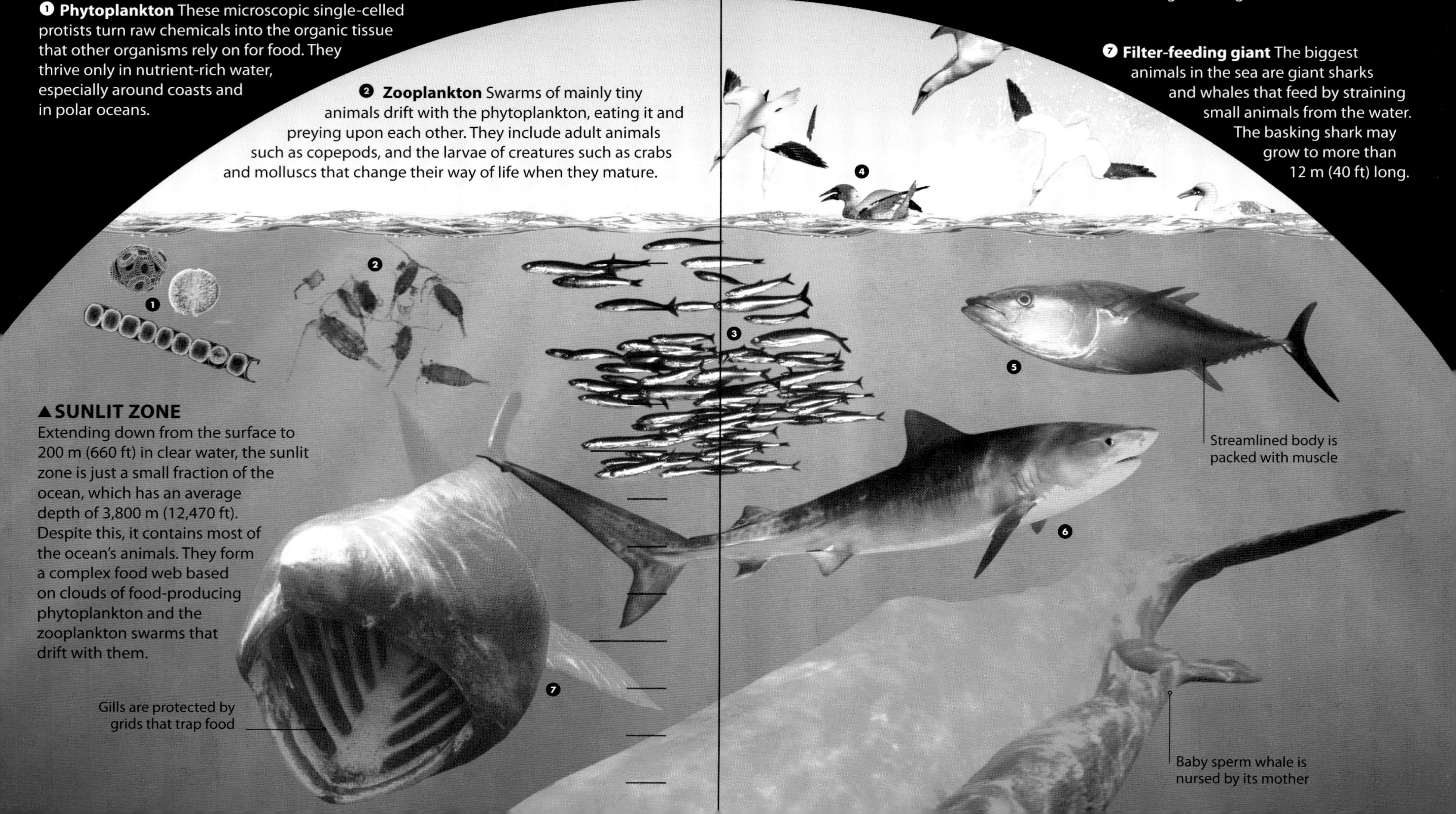

▲SUNLIT ZONE

Extending down from the surface to 200 m (660 ft) in clear water, the sunlit zone is just a small fraction of the ocean, which has an average depth of 3,800 m (12,470 ft). Despite this, it contains most of the ocean's animals. They form a complex food web based on clouds of food-producing phytoplankton and the zooplankton swarms that drift with them.

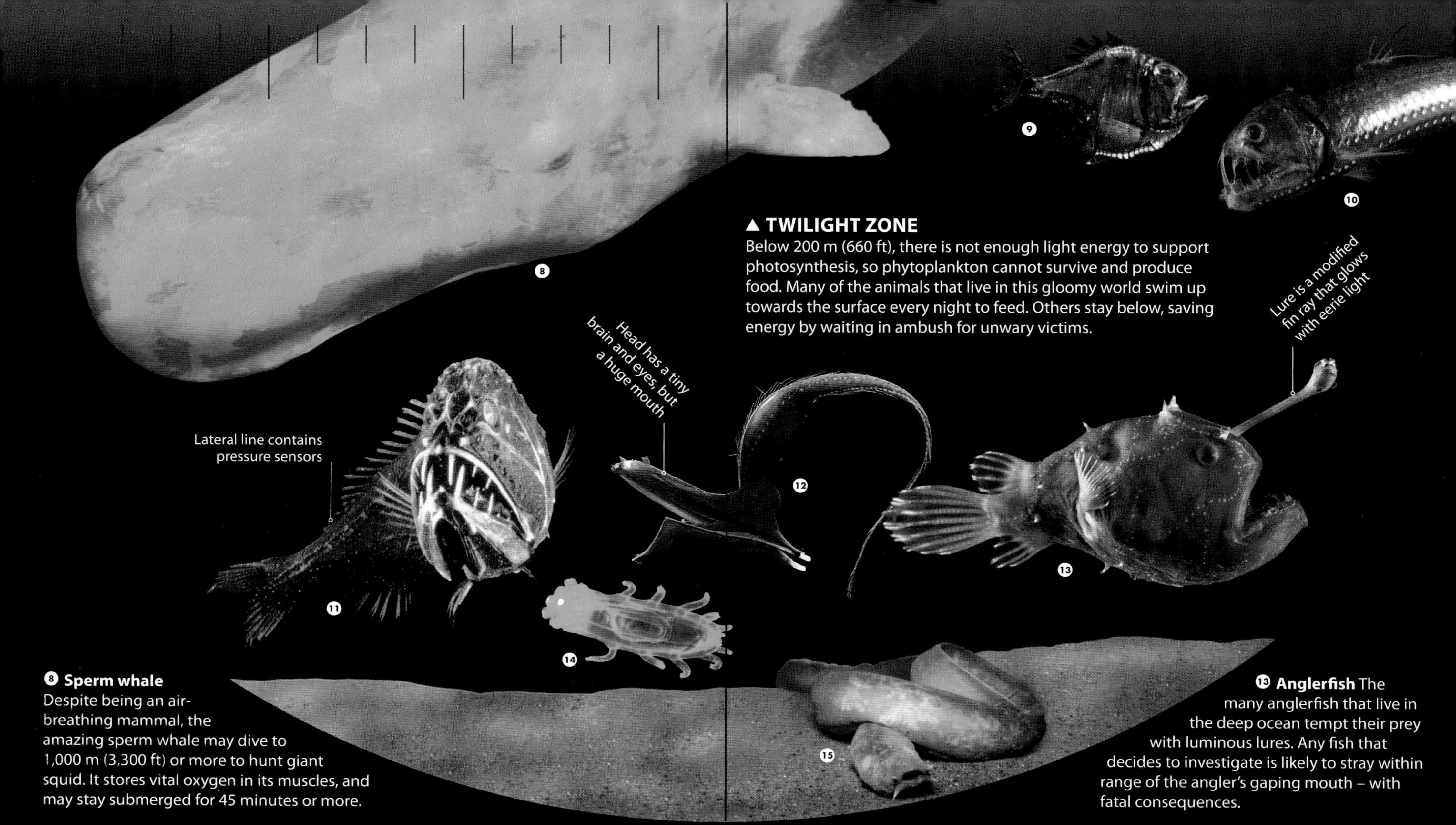

▲ TWILIGHT ZONE

Below 200 m (660 ft), there is not enough light energy to support photosynthesis, so phytoplankton cannot survive and produce food. Many of the animals that live in this gloomy world swim up towards the surface every night to feed. Others stay below, saving energy by waiting in ambush for unwary victims.

8 Sperm whale
Despite being an air-breathing mammal, the amazing sperm whale may dive to 1,000 m (3,300 ft) or more to hunt giant squid. It stores vital oxygen in its muscles, and may stay submerged for 45 minutes or more.

9 Hatchetfish These flattened fish eat small animals that live in the twilight zone by day but migrate to the surface at night. Their bellies glow with blue light that matches the glow from the surface, hiding their silhouette.

10 Viperfish Prey is scarce in the ocean depths, so like most hunters of the deep, the viperfish has extremely long, needle-like teeth to ensure that anything it catches has no chance of escaping.

▲ DARK ZONE

Below 1,000 m (3,300 ft), the last glimmer of blue twilight fades out, and the water is pitch black apart from the mysterious glow of the luminous animals that live here. Many fish are nightmarish hunters with long teeth and huge, gaping mouths. The deep ocean floor is populated by debris feeders that recycle the remains of dead animals drifting down from above.

11 Fangtooth Like the viperfish, the fangtooth has an impressive array of weapons for catching its victims. It has highly developed senses for detecting prey in the dark, including an acute awareness of pressure changes and vibrations in the water.

12 Gulper eel The bizarre gulper eels are nearly all mouth, with colossal gapes and stretchy, balloon-like stomachs. This enables some species to engulf animals that are their own size or bigger, providing them with enough food to last for several weeks.

13 Anglerfish The many anglerfish that live in the deep ocean tempt their prey with luminous lures. Any fish that decides to investigate is likely to stray within range of the angler's gaping mouth – with fatal consequences.

14 Sea cucumber Most sea cucumbers crawl over the ocean floor, sucking up the soft sediment, swallowing it, and digesting anything edible. But some deepwater species like this one can also swim a little.

15 Hagfish One of many deepwater scavengers, the slimy hagfish burrows into the carcasses of dead animals to eat them from the inside out. Its acute sense of smell enables it to locate food from far away.

CORAL REEFS AND ATOLLS

Tropical coral reefs are among the richest ecosystems on Earth. Their wealth is based on a partnership between corals, which are colonial animals related to sea anemones, and microscopic organisms living in their tissues that are able to make food by photosynthesis. Since these depend on light for their energy supply, the reefs are restricted to the clear, shallow, sunlit waters around tropical coasts and islands. They provide habitats for a dazzling diversity of marine life, ranging from tiny reef fish to giant clams.

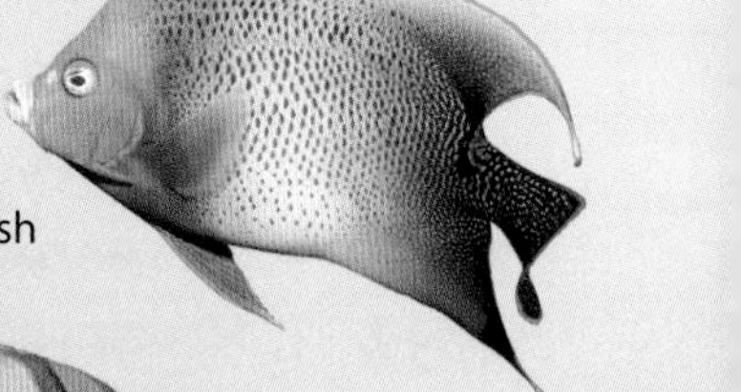
Blue angelfish

Copperband butterfly fish

1 BARRIER REEFS AND ATOLLS

Many coral reefs have formed around extinct volcanoes that are steadily subsiding under their own weight. The living coral keeps growing upwards as the bedrock of the island sinks, to create an offshore barrier reef sheltering a shallow lagoon. When the original volcanic island finally sinks from sight, all that remains is a ring of coral, often capped with sandy islands, known as an atoll.

2 STONY CORALS

Coral polyps are small cylindrical animals crowned with a ring of stinging tentacles, but they live in interconnected colonies that form branches, broad plates, massive blocks, and other shapes. The colonies are supported by skeletons of limestone secreted by the coral tissues. When individual corals die, the limestone remains. Living coral grows on top of the dead coral, so the limestone gradually builds up into rocky reefs.

Indo-Pacific sergeant

❸ REEF FISH

The total weight of fish, or biomass, on a coral reef is not large compared with some other marine habitats, but there is an amazing diversity of species. They have evolved because there are so many different ways to make a living on the reef. Some, such as parrotfish, eat the coral itself. Others nibble at algae, catch plankton, or prey on each other.

Grey reef sharks

❹ INVERTEBRATES

All kinds of colourful invertebrates live on coral reefs, including delicate prawns, flamboyant sea slugs, and deadly venomous cone shells. The biggest is the giant clam which, like corals, has masses of photosynthetic organisms called zooxanthellae living within its tissues. These provide the clam with sugar in exchange for nutrients that the clam obtains by filtering plankton from the water.

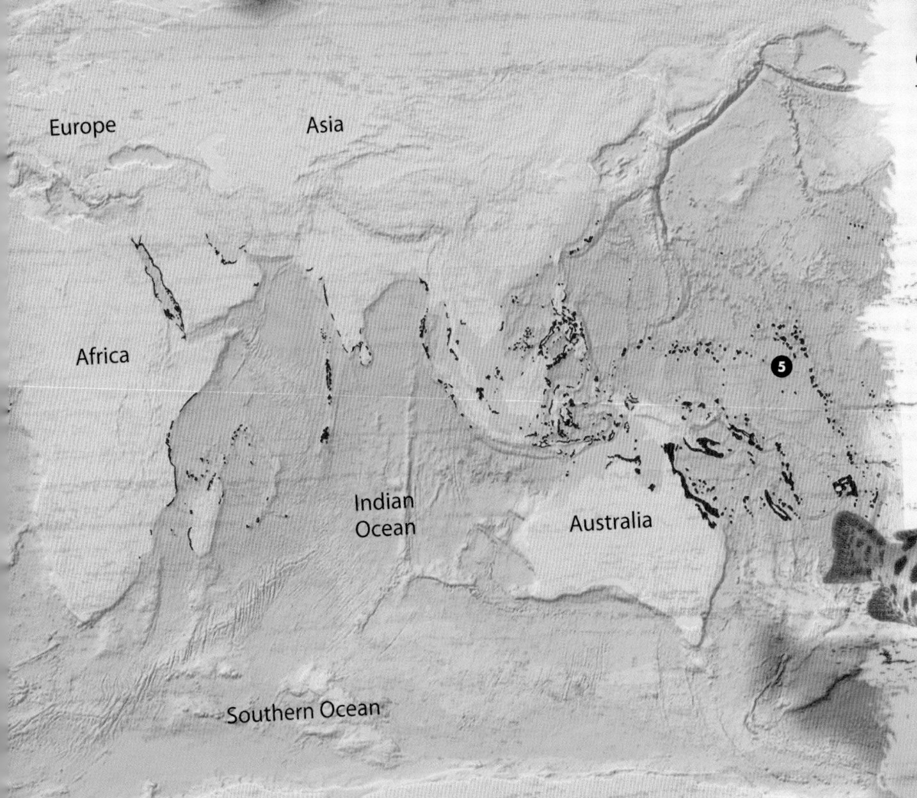

❺ CORAL ISLANDS

The tropical southwest Pacific is dotted with tens of thousands of coral islands. Most are too small to have names, and rise only a metre or two above the waves, but many are crowned with groves of coconut palm and other trees. These provide nesting sites for seabirds, while the beaches are used by breeding sea turtles.

Potato cod

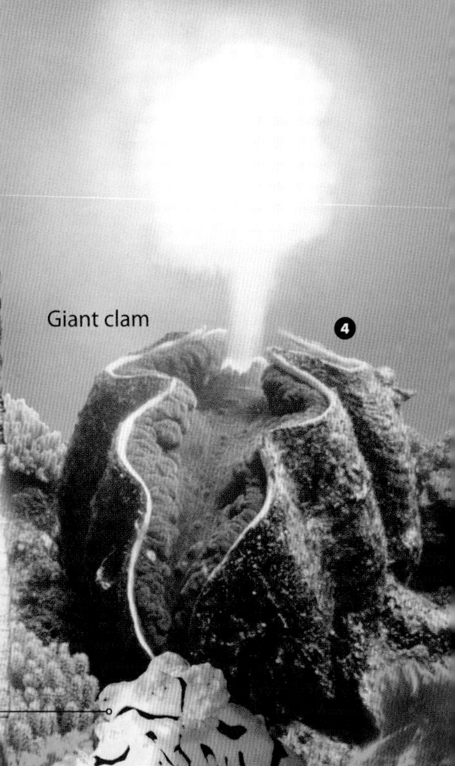

Giant clam

Brightly coloured sea slugs nibble at encrusting animals on the reef

❻ THREATS

Tropical stony corals thrive in sea temperatures of 20–29°C (68–84°F). If the water gets warmer than this, they may expel their microscopic, food-making partners and turn white, often with fatal results. Known as coral bleaching, this is posing an increasing threat to coral reefs as ocean temperatures rise. Another threat is the crown-of-thorns starfish, a coral-eater that can multiply rapidly and destroy large areas of coral.

Crown-of-thorns starfish

▼ CYPRESS SWAMP
Most trees cannot survive in waterlogged conditions, but some species like the American bald cypress have special "knee roots" that gather vital oxygen from above the water. They grow in flooded cypress swamps in the subtropical southern US states, famous for the rare, beautiful orchids that take root on the tree branches.

WETLANDS

Most wetlands are freshwater habitats where most of the water is hidden by dense vegetation. Many are transition zones between open water and dry forest or grassland. They range from overgrown lake and river margins to waterlogged forests with tall trees. Many support a wide diversity of wildlife. Others, such as acid peat bogs, are colonized by only a few specialized plants and animals. Yet even these are rich habitats compared to deserts, because they are so well supplied with the substance vital to all life – water.

▲ PAPYRUS SWAMP
The margins of many African lakes and rivers are choked with a type of giant sedge called papyrus, as seen here in the Okavango Delta in Botswana. The matted plants can also form floating islands. Virtually nothing else grows in these papyrus swamps, but they provide safe refuges for a great variety of animal life including waterbirds, crocodiles, and herds of hippos that spend their days in the water and emerge at night to feed on the surrounding grasslands.

▲ MARSH AND FEN
Low-lying waterlogged land supports grasses, sedges, and reeds that root in the mud, forming a marsh. As the plants die they do not decay properly in the waterlogged soil, but build up as peat. Over time, water-tolerant trees such as willow and alder take root, dry out the peat, and turn the marsh into fen woodland.

Cattle egret

▶ MANGROVES

Sheltered tropical coasts and river estuaries are colonized by mangroves – evergreen trees that can grow in salty, waterlogged soil thanks to root modifications like those of swamp cypresses. The mangrove forests are flooded at high tide, providing safe havens for many fish. Low tide reveals muddy swamps, alive with fiddler crabs and air-breathing fish called mudskippers.

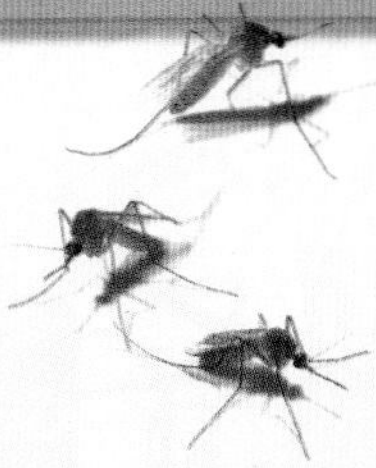

Mosquitoes

▶ ACID PEAT BOG

In cool, wet regions, spongy sphagnum moss grows on top of waterlogged plant remains to create acid peat bogs. Few other plants can grow in the acid, infertile conditions, but those that can include specialists such as carnivorous fly-traps, which feed on the mosquitoes that breed in the bog pools.

◀ TUNDRA SWAMP

In the far north, evergreen forest gives way to the open tundra that surrounds the poles. Here, the ground is permanently frozen at depth, forming a layer of permafrost. The surface thaws in summer, but the waterproof permafrost layer prevents the meltwater draining away, so the defrosted tundra becomes a waterlogged swamp. It resembles an acid peat bog, but colder, and only a few tough plants can survive the combination of waterlogged soils, icy winds, and winter freezing.

◀ TROPICAL SEASONAL WETLAND

During the tropical rainy season, the great rivers that drain the forests and savannas burst their banks to flood the landscape. In southern Amazonia this creates the Pantanal, which at peak flood covers 195,000 sq km (75,000 sq miles), making it the largest wetland in the world. The whole area becomes a habitat for aquatic animals, such as these spectacled caymans, the anaconda – the world's biggest snake – and the giant river otter.

Anaconda

▶ SALT MARSH

Muddy estuaries in temperate regions are colonized by low-growing salt-tolerant plants, forming tidal salt marshes. The regions nearest to the coast are dominated by fleshy plants and grasses, but other areas are more shrubby. They provide homes for a variety of small animals, including the endangered salt marsh harvest mouse of California.

Salt marsh harvest mouse

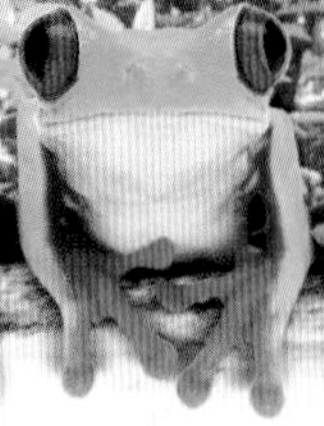

Red-eyed tree frog, Central America

FORESTS

Forests and woodlands are dense stands of trees growing so closely together that their crowns form a virtually continuous canopy, shading the ground below. Trees cannot grow so densely in dry climates, so forests are restricted to regions that experience regular rainfall, or where the climate is so cool that the ground never dries out. Other plants grow among the trees where they can get enough light. The trees also provide food-rich habitats for a wide variety of animals.

▼ TROPICAL RAINFOREST

Near the equator, heavy rain and high temperatures throughout the year create ideal conditions for tree growth, and these are the most luxuriant forests in the world. The trees are broad-leaved evergreens that grow to immense heights, creating a multi-layered habitat that teems with life – most of it living high above the forest floor.

Woolly monkey, Amazonia

▲ DRY WOODLAND

The delicate leaves of rainforest trees are destroyed by long droughts, so many trees that live in dryer climates, such as in Mediterranean and eucalypt forests, have evolved tougher types of leaves. The leaves of these Spanish cork oaks have thicker outer layers so they do not dry up. The bark of these trees has been harvested to be turned into cork.

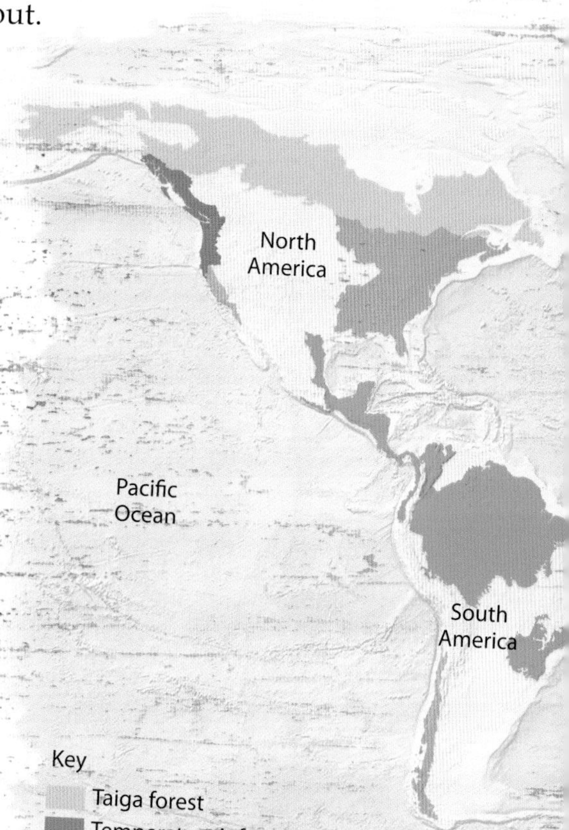

Key
- Taiga forest
- Temperate rainforest
- Tropical rainforest
- Temperate deciduous/mixed forest
- Dry woodland/eucalypt forest

Green rosella, Tasmania

◀ TEMPERATE RAINFOREST

Rainforests are not restricted to the tropics. Similar trees also grow in temperate rainforests, where the climate is cooler but still very wet, with mild, often frost-free winters. Forests of this type grow in Japan, New Zealand, and Tasmania, and include the giant redwood forests on the northern Pacific coast of North America.

Two-tailed pasha, southern Europe

◀ CONIFER FOREST

Coniferous trees such as cedar and cypress that grow in dry regions have leaves that are reduced to waxy needles to resist moisture loss. This leaf form also resists freezing, so needle-leafed conifers such as pine and spruce dominate the cold taiga forests that form a vast band around the north, through Alaska, Canada, Scandinavia, and Russia.

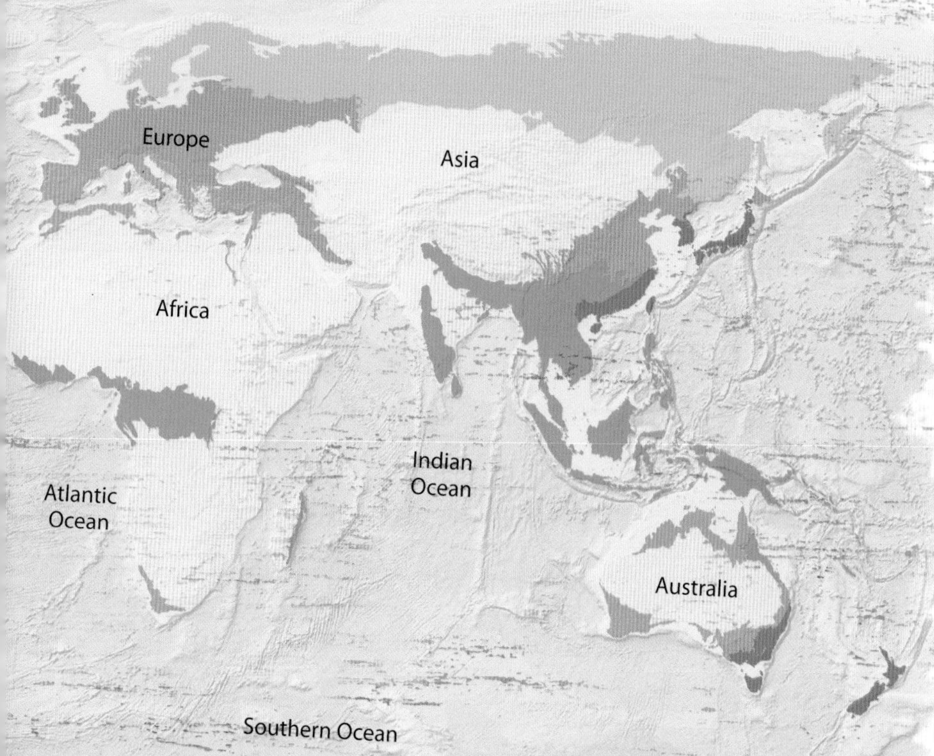

▲ BAMBOO FOREST

Many parts of the world have forests that are dominated by a particular type of tree. Unusually the forests of southwest China are dominated by bamboo, which is a type of giant grass. Along with rhododendron, it forms a dense undergrowth beneath the tall trees, and provides food for the bamboo-eating giant panda.

Fallow deer, UK

◀ DRY EUCALYPT FOREST

Most of the native trees of Australia are various types of eucalypt, with about 450 species altogether. They typically have fire-resistant bark and thick, leathery leaves that resist drying out in the hot sunshine. The leaves are full of oils that make them taste bad, but depite this they are the sole food of the koala, which is specially adapted to digest them.

▶ TEMPERATE DECIDUOUS FOREST

Some trees that live in temperate regions, such as oaks, beeches, and maples, have evolved thin, delicate leaves that make the most of the summer sun to photosynthesize. These leaves turn brown, die, and are discarded as winter closes in, and are replaced with a new set in spring.

▼ AFRICAN SAVANNA
The tropical grasslands of Africa are typically vast seas of grass dotted with drought-resistant acacia and baobab trees. Only a few of the world's grasslands, such as the Serengeti Plains of Tanzania, have retained their original wildlife. Vast herds of antelope and zebra migrate across the plains to find good grazing. They provide food for hunters such as lions and hyenas.

GRASSLANDS

In regions that are too dry for forests, but not quite dry enough to be described as deserts, the natural vegetation is grass. Other plants are dotted among the grasses, including scattered trees, but grass dominates the landscape. Temperate grasslands tend to be dry throughout the year, but tropical grasslands have long rainy seasons followed by long droughts. They support herds of large grazing mammals, many of which migrate over long distances to exploit seasonal flushes of lush growth.

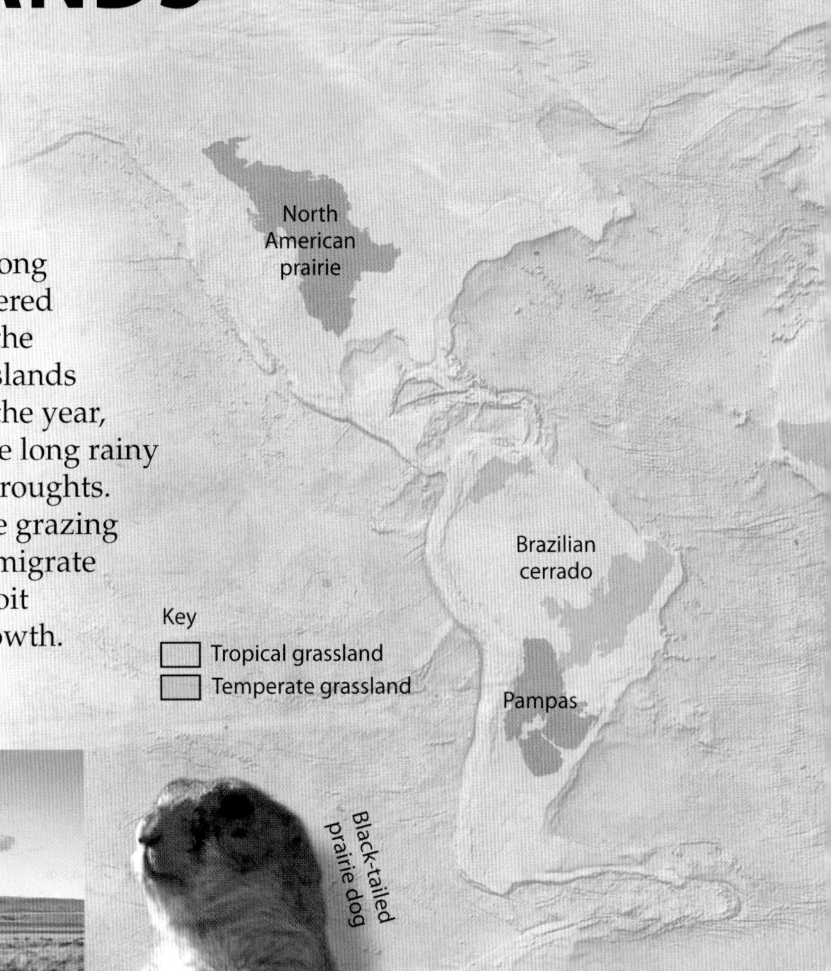

▲ PAMPAS
Many dry grasslands develop in the lee (sheltered side) of high mountain ranges that intercept all the rain carried on prevailing winds. In South America, the Andes strip the moisture from winds blowing off the Pacific, and the lands in the "rain shadow" to the east of the mountains form the cool, dry Pampas of southern Argentina.

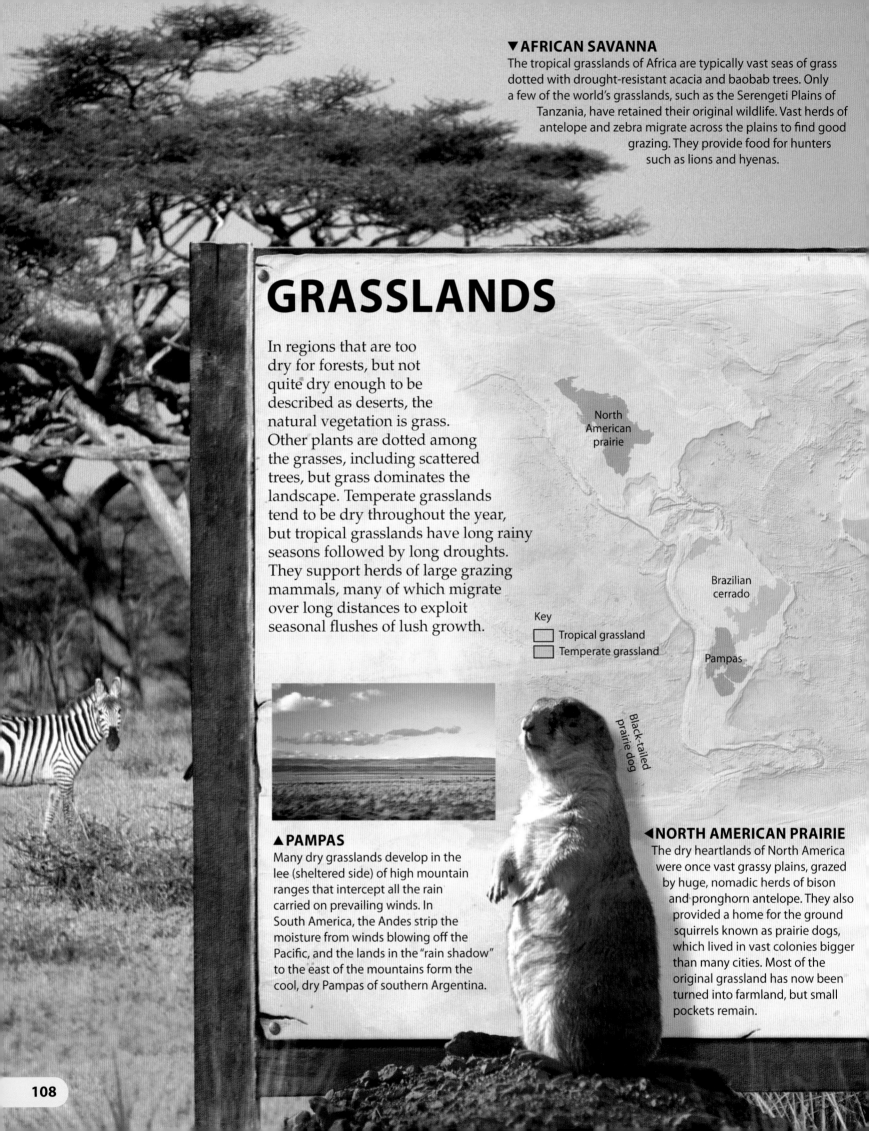

Black-tailed prairie dog

◀ NORTH AMERICAN PRAIRIE
The dry heartlands of North America were once vast grassy plains, grazed by huge, nomadic herds of bison and pronghorn antelope. They also provided a home for the ground squirrels known as prairie dogs, which lived in vast colonies bigger than many cities. Most of the original grassland has now been turned into farmland, but small pockets remain.

European souslik

◄ASIAN STEPPE

The temperate grasslands of central Eurasia have developed in the heart of the continent, and have hot, dry summers and cold, dry winters. Like many other grasslands they originally supported herds of big grazing animals, such as the saiga antelope and wild horses, but nowadays the most numerous wild mammals are small species such as this ground squirrel.

◄MOUNTAIN GRASSLANDS

Grasslands develop in mountains above the "tree line" or upper limit of tree growth. They resemble tundra, with tough, cold-adapted plants that can survive many months of snow cover and harsh, biting winds. They can be bleak places, but where there is a bedrock of nutrient-rich limestone, they are often bright with flowers such as this yellow alpine foxglove, being used as a perch by a false heath fritillary butterfly.

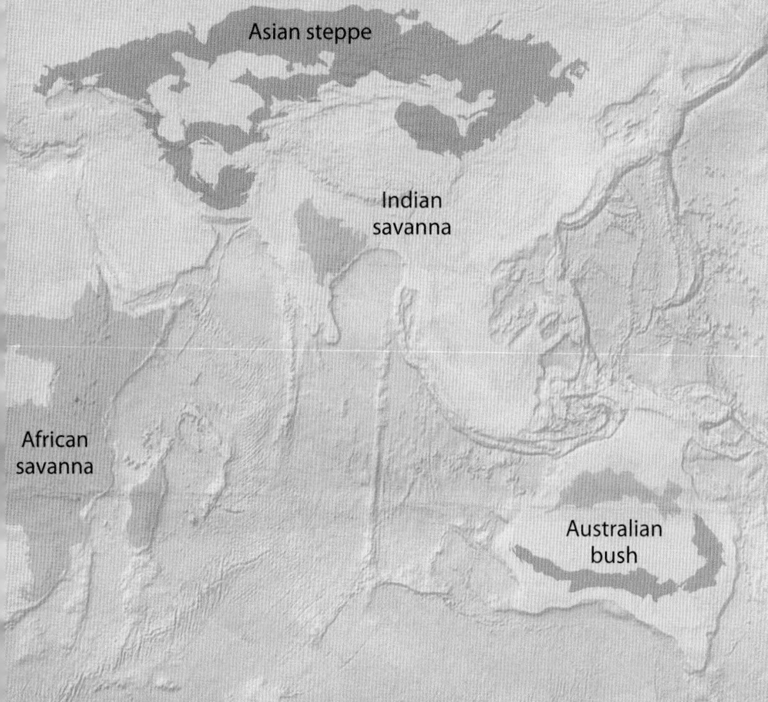

▲INDIAN SAVANNA

Like many grasslands, the savannas of India are now mainly farmland, but patches survive in hilly regions and on desert fringes. One of the few areas left lies in the foothills of the Himalayas in northern India, where monsoon rains fuel the growth of tall grasses that help tigers stalk their prey undetected.

▼BRAZILIAN CERRADO

The forests of Amazonia are flanked by two large tracts of tropical grassland – the Llanos in the north and the Cerrado in the east. The Cerrado is a rich habitat that grades into palm forest in wetter areas, and semi-desert in the drier south. It supports a wide variety of animals, such as ostrich-like rheas and the extraordinary giant anteater.

▲AUSTRALIAN BUSH

Dry grassland covers vast areas of Australia, grading into the deserts of the continent's arid interior. The main vegetation is spinifex, a tough form of tussock grass, dotted with eucalyptus trees and scrub. The grassland is regularly swept by fire, but the grasses and trees are adapted to survive this, and some plants even need regular fires to reproduce.

Giant anteater

DESERTS

Deserts develop in very dry regions at the hearts of continents, in areas sheltered from rain by high mountains, or in the subtropical desert zone where sinking dry air prevents clouds forming. The scant vegetation is dominated by drought-resistant plants such as cacti, euphorbias, and tough woody shrubs. The animal life consists mainly of insects, spiders, scorpions, and reptiles, but there are some birds and a few mammals. The few large animals are nomadic, and most of the smaller ones hide in burrows by day and come out only at night.

Saguaro can grow to 12 m (40 ft)

◀ATACAMA DESERT

The driest desert in the world, the Atacama lies along the northwestern coast of Chile, where the only moisture is delivered by fog rolling in from the Pacific. This supports sparse vegetation in places, providing food for animals such as these guanacos – relatives of llamas – but most of the desert is a barren wasteland.

◀SONORAN DESERT

One of a complex of deserts in the southwestern United States and Mexico, the Sonoran Desert is famous for its giant saguaro cacti and the drifts of short-lived flowers that bloom in the wake of winter rains. To the north lies the Mohave Desert, site of the infamous Death Valley – the hottest place in the US with a record high of 57°C (134°F).

Cactus wren perches on a saguaro flower

▶PATAGONIAN DESERT

Oceanic winds blowing towards the east over the southern Andes mountains lose all their moisture on the western flanks, so the land to the east gets very little rain. This creates the cool Patagonian Desert – a largely barren, stony landscape inhabited by a few tough animals such as this hairy armadillo.

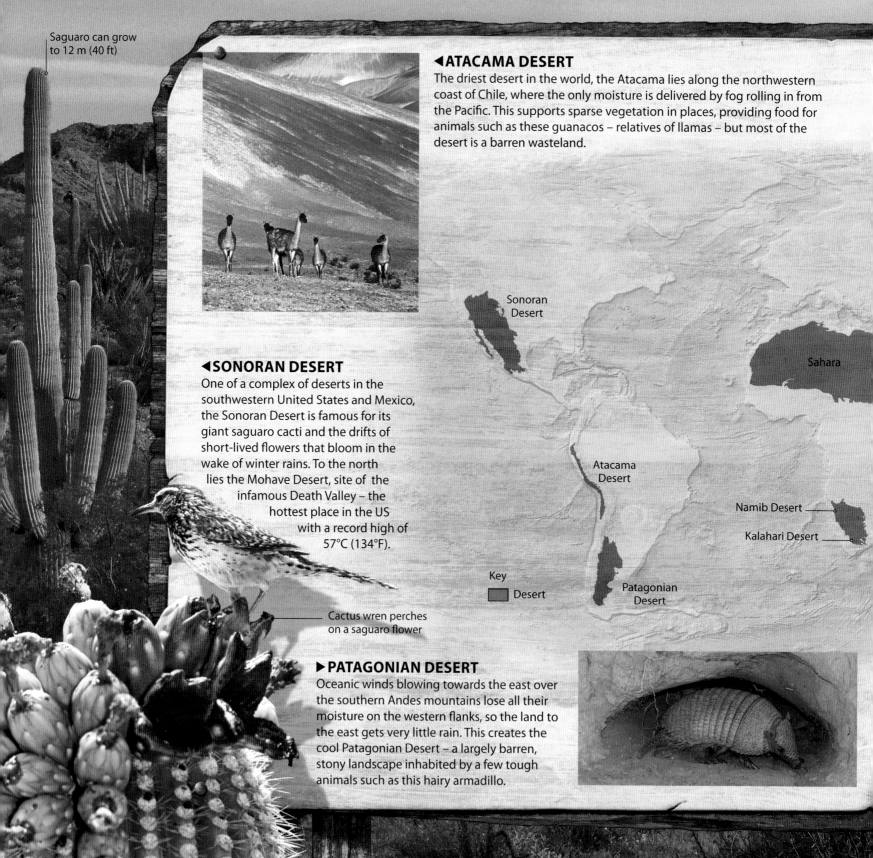

▶ KALAHARI DESERT

Lying at the heart of southern Africa, the Kalahari is a mixture of scorpion-infested desert with long sand dunes, and tree-dotted dry grasslands. The region contains the Okavango Delta, the remains of a huge prehistoric lake, that floods during the rainy season to create one of Africa's largest remaining wildlife havens.

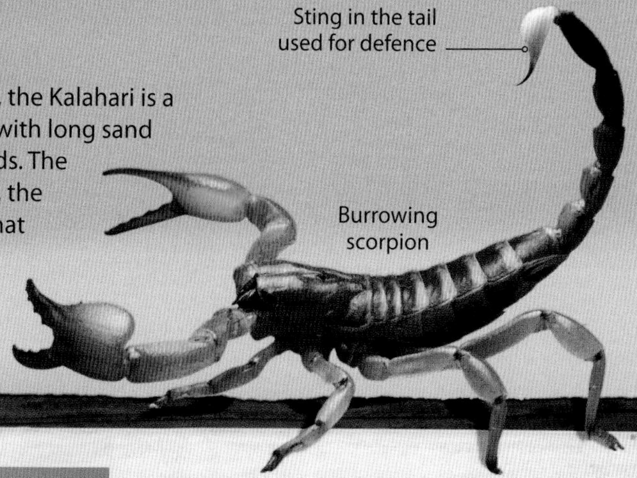
Sting in the tail used for defence

Burrowing scorpion

▼ GOBI DESERT

The Gobi Desert of Mongolia and northern China is a region of high, waterless, stone-littered plains that suffers blistering summer heat and freezing winters. It owes its dry climate to its distance from the oceans. Over vast areas there are very few plants, yet bactrian camels, wild asses, and gazelles survive by wandering widely in search of food.

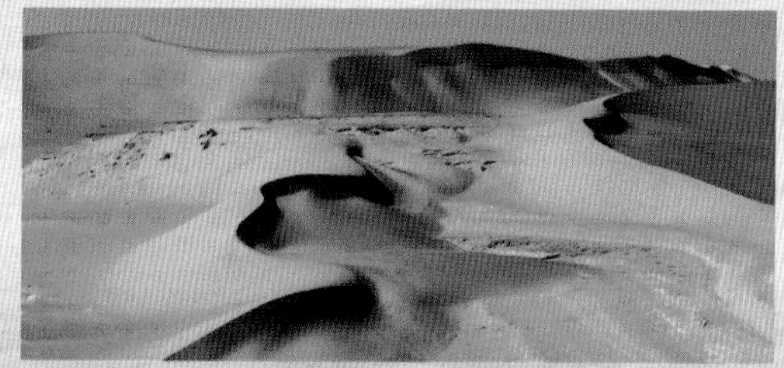

◀ ARABIAN DESERT

This is the classic sandy desert, with great expanses of sand dunes that, in the "Empty Quarter" to the south, cover an area the size of France. There is very little wildlife in the heart of the desert, but the sands lie above oil-rich sediments that have brought wealth to the few people who live here.

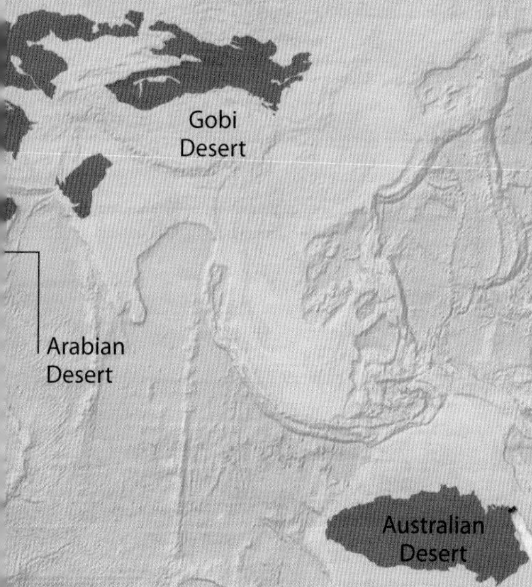
Gobi Desert
Arabian Desert
Australian Desert

▲ SAHARA

By far the world's largest desert, the Sahara has a total area of well over 9 million sq km (3.5 million sq miles). It has immense "sand seas" with dunes up to 300 m (970 ft) high, and vast tracts of gravel and bare rock. Scattered oases of moist ground support palm trees and spiny shrubs, and provide vital water for desert animals and people.

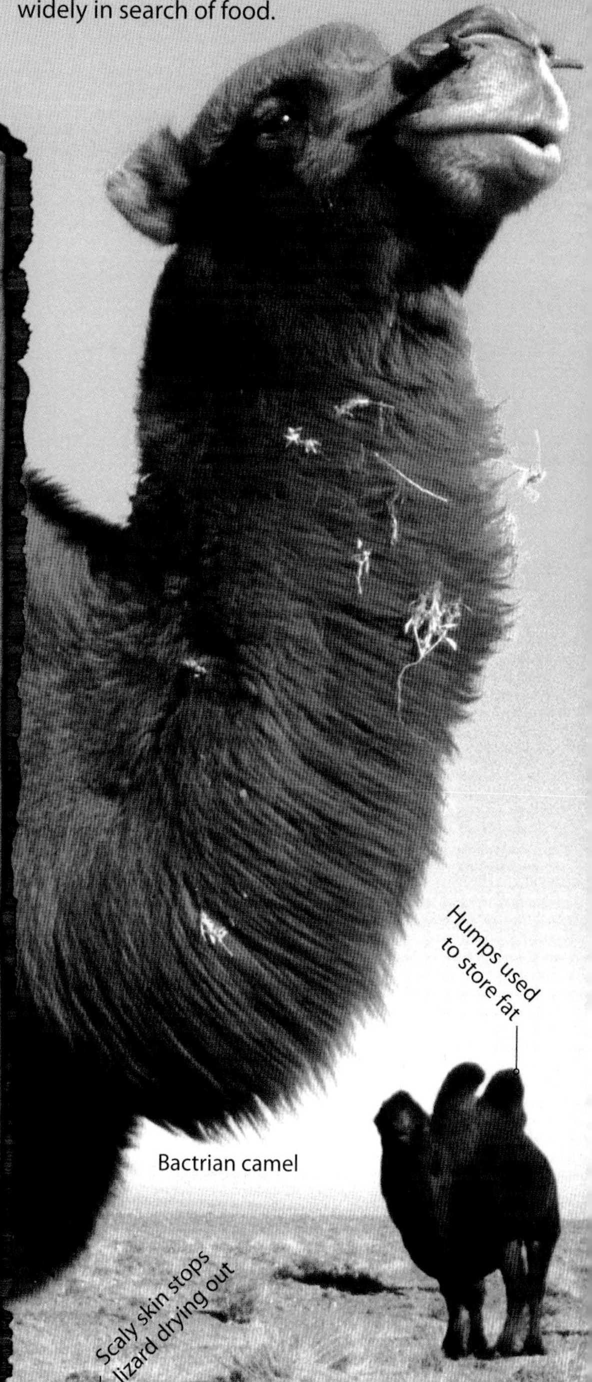
Humps used to store fat

Bactrian camel

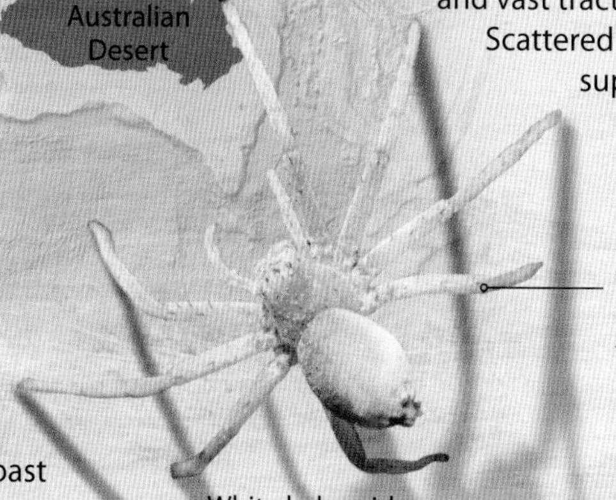
White lady spiders communicate by drumming the sand with their legs

White lady spider

▶ NAMIB DESERT

Lying along the Atlantic coast of Namibia, this is the African equivalent of the Atacama – a coastal desert created by the prevailing winds blowing from the shore to the ocean. Cold air that does blow in off the sea brings fog that supports the few plants and animals in the region, such as the white lady spider.

Scaly skin stops lizard drying out

Thorny devil

◀ AUSTRALIAN DESERT

Some 40 per cent of Australia is desert, with vast expanses of red sand and bare rock, dotted with scrub. It is inhabited by venomous snakes, lizards such as the ant-eating thorny devil, nomadic birds, and native marsupial mammals – many of which are now very rare owing to competition from introduced rabbits.

RECLAIMED LAND
The massed flowers of tulips create a dazzling spring spectacle on the bulb fields near Lisse, in the Netherlands. This geometrical landscape is completely artificial, created on land reclaimed from the sea.

Human influence

FARMING

People first started farming the land in the late stone age. Since then, farming has had a bigger impact on the landscape than any other human activity, eliminating forests, wild grasslands, and wetlands to create fields to grow crops and raise animals. In traditional mixed farming, animals are run over the land to fertilize the soil, and a variety of crops are grown in rotation to prevent the build-up of disease. However, animals may be raised without growing any crops. The use of artificial fertilizers and pesticides now enables one valuable crop to be grown repeatedly on the same land – although this can be damaging to both the soil and wildlife.

2

1

1 SLASH AND BURN

The most basic form of farming involves clearing the land of trees and other wild plants, burning the wood, spreading the nutrient-rich ash on the ground, and planting crops. When the fertility of the soil declines, the farmers move elsewhere. This "slash and burn" technique has been used for thousands of years, and is still employed in tropical forests. It can work well on a small scale, but if large areas are cleared there is less scope for moving on. The soil becomes exhausted and the land soon becomes waste ground.

2 RANCHING

One of the most basic forms of farming involves running herds of domestic animals over large areas of land, and allowing them to graze the wild plants. The land is often not fenced in any way, and managing the animals may involve rounding them up from a wide area using horses, as here in Ecuador. Although crops are not planted, such ranching often involves clearing forests and eliminating wild grazing animals and predators. The grazing itself alters the nature of the vegetation, suppressing most plants and gradually creating grassland.

3

3 MIXED FARMING

Confining farm animals such as sheep or cattle to a fenced field ensures that all their dung falls within a well-defined area and fertilizes the land. The field can then be used to grow crops. This can be repeated indefinitely, especially if the crops are varied so that they take different nutrients from the soil. Some crops are grown for the animals, while others are harvested and eaten or sold.

4 MONOCULTURE

Modern fertilizers allow the same crop to be planted on a field year after year, without the need for farm animals. This enables farmers to specialize in the crops that yield most profit, so the whole farm may be given over to growing a single product such as wheat. Unfortunately, such monocultures are hostile to wildlife, partly because weeds and insects are controlled by chemicals, and this has brought many species close to extinction.

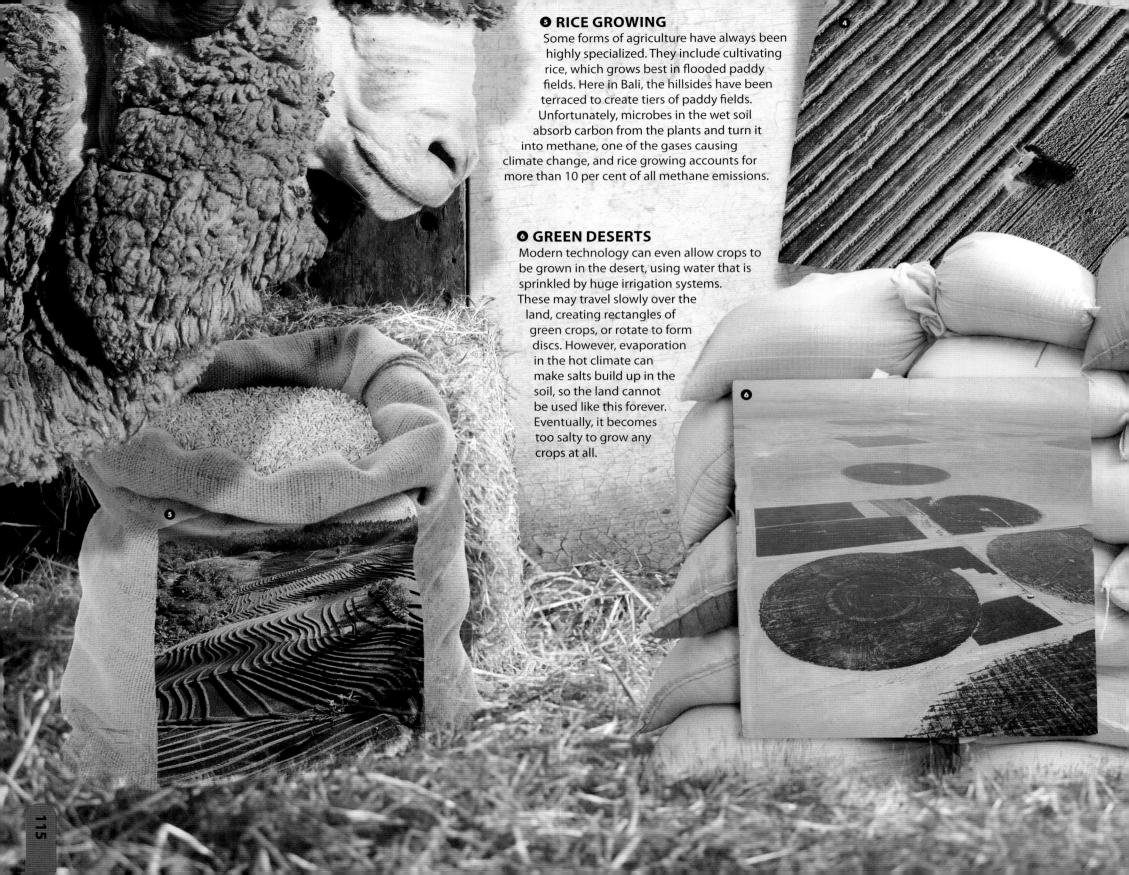

❺ RICE GROWING

Some forms of agriculture have always been highly specialized. They include cultivating rice, which grows best in flooded paddy fields. Here in Bali, the hillsides have been terraced to create tiers of paddy fields. Unfortunately, microbes in the wet soil absorb carbon from the plants and turn it into methane, one of the gases causing climate change, and rice growing accounts for more than 10 per cent of all methane emissions.

❻ GREEN DESERTS

Modern technology can even allow crops to be grown in the desert, using water that is sprinkled by huge irrigation systems. These may travel slowly over the land, creating rectangles of green crops, or rotate to form discs. However, evaporation in the hot climate can make salts build up in the soil, so the land cannot be used like this forever. Eventually, it becomes too salty to grow any crops at all.

4

5

6

NING

ınds of years, people have mined native
:h as gold, silver, and copper, and turned
tools, weapons, and ornaments. At some
y discovered that heating far more abundant
s in a charcoal furnace separated the pure
d this led to the widespread use of materials
Other minerals such as flint, building stone,
tones have also been mined since prehistory.
h as coal, oil, and natural gas have been
more recently. The three main techniques
ying, deep shaft mining, and drilling into
ıd to tap buried oil and gas reserves.

❶ STONE QUARRY

Building stone has always been a valuable resource. Originally chipped out and shaped using hand tools, it is now extracted using carefully placed explosive charges, or sliced out by machines. The stone being quarried here in Italy is Cararra marble, one of the finest of all stones. It has been used since Roman times for prestige building projects and sculptures such as the work of Michaelangelo.

❹ PANNING FOR GOLD

The fact that gold exists naturally in its native form makes it possible for people to extract it using the most basic methods, such as panning. This involves swirling water through gold-bearing sediments to carry away the lighter particles and leave the heavy gold. Gold is so rare, however, that days of work by these panners in Vietnam are likely to yield just a few grains of the precious metal.

1

4

2

❷ OPEN-CAST MINE

Where minerals occur near the surface, they can be extracted by digging out a deep pit, or open-cast mine. The Bingham Canyon mine in Utah has been under excavation since 1908 and is now the largest artificial hole on Earth. The pit itself is 1.2 km (0.75 miles) deep and measures 4 km (2.5 miles) across.

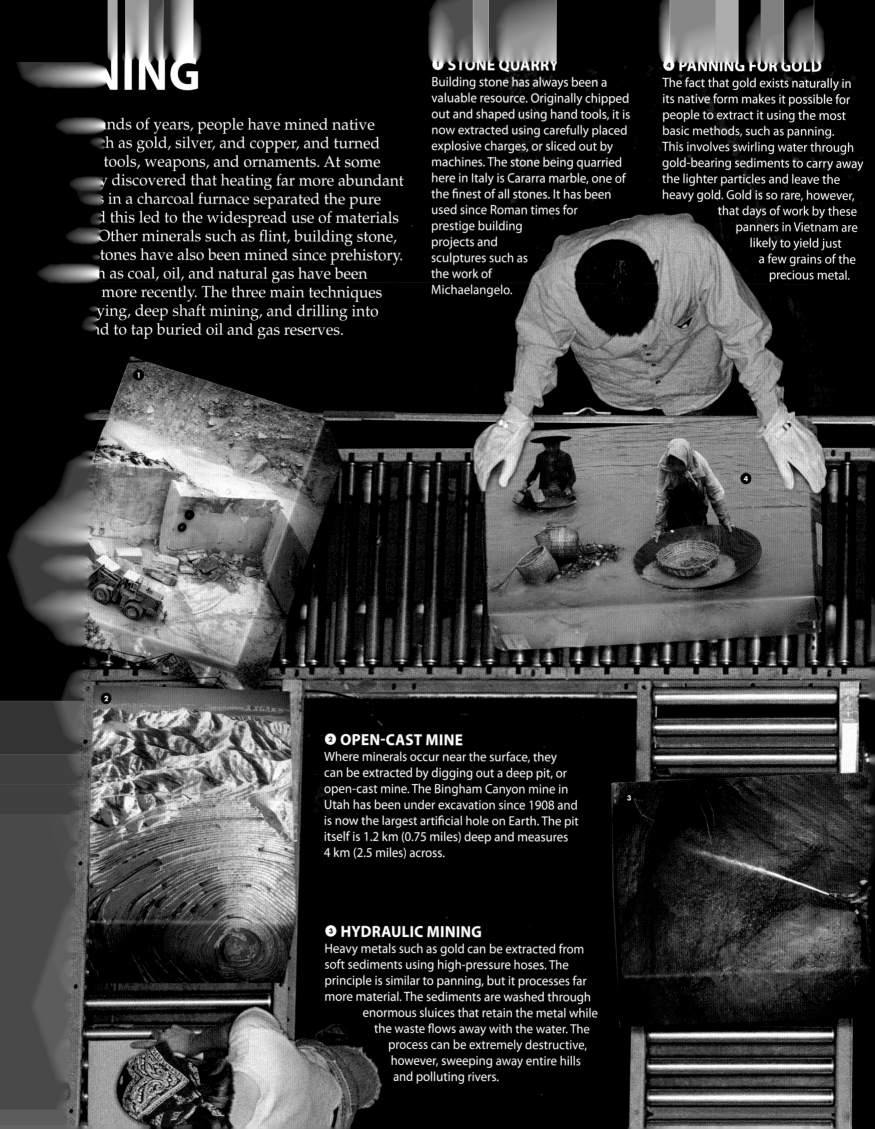

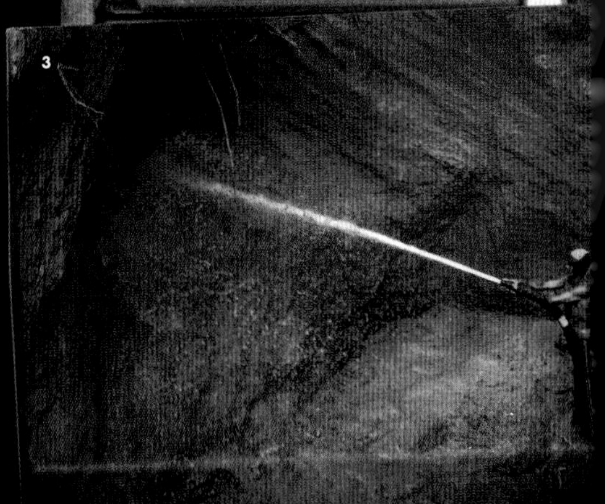

3

❸ HYDRAULIC MINING

Heavy metals such as gold can be extracted from soft sediments using high-pressure hoses. The principle is similar to panning, but it processes far more material. The sediments are washed through enormous sluices that retain the metal while the waste flows away with the water. The process can be extremely destructive, however, sweeping away entire hills and polluting rivers.

and used to make the concrete that is so essential to the construction industry. Gravel is also gathered from the sea bed using large dredgers. Some particularly pure forms of quartz sand are quarried for glass-making, and fine clays are mined for use in ceramics and papermaking.

❺ EMERALD MINE

Most mining is carried out on an industrial scale, using big, expensive machines. But in some parts of the world, valuable gold and gemstones are still mined at least partly by manual labour. At the Muzo emerald mine in Colombia, South America, one day a month is set aside for the swarms of workers to try their own luck, using simple picks and even their bare hands, and possibly dig out a fortune in gemstones.

❺

❽

❻ COAL MINE

The most dangerous and expensive type of mining involves sinking deep shafts and long galleries to extract minerals from far below the surface. A lot of coal is mined in this way, using big machines like this one in a mine in Germany. The mines must be drained of water, ventilated to remove gas, and cooled to reduce the high temperatures that exist deep below ground.

❻

❼ OIL RIG

Crude oil is a relatively light liquid that seeps up through porous sediments until it reaches a layer of rock that it cannot pass through. It accumulates in underground reservoirs, often topped with natural gas. Both can be extracted by drilling through the rock, but locating big reservoirs is not easy. Many occur below shallow sea beds, and are exploited using offshore rigs like this one.

❼

INDUSTRY AND TRANSPORT

While farming and mining have had the most dramatic impacts on the landscape, industry and transport have probably done more to change people's lives. The products of industry are now used routinely almost worldwide, and most countries have transport networks that both distribute these products and allow people to move easily from place to place. Along with power supply networks, communications, water supplies, and drainage systems, they form the "infrastructure" of civilization that is now taken for granted in the developed world. Modern cities – and indeed modern life – could not exist without it.

◀ POWER SUPPLIES
Industry, homes, and some forms of transport depend on a reliable electricity supply. Some is generated using wind or solar energy, or the power of flowing water. Other plants use nuclear reactors to heat water and drive steam turbines. Most, however, burn gas or coal, and get through vast amounts of fuel. A typical coal-fired plant burns enough coal every day to fill at least 100 of these big rail trucks.

◀ SHIPPING
Shipping is one of the oldest forms of transport, yet still one of the most efficient for heavy, bulky goods. In the past, ships were loaded at city docks, but today many cargoes are put into containers at the factory and sent by rail and road to a dedicated cargo terminal. Here, the containers are stacked onto ships like this one – which can carry up to 7,500 containers – for delivery to similar cargo terminals all over the world.

▶ RAILWAYS
Since the mid-19th century, railways have been vital arteries of commerce. They are still important for carrying heavy items, such as these containers, each one of which would be a full load for a road-going truck. The smooth, relatively flat railway enables very heavy loads to be moved using relatively little energy. However, each track is very expensive to build.

▲ ROAD FREIGHT
A lot of the heavy freight that was once carried by rail is now transported by road, often using giant trucks like this tanker. This is a less efficient use of fuel than rail transport, but it has the advantage of delivering goods directly to a destination, rather than to a rail terminal that can be a great distance away. The weight of such road trucks is immense, however, increasing highway maintenance costs.

▼ HIGHWAY NETWORKS

All developed countries now have complex networks of multi-lane highways like this, as well as local road systems. The driving force behind this development has been private car ownership. Traffic congestion and pollution are now becoming serious problems, however, and car use may soon lose some of its appeal.

▲ AIRPORTS

Air travel for both business and leisure is now a part of normal life for many people, especially in big countries such as the United States where cities are a long way apart. Airports make a big impact on the landscape, however, and aircraft noise and pollution are serious problems that are only partly addressed by improved aircraft design. The massive growth in leisure air travel has also had profound effects on many tourist destinations, turning coastal communities into hotel resorts and virtually eliminating many traditional ways of life.

▶ CITY TRANSPORT

Many cities have rapid transport systems that enable people to get around easily without using their cars. They include surface tramway systems like this one in southern France, and subways that run beneath the streets. Both use metal tracks and electric power, which keeps their energy requirements as low as possible. This is likely to become increasingly important in the future as energy costs rise.

rather than wide roads suitable for vehicles. The town is sited between two oases that provide vital water, and surrounded by farmland and olive groves that, until recently, provided the main wealth of the citizens.

1

Some 7,000 years ago, the development of farming in ancient Mesopotamia – now Iraq – produced a surplus of wealth that encouraged the growth of the first cities. Since then, city living has spread around the world, but until recently most people still lived in small communities. Today, more than half the world's population lives in cities, some of which have grown to colossal size. Many historic cities are surrounded by new development, and many have been transformed by high-rise architecture.

❷ ATHENS

The idea of the city as a centre of civilization was born in city states such as Athens about 2,500 years ago. The politicians of Athens are widely credited with inventing modern democracy. Many buildings of the era survive, including the Parthenon, seen here, which was built in about 440 BCE and still dominates the city.

2

❸ MACCHU PICCHU

This spectacular city was built by the Incas of Peru in about 1460. Although sited high in the Andes, it has reliable water sources and enough terraced farmland to support all the people who might have lived there. It was abandoned about a century after it was built – probably because of disease – and is now a ruin.

❹ CARCASSONNE

In the past, many rich cities were fortified to protect them from raiders. Carcassonne in southern France still retains its double ring of ramparts. From 1250, the town was extended beyond the fortifications, but this lower city was later destroyed by an invading army – demonstrating the value of the ancient city walls.

❺ VENICE

The richest cities were built on the wealth acquired through trade. During the Middle Ages, trade with the east brought rich rewards to Venice, a city built on 118 islands in a shallow coastal lagoon in northern Italy. Its many palaces and churches, rising directly from the water of its canals, make it one of the world's most beautiful cities.

❻ PARIS

Most old cities have been built up little by little, resulting in winding, narrow streets and a great variety of buildings. In the 19th century, much of Paris, the capital of France, was replaced with a planned city built around a geometrical network of wide avenues. Similar planning is now commonly used in new cities, often with the addition of open green spaces and road systems designed for use by high-speed traffic.

5

6

30 million inhabitants. It was virtually destroyed in 1923 by an earthquake. Since then, it has been rebuilt in the high-rise style typical of the world's richest cities. The steel-framed towers are more earthquake-proof than traditional masonry buildings.

❽ SHANTY TOWN

Cities are wealthy places that attract people looking for work. Many cannot afford to live in the city centres, and in some countries rich cities are surrounded by squalid shanty towns housing poor workers and their families. They have no proper drainage or water supply, and suffer high rates of disease.

8

7

3

4

ENVIRONMENT AND CONSERVATION

Over the last 100 years, the world's population has risen from 1.5 billion to more than 6 billion. All these people have to live somewhere, and must eat. They also consume energy, and most now demand the luxuries of modern technology. As a result, vast areas of former wilderness have been built over or turned into farmland. Every day huge quantities of coal, oil, and gas are burnt as fuel, and colossal amounts of waste and pollution are generated. Both the world's wildlife and the stability of the climate are under threat, and our future depends on solving the problem.

❶ INDUSTRIAL POLLUTION

The factories and power plants of the industrialized world release masses of waste gas into the atmosphere every day. Much of this is carbon dioxide and nitrous oxide, which cause global warming. Other pollutants include sulphur dioxide, which combines with water vapour in the air to form acid rain, and soot particles that create choking smog.

❷ TRANSPORT EMISSIONS

Many forms of transport – particularly on the roads and in the air – rely on burning hydrocarbon fuels derived from oil. This releases large amounts of waste gases into the air, particularly carbon dioxide. Modern cars are designed to minimize this, but there are more cars on the roads every year. Aircraft emissions at high altitude have a particularly serious impact.

❸ RUBBISH

Until the mid-20th century, most of the rubbish we produced could be broken down by natural decay. Most plastics, by contrast, are almost indestructible unless burnt, which causes pollution. As a result, many countries are suffering a mounting rubbish problem. New York City alone produces 12,000 tonnes (tons) of domestic waste every day.

❹ CONTAMINATED RIVERS

Fresh, clean water is a vital resource, but all over the world streams and rivers are being polluted by industrial waste and sewage. This can poison wildlife and cause serious diseases such as cholera. Fertilizers draining off farmland into rivers upset the balance of nature. Deforestation also allows soil to be swept into rivers by heavy rain, choking the water.

❺ POLLUTED OCEANS

The oceans are vast, but they are still affected by pollution. Oil spills at sea are deadly to wildlife like this penguin, and the oil that washes up on coasts is equally destructive. Drifting plastic rubbish kills many seals, turtles, and seabirds, and engine noise from ships may make whales lose their way and become fatally stranded on beaches.

❻ DEFORESTATION

Over the past 50 years, a third of the world's rainforests have been felled and burned, and the rate of deforestation is increasing. This is destroying one of the world's richest habitats, and placing thousands of species of plants and animals in danger of extinction. It is also adding a huge amount of carbon dioxide to the atmosphere, contributing to climate change.

❼ CLIMATE CHANGE

Pollution of the atmosphere with carbon dioxide and other greenhouse gases is warming it up, raising world temperatures. Polar ice is melting, and by 2050 – if not before – there may be no ice at the North Pole in summer. Polar bears could become extinct, and if the polar ice sheets melt, sea levels could rise by up to 25 m (82 ft), drowning the world's coastal cities.

❽ CONSERVATION

Humanity relies on the web of life that produces our food and makes the air fit to breathe. We can help secure its future by protecting wildlife and wild places, and working to reduce climate change. Conservation can also provide tourist income for nations such as Kenya that still have spectacular wildlife.

❾ SAVING ENERGY

People in the industrialized world use a lot of energy every day, and most of it is generated in ways that add to climate change. We can reduce energy use by living in houses that need less heating or air conditioning, and which generate their own power. These "zero-carbon" homes in London, UK, are designed to produce the energy they need from sources such as solar panels.

❿ THINKING FOR THE FUTURE

Many environmental problems have been brought about by using scarce resources to produce things that are thrown away, or by wasting energy moving goods around the world. Many people now try to re-use and recycle more, and by buying local produce in markets such as this one they save energy and help fight climate change.

Glossary

ACCRETION
The process by which small particles cling together to make larger objects, including planets and asteroids.

ALGAE
Plant-like protists that can make food using solar energy. Most are single-celled, but they include seaweeds.

ALLOY
An artificial mixture of two different metals.

AMPHIBIAN
A vertebrate animal, such as a frog, that lives on land but loses moisture easily and typically breeds in water.

ANTICYCLONE
A high-pressure weather system in which sinking cool air creates cloudless skies.

ASTEROID
A relatively small, irregular rocky body orbiting the Sun.

ATMOSPHERE
The layers of gas that surround Earth, retained by gravity.

ATOM
The smallest particle of an element such as iron. Compound substances, such as water, have more than one kind of atom.

BACTERIA
Microscopic organisms with a simple single-celled structure.

BIOSPHERE
The web of life that exists on or near Earth's surface.

CALDERA
A giant crater formed when a volcano collapses into its magma chamber after this has been emptied by an eruption.

CARBOHYDRATE
A substance, such as sugar or starch, that is made of carbon, hydrogen, and oxygen by a living organism, such as a plant.

CARBON DIOXIDE
A gas that forms a very small fraction of the atmosphere. Living things, such as plants, use it to make carbohydrate food.

CIRQUE
A crater-like depression near a mountain peak, carved out by ice building up to feed a glacier.

CLIMATE
The average weather of any region, and its typical seasonal weather pattern.

COMET
An orbiting body made of ice and dust. Some comets pass close to the Sun at rare intervals, and its radiation makes them stream long tails.

COMPOUND
A substance containing two or more elements, formed by a chemical reaction that bonds their atoms together.

CONDENSE
To change from a gas to a liquid.

CONTINENTAL SHELF
The submerged fringe of a continent, forming the relatively shallow floor of a coastal sea.

CONVECTION
Circulating currents in gases or liquids, such as air and water, and even hot, mobile rock, driven by differences in temperature.

CRYSTAL
A gem-like structure that may form when a liquid becomes a solid. Its shape is determined by the arrangement of its atoms.

CYANOBACTERIA
Bacteria that can use solar energy to make sugar from carbon dioxide and water.

CYCLONE
A weather system with clouds, rain, and strong winds caused by air swirling into a region of rising warm, moist air.

DEPRESSION
Another word for a cyclone.

DROUGHT
A long period with no rain.

ECOSYSTEM
An interacting community of living things in their natural environment.

ELEMENT
A substance that is made up of just one type of atom.

EROSION
Wearing away, usually of rock, by natural forces such as flowing water or ocean waves breaking on the shore.

EVAPORATE
To turn from a liquid into a gas or vapour.

EVAPORITE
A solid such as salt that is left behind when a liquid solution, such as saltwater, evaporates.

FAULT
A fracture in rock, where the rock on one side of the fracture has moved relative to the rock on the other side.

FERTILIZER
A mixture of plant nutrients used to promote plant growth.

FJORD
A deep coastal valley eroded by a glacier, that is now flooded by the sea.

FOSSIL
The remains or traces of a living thing that have been preserved, usually in stony form and in sedimentary rock.

GALAXY
A vast mass of many millions of stars in Space, often circulating around a central nucleus.

GLACIER
A mass of ice formed from compacted snow that may flow slowly downhill.

GRAVITY
The attractive force between objects in Space. The greater the mass of the object, the more gravity it has.

GREENHOUSE EFFECT
The way certain gases in the atmosphere absorb heat radiated from Earth, warm up, and keep the planet warmer than it would otherwise be.

HOTSPOT
A zone of volcanic activity caused by a stationary plume of heat beneath Earth's crust. Where the crust is moving, the hotspot creates chains of volcanoes.

HYDROTHERMAL VENT
An eruption of very hot, mineral-rich water from the ocean floor, normally from a volcanically active mid-ocean ridge.

IGNEOUS
A rock that has been formed by the cooling of molten magma or volcanic lava. Most igneous rocks are composed of interlocking crystals and are very hard.

LAVA
Molten rock that erupts from a volcano.

LIMESTONE
A rock made of calcite (lime) that is easily dissolved by slightly acid rainwater. Most limestones are formed from the skeletons of marine organisms.

MAGMA
Molten rock that lies within or beneath Earth's crust.

MANTLE
The deep layer of hot rock that lies between Earth's crust and the core. It forms 84 per cent of the volume of the planet.

MARITIME CLIMATE
A climate heavily influenced by a nearby ocean. Typically, it has mild winters, cool summers, and regular rainfall throughout the year.

METAMORPHISM
In geology, a process that turns one type of rock into another, usually involving intense heat, pressure, or both.

METEOR
A fragment of space rock or ice that plunges through the atmosphere and burns up as a "shooting star".

METEORITE
A fragment of space rock that survives its passage through the atmosphere and hits the ground.

MID-LATITUDES
The regions of the world that lie between the polar regions and the tropics, and have temperate, seasonal climates.

MINERAL
A natural solid composed of one or more elements in fixed proportions, usually with a distinctive crystal structure.

MOLECULE
The smallest particle of a substance that can exist without breaking the substance into the elements from which it is made. Each molecule is formed from atoms of those elements.

MONSOON
A seasonal change of wind that affects the weather, especially in tropical regions where it causes wet and dry seasons.

MORAINE
A mass of rock debris carried by a glacier, or piled up at its end.

NOMADIC
Moving constantly in search of food or other resources, but with no fixed route.

NUCLEAR FUSION
Fusing the atoms of two elements to create a heavier element.

NUTRIENTS
Substances that living things need to build their tissues.

ORBIT
The path taken by a body in Space that is travelling around a larger body, such as the Sun.

ORGANIC
Technically, a substance that is based on the element carbon, but usually meaning something that is – or was once – alive.

ORGANISM
A living thing.

PASTURE
Grassland used to feed animals, such as sheep and cattle.

PEAT
The compacted remains of plants that have not yet decayed, because waterlogging excluded oxygen vital to decay organisms.

PERMAFROST
Permanently frozen ground that covers vast areas of the Arctic.

PESTICIDE
A chemical used to kill the insects, fungi, and weeds that reduce farm productivity.

PHOTOSYNTHESIS
The process of using the energy of light to make sugar from carbon dioxide and water.

PHYTOPLANKTON
Drifting, microscopic, single-celled aquatic organisms that make their food using a process called photosynthesis.

PLANET
A large body made of rock and/or gas that orbits a star, but is not big enough to generate its own light by nuclear fusion.

PLANKTON
A form of life that drifts in oceans, lakes, and other bodies of water. Most of it is microscopic, and lives near the surface.

PLATEAU
A broad area of land that lies at high altitude.

PLATE TECTONICS
The dynamic process in which the large plates that form the crust of Earth are constantly moving together or apart.

POLLUTION
Anything added to the natural environment that upsets the balance of nature.

PREDATOR
An animal that hunts and eats other live animals, which are known as its prey.

PROTIST
An aquatic or terrestrial organism that usually consists of a single, complex cell, such as the diatoms that drift in the ocean, but also including seaweeds. Protists comprise one of the five kingdoms of life.

RESERVOIR
A natural or artificial store of liquid, usually water.

RIFT
A widening crack in rocks or Earth's crust, caused by the rocks pulling apart.

RIFT VALLEY
A region where part of Earth's crust has dropped into the gap formed by the crust pulling apart.

SAVANNA
Tropical grassland.

SCAVENGER
An animal that feeds on the remains of dead animals and other scraps.

SEDIMENT
Solid particles, such as stones, sand, and mud that have been transported by water, wind, ice, or gravity, and have settled, usually in a layer.

SEDIMENTARY ROCK
Rock formed from compressed and hardened sand, mud, or other sediments.

SILICA
A compound of silicon and oxygen that is an important component of most rocks, and the main ingredient of glass.

STRATA
Layers of sedimentary rock.

SUBDUCTION ZONE
A region where one tectonic plate of Earth's crust is diving beneath another, creating an ocean trench, causing earthquakes, and generating molten rock that erupts from volcanoes.

SUPERHEAT
To heat a liquid, such as water, under pressure, so it gets hotter than its normal boiling point.

TEMPERATE
A climate that is neither very hot nor very cold, or a region that has such a climate.

TRANSFORM FAULT
A plate boundary between two slabs of Earth's crust where they slide sideways relative to each other.

TRIBUTARY
A stream that flows into a river, or a small glacier that flows into a bigger one.

TROPICS
The hot regions to the north and south of the Equator, between the Tropic of Cancer and the Tropic of Capricorn.

TROPOSPHERE
The lowest layer of Earth's atmosphere.

TSUNAMI
A fast-moving and powerful ocean wave generated by an earthquake on the ocean floor, or by the collapse of an oceanic volcano.

TUNDRA
The cold, largely barren, treeless landscape that lies on the fringes of the polar ice sheets.

ULTRAVIOLET RADIATION
A form of light that can damage living tissue. It is invisible to humans, but not to some other animals, such as insects.

UNIVERSE
The entirety of Space, including all the galaxies.

VISCOUS
Refers to a fluid that is sticky and thick, like glue or treacle.

WATER VAPOUR
The invisible gas that forms when energized water molecules escape into the air.

ZOOPLANKTON
Animals that mainly drift in the water, although some may also swim actively.

Index

Bold page numbers refer to main entries

Acknowledgements

DK would like to thank:
Kieran Macdonald for proofreading, Chris Bernstein for preparing the index, Fran Vargo for additional picture research, Dave King for photography, Richard Ferguson for paper engineering, and Simon Mumford for cartography.

The publisher would like to thank the following for their kind permission to reproduce their photographs:

Key: a–above; b–below/bottom; c–centre; f–far; l–left; r–right; t–top

4 Corbis: Yann Arthus-Bertrand (r); zefa/Frank Krahmer (bl). Landov: UPI Photo (tl). **5** Corbis: Yann Arthus-Bertrand (l); epa/Ed Oudenaarden (r). **6-7** Landov: UPI Photo. **8-9** NASA: JPL-Caltech. **10** Corbis: Denis Scott (r). NASA: JPL (cl) (cr). Science Photo Library: Californian Association for Research in Astronomy (l). **10-11** NASA: SOHO (c). **11** NASA: JPL (cl) (cr) (r); USGS (l). 12 NASA: JPL (bc) (br) (tr). Science Photo Library: Royal Observatory, Edinburgh/AAO (l). **12-13** Corbis: Jonathan Blair. **13** NASA: Hubble Space Telescope (tr). The Natural History Museum, London: (bc) (br). Science Photo Library: Manfred Kage (cr); Walter Pacholka/Astropics (tl). **14** Corbis: Bettmann (tc). NASA: (bl) (br). Science Photo Library: RIA Novosti (tl). **14-15** NASA. **15** Corbis. NASA: (bl) (bc) (1/c) (2/c) (3/c) (4/c). Science Photo Library: John Sanford (t). **16** iStockphoto.com: Claude Dagenais (bl); Snezana Negovanovic (b). Science Photo Library: Bonnier Publications/Henning Dalhoff (tr); Mark Garlick (bc). **16-17** iStockphoto.com: Branko Miokovic. **17** iStockphoto.com: Nicholas Belton (tr); Onur Döngel (ca); Alisa Foytik (br); Igor Terekhov (bl). Science Photo Library: Mark Garlick (c). **18** iStockphoto.com: Angelo Gilardelli (b/background); Linda Steward (b). NASA: (t). The Natural History Museum, London: (cr). Photolibrary: Animals Animals/Breck P. Kent (c). Science Photo Library: Joyce Photographics (cl). **19** DK Images: © Satellite Imagemap Copyright 1996-2003 Planetary Visions (tc). **21** iStockphoto.com: Jon Helgason (t). **23** Alamy Images: Lyroky (t). **24** Corbis: Gallo Images/Roger De La Harpe (bl); Didrik Johnck; NASA (cl). FLPA: Terry Whittaker (br). **25** Alamy Images: Ian Paterson (c). Photolibrary: Imagestate/Randa Bishop (cl); Stefan Mokrzecki (b). **26** James Jackson, Department of Earth Sciences, University of Cambridge: (t). Marli Miller / Department of Geological Sciences, University of Oregon: (br). Science Photo Library: W.K. Fletcher (cl). **26-27** Getty Images: AFP. **27** Alamy Images: Images of Africa Photobank/David Keith Jones (tl). FLPA: Imagebroker/Konrad Wothe (tr). Science Photo Library: Dr Ken MacDonald (b). **28** Corbis: Comet/Lloyd Cluff (bl). Science Photo Library: Gary Hincks (cr). **28-29** iStockphoto.com: Beacon Hill Photography. **29** Corbis: George Hall (tr); Lucid Images/Mark Downey (tl); Sygma/Xinhua (br); Michael S. Yamashita (bl). **30** Alamy Images: Mark Lewis (t). DK Images: Andy Crawford/Donks Models - modelmaker (br). iStockphoto.com: Floortje (bl). Science Photo Library: US Geological Survey (cr). **30-31** iStockphoto.com: MBPhoto. **31** Alamy Images: Roger Coulam (crb); Zach Holmes (c). Getty Images: Science Faction/G. Brad Lewis (bc). NASA: Aster (t). **32** Alamy Images: INTERFOTO Pressebildagentur (cr). Getty Images: Photographer's Choice/Francesco Ruggeri (b); Stone/G. Brad Lewis (cl). **32-33** Science Photo Library: Stephen & Donna O'Meara. **33** Corbis: Comet/Gary Braasch (cl); NASA/Roger Ressmeyer (br); Sean Sexton Collection (cr); Sygma/Pierre Vauthey (c). **34** Alamy Images: David Muenker (bl); WoodyStock (tr). Corbis: Frans Lanting (br). **35** Alamy Images: James Kubrick (tr); David Muenker (tl). Corbis: Ralph White (br). Photolibrary: age fotostock/Juan Carlos Munoz (bl). **36-37** Corbis: zefa/Frank Krahmer. **38** Alamy Images: Jack Clark Collection/Phil Degginger (3). The Natural History Museum, London: (6). **39** Alamy Images: GC Minerals (7). Dreamstime.com: Lightprints (tl). The Natural History Museum, London: (8) (9). Science Photo Library: Mark. A. Schneider (10). **40** Alamy Images: WILDLIFE GmbH (10/t). Corbis: Visuals Unlimited (8/l). Dreamstime.com: Araminta (1/r); Egis (4/l); Elnur (9/b); Fordphotouk (5/b); Galdzer (2/r); Holligan78 (8/r); Mhryciw (3/l); Ptaxa (6/b). The Natural History Museum, London: (4/r). Science Photo Library: Jean-Claude Revy, ISM (1/l); Ben Johnson (2/l) (3/r) (6/t). **40-41** Alamy Images: Mira. **41** Corbis: Visuals Unlimited (11/l). Dreamstime.com: Bernjuer (7/l); Brent Hathaway (11/r). Science Photo Library: Arnold Fisher (7/r). **42-43** Alamy Images: Hemis/Emilio Suetone. **44** Alamy Images: David Muenker (bl). Photolibrary: Imagestate/Gavin Hellier (cr). **44-45** www.dinodia.com: (t). **45** Graeme Peacock, www.graeme-peacock.com: (b). Photolibrary: JTB Photo (tr). **46** Dreamstime.com: Milosluz (bc). FLPA: Mark Newman (br). Getty Images: Image Bank/Karin Slade (bl). Photolibrary: Jon Arnold Travel/James Montgomery (t). Science Photo Library: Fletcher & Baylis (cb). **47** Corbis: Visions of America/Joseph Sohm (cla). Dreamstime.com: Dannyphoto80 (br/goggles); Dingelstad (bl/gloves); Christopher Dodge (bc/tools). FLPA: Imagebroker/Thomas Lammeyer (cra). Getty Images: Image Bank/David Sanger (clb). Photolibrary: Robert Harding Travel/James Emmerson (tl). **48** Alamy Images: nagelestock.com (tl); Robert Harding Picture Library Ltd/Ellen Rooney (br). USGS: (bl). **48-49** ESA: (c). iStockphoto.com: Valeria Titova. **49** FLPA: David Hosking (bl). Photolibrary: Robert Harding Travel/Tony Waltham (tl). stevebloom.com: (tr). **50** Tony Waltham Geophotos: (1) (2) (3) (4) (5). **51** Tony Waltham Geophotos: (6) (7) (8). **52** Corbis: Annie Griffiths Belt (tl). iStockphoto.com: pixonaut (t/background). The Natural History Museum, London: (bl). Science Photo Library: Lawrence Lawry (crb). 53 Camera Press: Gamma/Benali Remi (3). Science Photo Library: Tom McHugh (6); MSF/Javier Trueba (4); Smithsonian Institute (5). **54** Alamy Images: Wild Places Photography/Chris Howes (bc). Corbis: Louie Psihoyos (bc/inset); Scott T. Smith (br). Science Photo Library: Martin Bond (bl). **54-55** FLPA: Nicholas & Sherry Lu Aldridge. **55** Dreamstime.com: Joe Gough (bc/inset); Pancaketom (t/inset). Science Photo Library: Martin Bond (bl) (br); W.K. Fletcher (bc). **56** DK Images: Colin Keates/courtesy of the Natural History Museum, London (br). iStockphoto.com: mikeuk (bl). **56-57** The Natural History Museum, London: (c). **57** Science Photo Library: Jean-Claude Revy, ISM (bl). **58** Alamy Images: Danita Delimont (ftl). Dreamstime.com: Christopher Ewing (bc). Science Photo Library: Simon Fraser (tr); Edward Kinsman (cr); Michael Szoenyi (tl). **58-59** DK Images/Colin Keates/courtesy of the Natural History Museum (c). **59** Dreamstime.com: Homestudiofoto (tl); Picturephoto (tr). Science Photo Library: Joyce Photographics (cr) (ca); Doug Martin (br). **60** Alamy Images: blickwinkel/Schmidbauer (cr); blickwinkel/Schmidbauer (3). Dreamstime.com: Dusty Cline (3/worms). iStockphoto.com: Marcin Pawinski (cr); Csaba Zsarnowszky (bl). Photolibrary: Animals Animals/Doug Wechsler (b); Animals Animals/Doug Wechsler (2). Tony Waltham Geophotos: (cl) (1). **61** iStockphoto.com: Richard Goerg (r). Photolibrary: OSF/Iain Sarjeant (cr); OSF/Iain Sarjeant (5). Tony Waltham Geophotos: (bl) (br) (4) (6). **62-63** Corbis: Yann Arthus-Bertrand. **64** iStockphoto.com: Donna Poole (cl). Science Photo Library: Biosym Technologies/Clive Freeman (tr) (cra) (crb); ESA/DLR/FU Berlin/G. Neukum (bl). **64-65** Dreamstime.com: Martin Green. **65** Alamy Images: bobo (cb); JLImages (bc). Science Photo Library: (tr); John Mead (tl); Claire Ting (br). **68** Alamy Images: Leslie Garland Picture Library/Alan Curtis (b). Getty Images: Photonica/Kai Wiechmann (t). Photolibrary: age fotostock/Andoni Canela (c). **69** Alamy Images: Guy Edwardes Photography (t); NASA (br). Corbis: Ashley Cooper (c). iStockphoto.com: techno. **70** NASA (tl). Corbis: Comet/Dale Spartas (cr); Roger Ressmeyer (bl). **70-71** Corbis: Atlantide Phototravel/ Stefano Amantini. **71** Corbis: Torleif Svensson (cl). naturepl.com: Jeremy Walker (cr). **72** FLPA: Mark Newman (4). iStockphoto.com: Ryan Kelly (bc). **72-73** Alamy Images: Jupiterimages/Ablestock (b). **73** Alamy Images: John C. Doornkamp (1); Volvox Inc/Tsuneo Nakamura (5). Corbis: Tom Bean (2). FLPA: Minden Pictures/Colin Monteath (6); Malcolm Schuyl (7). iStockphoto.com: Andy Hwang (t). Photolibrary: Robert Harding Travel/Dominic Harcourt Webster (3). **74** Alamy Images: Leslie Garland Picture Library/Vincent Lowe (1/inset); Chuck Pefley (1). Corbis: JAI/Jon Arnold (2/inset); zefa/Juergen Becker (2). Photolibrary: Index Stock Imagery/Eric Kamp (3). Science Photo Library: Kaj R. Svensson (3/inset). **75** Alamy Images: Jeremy Inglis (6/inset); Wolfgang Kaehler (5/inset); Stan Pritchard (4/inset). Corbis: William Whitehurst (4). Photolibrary: Index Stock Imagery/Martin Paul Ltd. Inc. (5); Index Stock Imagery/Eric Kamp (6). **76** Corbis: zefa/José Fuste Raga (1). FLPA: Minden Pictures/Jim Brandenburg (2). Photolibrary: Index Stock Imagery/Craig J. Brown (3). **76-77** Alamy Images: Arco Images GmbH (t); David Cheshire. **77** Alamy Images: Arco Images GmbH (6); Kuttig-Travel (5); Nicholas Pitt (4). **78** Alamy Images: Anthony Baker (tc). Corbis: Arne Hodalic (tr); George Steinmetz (tl). Dreamstime.com: Jorge Folha (bc). iStockphoto.com: Jacqueline Hunkele (br). **79** Alamy Images: Wild Places Photography/Chris Howes (br/inset). Corbis: Macduff Everton (tr); Hans Strand (tc). Getty Images: Dorling Kindersley/Stephen Oliver (br). iStockphoto.com: Tina Rencelj (bl). **80** Alamy Images: Steve Allen Travel Photography (2). Corbis: Roger Ressmeyer (1). National Geographic Stock: Medford Taylor (bl). **80-81** Corbis: Image Source. **81** Alamy Images: Design Pics Inc/Carson Ganci (5); Stephen Frink Collection/Masa Ushioda (3); Stock Connection Distribution/Tom Tracy (6). **82** Alamy Images: John Morgan (3). Corbis: Lawson Wood (2). iStockphoto.com: Ryan Burke (tr). Science Photo Library: Karsten Schneider (1). **82-83** iStockphoto.com: bravobravo (background). **83** Alamy Images: Peter L. Hardy (6); Buddy Mays (5); Peter Titmuss (4). Corbis: NASA/Roger Ressmeyer (7). iStockphoto.com: appleuzr (tl); Philip Barker (cb); Ryan Burke (bl); Brandon Laufenberg (br). **84** Corbis: Tiziana and Gianni Baldizzone (cr). Dreamstime.com: David Hughes (bl). iStockphoto.com: DSGpro (cb). Science Photo Library: NASA (cl). **84-85** Alamy Images: moodboard. **85** Alamy Images: blickwinkel/Laule (tc); BrazilPhotos.com/Patricia Belo (bc). Science Photo Library: Dr Jeremy Burgess (bl). **86** Corbis: Brand X/The Stocktrek Corp (2); Ecoscene/Richard Glover (3). Science Photo Library: AGSTOCKUSA/Mike Boyatt (4); Claude Nuridsany & Marie Perennou (5). **87** Alamy Images: Pablo Paul (bl/inset). Dreamstime.com: Drx (br); Pyewackett (bl). Science Photo Library: Eurelios/Karim Agabi (cr). **88** Dreamstime.com: Marc Dietrich (ca) (crb); Barbara Helgason (tl) (cb); Beata Wojciechowska (clb). Photolibrary: Animals Animals/Stephen Ingram (crb/inset). Science Photo Library: Sally McCrae Kuyper (clb/inset) (ca/inset); Pekka Parviainen (tl/inset). **88-89** Dreamstime.com: Mark Emge (t); Sebastian Kaulitzki (b). iStockphoto.com: David H. Lewis (bc). **89** Dreamstime.com: Marc Dietrich (br); Barbara Helgason (tl) (c) (tr). Science Photo Library: Gustoimages (tl/inset); Stephen J. Krasemann (tr/inset); John Mead (br/inset); David Parker (c/inset). **90** Corbis: Tim Wright (br). Dreamstime.com: Jon Helgason (bl). Science Photo Library: Keith Kent (bl/inset); Jim Reed (tr). **90-91** Science Photo Library: Reed Timmer. **91** Corbis: epa/Skip Bolen (cl); Reuters/Mia Shanley (tr). Dreamstime.com: Ann piaia (br); Solarseven (cr). Science Photo Library: NOAA (tl). **92** Alamy Images: ICP-Pano (5). Corbis: Godong/Michel Gounot (3). FLPA: Minden Pictures/Michael & Patricia Fogden (2). iStockphoto.com: Jakub Semeniuk (bl). **92-93** iStockphoto.com: Luca di Filippo (bc); fotosav. **93** Alamy Images: Gavin Hellier (6); Robert Harding Picture Library Ltd/Tony Waltham (7). Corbis: Robert Harding World Imagery/John Henry Claude Wilson (4). iStockphoto.com: Robert Payne (br). Photolibrary: Picture Press/Thorsten Milse (8). **94-95** Corbis: Yann Arthus-Bertrand. **96** FLPA: Imagebroker/Alessandra Sarti (10); Minden Pictures/Norbert Wu (8). Science Photo Library: Alexis Rosenfeld (7); Peter Scoones (9). **96-97** Alamy Images: Marvin Dembinsky Photo Associates. **97** Science Photo Library: Michael Abbey (6); Christian Jegou Publiphoto Diffusion (11); Eye of Science (3); Steve Gschmeissner (5); Laboratory of Molecular Biology/Dr A. Lesk (2); Friedrich Saurer (12); Claire Ting (4). **98** Alamy Images: Andrew Darrington (bc); Scenics & Science (c). Ardea: Jean Paul Ferrero (crb). FLPA: Ron Austing (bl); Imagebroker/Alessandra Sarti (clb). Photolibrary: Flirt Collection/Chase Swift (br). Science Photo Library: Jeff Lepore (cla); David Scharf (tr). **99** Alamy Images: Martin Harvey (b); Robert Harding Picture Library Ltd/Jack Jackson (br/inset b). Ardea: David Dixon (clb); Jean Michel Labat (br/inset crb); Duncan Usher (bl). Dreamstime.com: Sara Robinson (br). FLPA: Imagebroker/Andreas Rose (br/inset t); Panda Photo (br/inset cra). Science Photo Library: Dee Breger (tl); A.B. Dowsett (tr); Eurelios/Philippe Plailly (cra); Steve Gschmeissner (cla) (ca); Maximilian Stock Ltd (tc). **100** Alamy Images: digitalunderwater.com (7); Stephen Frink Collection/Masa Ushioda (6). Ardea: Roy Glen (1); Valerie Taylor (4). Corbis: Visuals Unlimited (1/tl). Dreamstime.com: Eline Spek (r). FLPA: Gerard Lacz (3); D. P. Wilson (1/r). Science Photo Library: Steve Gschmeissner (1/bl); Andrew Syred (2). **101** Ardea: Pat Morris (15). Corbis: Reuters/NOAA (14). FLPA: Minden Pictures/Bruce Robison (11); Minden Pictures/Norbert Wu (12). naturepl.com: Doug Perrine (5); David Shale (9) (10) (13). **102** Ardea: Auscape/Dr David Wachenfeld (bc) (crb); Francois Gohier (2); Jean Michel Labat (cra); Ken Lucas (cb); D. Parer & E. Parer-Cook (1); Gavin Parsons (tl) (bl) (br) (tr); Valerie Taylor (3). **103** Ardea: Kurt Amsler (bc) (crb); Auscape/Dr David Wachenfeld (6); D. Parer & E. Parer-Cook (cr); Valerie Taylor (t) (bl) (br) (c). **104** Alamy Images: M. A. Battilana (bl); Konrad Zelazowski (cl). FLPA: David Hosking (cra). Photolibrary: OSF/Richard Packwood (crb). **104-105** FLPA: Minden Pictures/Tim Fitzharris. **105** Alamy Images: Mike Kipling Photography (cr). Ardea: B. Moose Peterson (br). Corbis: Momatiuk - Eastcott (clb). Dreamstime.com: Nathalie Speliers Ufermann (cla). Science Photo Library: Jim Edds (tr). **106** Alamy Images: Arco Images GmbH/F. Scholz; Redmond Durrell (tc). FLPA: David Hosking (bl); Jo Halpin Jones (cr); Minden Pictures/Pete Oxford (br). **107** FLPA: Elliott Neep (br); Bob Gibbons; Tony Hamblin (tr); Minden Pictures/Gerry Ellis (tl); Minden Pictures/Katherine Feng (cb); Martin B. Withers (bl). **108** Corbis: zefa/Schmitz-Söhnigen (c). FLPA: David Hosking (br); Winfried Wisniewski. **108-109** iStockphoto.com: Patricia Hofmeester (c). **109** FLPA: Andrew Bailey (tr); Elliott Neep (cr); David Hosking (tl); Imagebroker/Alessandra Sarti (bl, x); Minden Pictures/Tui de Roy (br). **110** Alamy Images: Kevin Schafer (br). FLPA: S. & D. & K. Maslowski (bl); Minden Pictures/Tim Fitzharris; Minden Pictures/Tui de Roy (cl). **111** Alamy Images: Martin Harvey (cb); Jon Arnold Images Ltd/Jon Arnold (cr); Thomas Lehne. FLPA: Frans Lanting (tc); Minden Pictures/Michael & Patricia Fogden (bc); Ariadne Van Zandbergen (cl). **112-113** Corbis: epa/Ed Oudenaarden. **114** Corbis: Sygma/Herve Collart (1). FLPA: Minden Pictures/Pete Oxford (2). Photolibrary: Robin Smith (3). **114-115** Corbis: Denis Felix (b). **115** Alamy Images: Richard Cooke (4); Trip (6). Corbis: Louie Psihoyos (5). Dreamstime.com: Astroid (tr); Andrew Kazmierski (tl). iStockphoto.com: Dieter K. Henke (bc); studiovancaspel (br). **116** Corbis: Gary Braasch (1); H. David Seawell (2). Getty Images: Aurora/Robert Caputo (3/l). Photolibrary: Robert Harding Travel/Sybil Sassoon (4). **116-17** Corbis: Brand X/Andersen Ross. **117** Alamy Images: INSADCO Photography/Willfried Gredler (8); Trip (5). Photolibrary: Imagestate RM/Stephen New (7). Still Pictures: Argus/Peter Frischmuth (6). **118** Alamy Images: Martin Jenkinson (t); Transtock Inc/Steve Crise (b). Corbis: epa/Hapag-Lloyd (l); zefa/Roland Gerth (r). **118-119** Corbis: Justin Guariglia. **119** Alamy Images: David R. Frazier Photolibrary, Inc (tr). Corbis: Ron Chapple (tl); Comet/Jean-Pierre Lescourret (b). **120** Alamy Images: nagelestock.com (2). Corbis: Yann Arthus-Bertrand (6); Hemis/Hervé Hughes (1); Sergio Pitamitz (5). **120-121** Alamy Images: Jon Arnold Images Ltd/Walter Bibikow. **121** Corbis: Darrell Gulin (3); Sygma/Les Stone (8). Getty Images: National Geographic/Jonathan S. Blair (4). **122** Alamy Images: Lou Linwei (2). Corbis: Flirt/W. Cody (1); Martin Harvey (5); Michael St. Maur Sheil (4). **122-123** Alamy Images: Simon Stirrup. **123** Alamy Images: Andrew Butterton (9); Images of Africa Photobank/David Keith Jones (8); Jacques Jangoux (6); Terrance Klassen (10); Stuart Yates (7)

For further information see:
www.dkimages.com